Age of Agility

Age of Agility
The New Tools for Career Success

ANDREW J. WILT

AGE OF AGILITY: THE NEW TOOLS FOR CAREER SUCCESS

Library of Congress: 201-79-58361
ISBNs: 978-0-9984152-0-8 (paperback), 978-0-9984152-1-5 (ebook)

Age.·.Agility.·.

Book design by Vanger: http://vangerlaszlo.blogspot.rs/
All watercolors in Dock Model are by Kittie Wilt
Photos in "Workspace" chapter by Alina Kaiser
Author photo by Megan Wilt
Book edited by Josh Veal—joshdveal@gmail.com

FIRST AMERICAN EDITION

Printed in the United States of America
9 8 7 6 5 4 3 2

I appreciate you taking the time to read my work. Please consider leaving a review wherever you bought the book and telling your friends to help spread the word. Have something to tell me? Find me at andrewjwilt.com

Thank you for supporting indie business writing and publishing!

DEDICATION

For my mentors, Andy Ruth and Andy Catlin. It took a few years for the hot water to reach the top floor. Thank you for your guidance and support. Most of all, thank you for your patience.

Agile

adjective ag·ile \ ˈa-jəl, -ˌjī(-ə)l\

Definition of AGILE

1: marked by ready ability to move with quick easy grace AN AGILE DANCER

2: having a quick resourceful and adaptable character AN AGILE MIND

Merriam-Webster

Intelligence is the ability to adapt to change.
— STEPHEN HAWKING

CONTENTS

ACKNOWLEDGMENTS

Soft Skills

Most of this book was inspired by conversations with Andy Catlin and Andy Ruth between 2009 and 2016. Andy Catlin met with me weekly for coffee from 2009 until 2012 when I decided to move to Seattle, WA. In Seattle, I found a new coffee buddy, Andy Ruth, who became my soft skills mentor. The mentoring turned into a two-year business analyst apprentice position with his company, Sustainable Evolution Inc. After completing the program, I hung around the SEI crowd for an extra year and in 2016, I moved to Minneapolis, MN, to develop the apprenticeship education model I learned at SEI. Both Andy Catlin and Andy Ruth have gone out of their way to make time for me whenever I have a question or want to talk about something that is on my mind. They are the true masters of the skills in this book—all I had to do was listen.

The Writing

My wife, Megan, is always my first reader. Whether it's poetry, fiction, blogs, nonfiction, or the weird bizarro thing I sometimes do, her eyes are the first to see it. This may sound like a lot of fun, but she might tell you it's not as glamorous or romantic as it sounds. While I'm pacing around the living room, bright-eyed and bushy-tailed, practicing imaginary interviews and lectures in sold-out auditoriums, Megan is in the bedroom sifting through the jumbled Scrabble board I call a first draft. And then she has the very difficult task of telling me my writing is not there yet without completely ruining my spirits. Megan, I am so lucky to have a partner who is kind, honest, and compassionate.

Additional thanks to the following people who offered love and support from the beginning (a-z): Garry Alcedo, Jason Benchimol, the Biddies and their significant others, Heather Bulliss, Douglas Cole, Garrett Dennert, Chris(topher) Dier-Scalise, James Habiger, Rue Lazzaro, Caleb Kaiser, Allie Mae Kelly, the Koester family, Rosalind Koff, Seyon Makuannen, Elliot Malcolm, Katie McDonald, Jason Michalek, Taylor Normington, Meara O'Neill, Vincent James Perrone, Sam Pierce, Honor Posey-Marquez, Joshua P. Preston, the Pumper family, Emily & Mark Schumacher, J.C. Sevcik, Robert Standefer & Zoe Kingson, Margarita E. Wilde, the Wilt family, and T.J. Wood.

Finally, a big thank you to those who cannot be named, but nevertheless, made an important impression on my life. Writing friends, college friends, musicians, and bookworms from Michigan and Washington. We made a lot of memories, and when I think of them, I smile.

WHY READ THIS BOOK?

Before you click the shopping cart button in your web browser or make your way up to the cash register at one of the few remaining bookstores hanging around your neighborhood (thank you for supporting your local booksellers), let me pause you where you are while you still have your money safely in your pocket. Before you move the money in your pocket to my pocket, I want you to know what you're getting yourself into.

How do I find and sustain a career that I am excited to wake up for, am passionate about, pays the bills, and doesn't burn me out?

This is the question I am going to answer in the next three-hundred or so pages. Unfortunately, this book will not tell you what that career is, but it will give you a good direction to start in. It will provide you with the necessary tools to navigate your life and work. I wrote this book in response to what was promised when you were told the one-word answer to having a successful life and career: college.

The biggest lie we were told is that a college education will prepare us for a lifelong career. If you go to college or put in your four years and earn a bachelor's degree, you will have a rewarding and stimulating career with a comfortable salary and benefits. The reality is, there is a huge skill gap between the classroom and the workplace, and this skill gap is the main reason why I watched countless friends struggle post-college to find a meaningful career. I saw my friends fall into one of three groups.

The first group consists of my friends who are still struggling to find a full-time job in the field they went to school for. While they sent out resumes and cleaned up their LinkedIn profiles, an entire generation of college graduates moved back home to live with friends or relatives because they couldn't afford to pay rent, as we are, on average, $35,000 in debt to student loan companies.

The second group of friends found full-time work using their degrees and entered a competitive, fast-paced culture their school did not prepare them for. It was trial by fire. Sink or swim. They reported to drill sergeant managers and had a hard time forming connections with co-workers. There were too many emails, too many action items, and the challenges they faced were beyond their skill level. Their schedules were unmanageable, and they had little time for life outside of work. Shortly into their college-promised career, many were burned out and questioned if they made a mistake choosing their major and career path.

The rest of my friends, representing a smaller number than the previous friend groups, discovered the skills to be successful in a career after school through their experiences in college, but did so outside of the classroom. They made connections with peers, professors, and mentors who bridged the gap between school and work. For this group, the classroom didn't lead them to a career they love, the university ecosystem allowed them to form connections and build relationships with people who were aware of this gap and the necessity to fill it. To be clear, a university setting isn't the only place where these connections exist. I have other friends who dropped out of school, went directly to work after high school, or spent time in the military. All of them were able to make connections in the environments they were in.

This book addresses the skill gap the last friend group was enlightened to by industry leaders and mentors. They learned skills that are not taught in school but are expected when you enter the workplace and begin your career. They also learned the skills needed to find a job that aligned their passion with their strengths, and once they landed a job, they used their knowledge and network to successfully transition to the demands of the 21st century workplace. Most importantly, this group learned how to learn. Instead of following their textbooks to the letter, they recognized the difference between book learning and practical application in the field. These friends were excited to enter a culture of curiosity where they could move with change, not against it.

Why were these things never taught to me in school?

Great question. We are living in an Age of Agility, meaning, business and industry are changing so quickly, books cannot be printed fast enough to stay current. In school, many of us were taught from outdated textbooks by professors who tried to stay up-to-date on current trends, but often could not because of all the hats they wear. As a result, we were not prepared for a career after school. Instead of placing a focus on trying to print books faster to learn hard industry skills, students should be taught how to learn so they can move as the industry moves. The skills in this book will teach you how to observe, think, and communicate effectively so you can move with change instead of responding to it.

WHO SHOULD READ THIS BOOK?

If you are a recent college graduate looking for a career doing something you love, that will pay you fairly, and will not burn you out, I wrote this book for you. If you are confident, motivated, love a challenge, and can't sit behind a desk for another year (or four years), I wrote this book for you. Finally, this book is for my peers who are displaced workers, underemployed, or sick and tired of their job(s). If I didn't have the influence of some great mentors in my life, I would still be working next to you in West Michigan, running between two or more part-time jobs, angry, frustrated, and tired. Since you would have shared it with me, I am now sharing it with you.

WHAT'S IN THE BOOK?

I wrote this book with a particular structure in mind, but that doesn't mean you have to read it cover to cover. If you are looking to only build skills in a certain area, feel free to flip through the table of contents and find what tool you want to learn. If you want the full experience, here is a roadmap of how the book is structured.

The book is composed of small bite-sized chapters intended to be read slowly so you reflect on the content in each section. To set a tone of reflection and contemplation, my first chapter is about carrying a notebook. As a student of life, having a journal or notebook is critical when learning new topics because it externalizes your thoughts, which helps you process, make connections, and ingrain new information into your life. After the chapter on journaling, you will learn the foundational skills the rest of the book is built on, hence the name, "Laying a Foundation". You will learn about how to deal with change, talent barriers, and failure, because how you respond to these three topics is critical to your success.

Next, you will learn how you learn. Since we all see the world differently, knowing how you learn, how to work with others, and how much information you can take in at once will propel you forward in your career. These chapters will prompt you to think about your strengths and weaknesses, and with this knowledge, you can start thinking about what you want out of life and where you could be most successful. For example, do you want to be a leader, or did it ever cross your mind that you don't have to be a leader to be successful? In the sections that follow, you will learn ways to brainstorm possible career choices by looking for the intersection between where your passion meets your skills. The goal isn't to have a career pinned down at this point, but to at least have a direction you can start exploring.

Once you have a direction, you will learn about what motivates you, so you can create small, manageable goals. You will also learn how to manage your time, yourself, and strategies to get in gear if you can't get started. Most of your goals will include other people, so Part 1 ends with learning how to build and manage relationships. The tools in this section include emotional intelligence and empathy-driven communication.

If that sounds like a lot, you're right. Part 1 is the largest section, and provides the necessary foundation for Part 2: Building Structure. Part 2 takes the foundational skills in Part 1 and builds structure around them by showing you how you can incorporate them into your day-to-day life. In this section, you will learn how to intertwine your new foundational skills into routines and daily habits. You will learn about a model devised to help you sustain these skills and balance them amongst each other. The model, called the Dock Model, is the ultimate work/life balance tool to managing your personal life and career. The model covers how managing your health can improve your mood and productivity; how practice works; the benefits of play as adults; and how to use reflection as a check-in for your goals and career path.

In Part 3, Reinforcement, you will learn how to excel in the career path you have chosen by fine-tuning the soft skills you learned about in Part 1 and 2, as well as many other workplace-specific skills. These include: mentoring, interviewing, working with tough colleagues, and what to look out for in a company (cult)ure. The rest of Part 3 is about skills and tools you didn't learn in school that are necessary to bridge the gap to the workplace and help you thrive in your career. These are: blogging, creating a productive workspace, building the right kind of confidence, combating overthinking, learning a lot quickly, and how using a budget will give you more control over your future. Finally, I end with the four rules I keep in the forefront of my mind to guide my thoughts and behaviors at home and work.

My goal for this book is to add immediate value to your life, and this value is two-sided. I hope to introduce new skills and concepts to you AND acknowledge the tools you already know but might need a friendly reminder to start using again. My sincere hope is to reframe how you see yourself and your career, so you can be successful in both.

HOW TO USE THIS BOOK

Warning! Do not read this book all at once.

Many of these chapters started as blog posts and were intended to be consumed as single servings. If you try to read this book all in one sitting, you will miss something or get a headache. Probably both. My advice is to read one chapter a day, so you have time to reflect on and interact with the concepts introduced in each section.

I cover a little about a lot. This is a big picture manual for you to dig deeper with, and that's why I have included a suggested reading and listening list at the end of the book. You can think of this book as a toolkit and if you do, I hope you are also thinking about building your own personal toolkit as you read. A good toolkit will prepare you for tough projects and unforeseen circumstances. When the excrement hits the air conditioner (this is not an *if*, it is a *when*), you will be able to evade panic and conduct yourself from a place of ease and comfort. I think Stephen King said it best in his book, *On Writing*:

When the screen was secure, Uncle Oren gave me the screwdriver and told me to put it back in the toolbox and "latch her up." I did, but was puzzled. I asked him why he'd lugged Fazza's toolbox all the way around the house, if all he'd needed was that one screwdriver. He could have carried a screwdriver in the back pocket of his khakis.

"Yeah, but Stevie," he said, bending to grasp the handles, "I didn't know what else I might find to do once I got out here, did I? It's best to have your tools with you. If you don't, you're apt to find something you didn't expect and get discouraged."

With a box full of tools, you will be prepared for anything that comes your way. This also means you should take out tools from time to time and make sure they are sharp and polished. After some time has passed, go back over the skills in this book (or dig deeper with the suggested reading and listening) so you can stay current. When Benjamin Franklin was 20 years old, he developed a system of 13 virtues for character development. He would spend one week on each virtue and when he finished number 13, he would start back at number one. Doing this, he would cycle through the virtues four times a year. Likewise, interacting with the skills in this book regularly will keep them in the forefront of your mind so they are readily available when you need to use them.

Finally—and this should go without saying, but let me give you permission in case you need it—this is *your* book, so get rough with it. Feel free to dog-ear sections, highlight passages, and take notes, adding your own experiences to the text. Far too often we hold books on a pedestal instead of using them as the tools they are. If you want to respect a book, use it and get wild with it—that's why the author wrote it.

If any of this sounds like it is up your alley, I would be honored if you bought my book.

! ! ! ! !

BEFORE READING

This page is yours. Dog-ear it, write on it, or rip it out. Break all the rules your elementary school librarian taught you. Grab a crayon and scribble an expletive on this page. Go for it, because that's the quickest way you are going to learn the skills in this book: by questioning everything you ever learned about growing professional skills in business.

! ! ! ! !

Introduction

THE AGE OF AGILITY

My life is a vocation; I can't imagine doing anything else. I have the freedom to explore whatever idea I want, take really random gigs and projects which change my life in some way.
— DOUGLAS COUPLAND

I am the master of my fate,
I am the captain of my soul.
— WILLIAM ERNEST HENLEY, *Invictus*

Life-long careers are something of the past. Only two generations ago, people took for granted that they would retire from the first company they started working for right out of school. After serving in the U.S. Air Force, my grandfather found a job in the same city he grew up in, Kalamazoo, Michigan, where he also earned his bachelor's degree. He was with the company for over 30 years before retiring. My wife's grandfather retired from the same company he started working at in high school. Now, it's hard finding someone who has been with the same company for more than a decade. According to the U.S. Bureau of Labor and Statistics, the median length of an employee as a salary worker in 2016 was 4.2 years. And if you take a closer look at the data, people are not only changing jobs, they are changing the industries they work in.

In the Age of Agility, you can't rely on what you have always done in the past. Let's say you have a job putting square blocks (your skills) into square holes (industry). You go to school and study square blocks and get an internship at a company that specializes in right-angle design. Shortly after your internship, you get a job in the field. At your job, you are one of the best at putting square blocks in square holes—congratulations. A few months later, you start to realize that you are not getting the same results you used to. The blocks are not fitting right, and you have to push on them and still, they barely squeeze through. More time goes by, and the blocks don't fit into the holes at all! The hole is changing into what looks like a circle! All your teachers in school and your managers at your internship said that there were ONLY square holes. Circle holes simply don't exist. In fact, you remember a well-liked professor telling you circle holes cannot exist. You try everything to get the blocks to fit, from putting a new flexible coating on the blocks to making them smaller by breaking them in half. And then you get it! You realize that in the Age of Agility, need to change your skills as the industry changes. If the holes are round, your blocks should be too, and they should be able to form into any shape the hole changes into. That's what it means to be agile. To move with and anticipate changes in industry.

A few years ago, futurist Thomas Frey famously tweeted: "As a rule of thumb, 60% of the jobs 10 years from now haven't been invented yet." This means that the job you have now will look different in the next decade. As an exercise, think about how your life has changed in the last 10 years. Technology has changed how we communicate, how we buy products, and how we learn. Leaps in technology are happening more frequently and are having just as big of an impact on the market place as the internet did. Living in the Age of Agility also means that having a hard-set 10-year goal will work against you, because it needs to be able to change as the industry changes. Instead, you should have a well-defined 10-year path to give you direction, and expect your end-goal to change in some way. If you put up too many fences around your goal, you will end up creating a product, service, or technology that is outdated. To drive this point home, here's a simplified example in recent memory.

When I was a kid, I remember walking into my family doctor's office and seeing rows and rows of folders stacked on library shelves behind the receptionist. Each folder was color-coded and in alphabetical order. This was 15 years ago. Let's say in the early 2000's, someone decided that their 10-year plan was to revolutionize the paper filing system for medical records to make it easier for healthcare staff to pull a patient's medical information. With this goal in mind, they spend years making the perfect filing system for paper medical records. Flash forward to 2012. Ten years go by and they have done it! It's the most effective retrieval system for paper charts ever invented. It's accurate, easy to use, and takes up 40% less space. All the while, paper became obsolete and now digital copies of medical records are all the buzz. A perfect piece of technology was created for a demand that is no longer needed. Since the end goal was too well-defined, the path could not change when industry changed. Instead they should have anticipated the change in technology and adopted this into their strategy.

THAT is the Age of Agility. The skills in this book will bridge the gap from school to work and they will also prepare you to anticipate change in your career, so you can adjust your course respectively. Your future is undefined, and so is the career you will retire from. You don't need an end goal to put on a pedestal (those were only vague ideas you told your grandmother, so she could brag about you to her friends), but you do need to know the skills to get you there. These skills will define your path.

JOURNAL

Always carry a notebook. ... THAT is a million dollar lesson
they don't teach you in business school!
— ARISTOTLE ONASSIS

Before we dig into specific skills, I want to start with a tool. Whether
you are in school, working, or in the middle of the very tough task of
finding where you fit into the world, this is something you can start
doing RIGHT NOW that will immediately add value to your day. All
you need is a pen and a piece of paper. That's it. Call it your journal,
sketchbook, notes for a later project, or your external memory. Mine,
I call my Muse Book, because I use it to write down any interesting
thought that pops into my head throughout the day. Usually the ideas
are so sudden, it's as if they were sent from one of the Greek muses.

Here's the catch: Your notebook should be a "paper and pen"
notebook (or mimic the motion with a tablet and a stylus) and not a
keyed device such as a smartphone or laptop—you need to be able to
interact with what you write down on a deeper sensory level. It needs
to be tactile. Touching the page and holding a pen engages your
whole body as each letter you write looks and feels a little different
each time you write it. With a keyboard, you are using repetitive
memory-based movements, and all the letters feel the same as you
type. When you write each letter by hand, everything slows down, so
you have more time with the idea. This means having more time to

30

commit it to memory by making associations with other thoughts you have, because more of your brain is engaged. In our fast-paced world (that is only getting faster) long-hand is the one thing you have absolute control over. Also, did I mention it doesn't have a battery? And it can't be accidently deleted when you update to a new phone?

Why? What's the Point?

When you look back at the ideas you wrote down throughout the day, you can take a step back and connect the dots. Moment by moment, we see, hear, and observe the world around us, but we don't have context until we are removed from the event or situation. When naturalist Charles Darwin returned from his five-year voyage on the Beagle in 1836, he started writing in his journal about the transmutation of species. It wasn't until 1858, more than 20 years later, when he connected all the dots and wrote his theory of natural selection in evolution.

What Should You Write?

Write or draw anything you want in your notebook. You can draw pictures, write music notes, or jot down clumsy ideas. If a few words sound good together, write them down. If the architecture of a building stands out to you, draw it. When you get frustrated with an ordinary object or situation, think about how you would eliminate the problem and draw what the solution might look like.

There are four types of things I write down in my Muse Book. Feel free to borrow, steal, or add to my categories in your own notebook. The *first* type is observations I see as a researcher of the world. The *second* is ideas I am working on: I use the blank page as a way of playing with an idea, so I can explore possible ends and pitfalls. The *third* is interesting things I hear people say in conversation: things I want to make a note of to look up later or phrases that strike me as interesting. Finally, the *fourth* is my sudden moments of insight. In Elizabeth Gilbert's book on creativity, *Big Magic*, she writes about the American poet Ruth Stone, who describes these moments of insight perfectly. When Stone was growing up on a farm in rural Virginia, she would sometimes "hear a poem coming towards her…" When this happened, she would run to the house as fast as she could, so she could write it down before the poem passed through her. Gilbert writes:

Sometimes… [Ruth] was too slow, and she couldn't get to the

paper and pencil in time. At those instances, she could feel the poem rushing right through her body and out the other side. It would be in her for a moment, seeking a response, and then it would be gone before she could grasp it–galloping away across the earth, as she said, 'searching for another poet.'

Your brain is constantly processing information beneath your consciousness. From time to time, a connection will pop up to the conscious level, but only briefly. It could be as odd as wondering what an old elementary school friend's basement looked like (didn't his dad collect hats?). Or it could be another random smashing of memory and observations that leads you to the perfect idea for a new business.

Whether you believe ideas are divine or not, they won't stick unless you write them down. Great ideas are all around us and we can catch them or let them pass us by.

The Notebook

Some notebooks nowadays are more of a fashion statement than a tool. If that's your dig, go for it. I use a 3x5 spiral notebook I usually find for 59 cents during the back-to-school sales. They're sturdy and small enough to fit into the back pocket of my blue jeans.

The Pen

Unlike notebooks, pens are important. Finding the right one is like finding the right wand in the Harry Potter series; some people love pens others cannot stand. I hate using the pens my wife, Megan, uses, and vice versa. In our household, blindly grabbing for a pen can be dangerous. When I accidently grab one of her pens, it feels limp in my hand, like I'm grasping the small tail of a rodent, and I get so distracted I lose focus. That said, if the pen isn't a good fit, you may forget your idea and the exercise will no longer be useful.

My favorites are the G2 Pilot and the Uni-Ball Signo 207. Megan, on the other hand, loves Pilot Better Retractable Ballpoint pens. Whatever your utensil of choice ends up being, it should feel comfortable in your hand and allow you to write so you can read your notes later.

When I reach the last page in my notebook, I go back to the first page and skim through what I wrote. This is the first time I allow myself to use technology. I open a Google Doc and transcribe my notes, page by page, so they are searchable and safe in the cloud. I close my notebook and hold it at my chest with one hand on top and the other on the bottom. Before adding it to the Rubbermaid Roughneck container in my basement with all my other notebooks, I thank it for its role in my life over the last few months. I walk upstairs and grab another notebook from the closet in my office and write a little note to the notebook on the first page. As silly as it sounds, I find this practice to be incredibly useful. I set my intentions for the notebook and it establishes our relationship.

With a notebook in your pocket, you become an observer of everyday life. Every idea in this book started in one of my Muse books.

Key Takeaways

o   If you don't write it down, chances are, you are going to forget it.

o   The process of putting your hand to the page is important as it gives you time to imprint what you are writing to memory, and as an added benefit, allows you to take a break from technology.

o   You need one space to collect all your ideas *as they happen.* When you revisit them, you can expand on them in another format or medium.

o   Unlike a smartphone or laptop, you won't get distracted by a notification when you open your notebook.

o   You are more likely to act on the things you write down.

GOAL FOR TODAY: Find a notebook and writing utensil you like. Practice taking it out during the day and jotting down whatever you are thinking about. Write freely and don't be too self-critical.

Part 1:
Laying a Foundation

1.1 WHAT MAKES US TICK

Now that you have the most important tool in your pocket, your journal, you are ready to take on the three toughest areas in building your foundation. They are:

o   How to make change work to your advantage

o   Mindset, emotional resilience, and why natural talent is overrated

o   How to stare down failure

These skills will give you the confidence to follow through with whatever you set your mind to. The more in tune you are to your inner ticking, the more control you will have over your future.

CHANGE

The only thing that is constant is change.
— HERACLITUS

We cannot choose our external circumstances, but we can always choose how we respond to them.
— EPICTETUS

We face change in every stage of our lives. Growing up and growing older, our bodies build and then dismantle. We move to a new city or change jobs. We make new friends and learn how to navigate new roads. Without thinking, we hit an update button on our computers or phones and learn the tricks of a new operating system. At work, we regularly see change with new procedures in response to technology, innovation, and globalization.

Sometimes change comes in the form of new routines we want to build into our lives to be healthier or more efficient with our time. Other times, it is in response to a change that is completely out of our control: a new policy or an unexpected event. Although we are faced with change daily, most of us don't know how it works, how to follow through with change, or if it's worth the time and effort *to* change.

The Internal Battle

Whenever we are faced with change or want to try something new, an internal battle begins. This struggle is explained in Plato's Dialogue, *Phaedrus*. In the text, Socrates tells us that the human soul is made up of three parts: a flying dark horse with wings (naturally), a winged light horse, and a charioteer.

According to the analogy, the conscious self (this is who you are when you think of yourself) is the charioteer, and you are the one who is driving the horses. Your winged horses represent the two sides of the lower consciousness, this is the emotional side that pulls you one way or another that you may or may not be aware of. The light horse is noble and loves things like victory and honor. The dark horse, on the other hand, is what you probably expect. It loves food and indulging in alcohol, sex, and material wealth. Neither is technically good or evil because both can lead you down the wrong path.

The dark horse's danger is obvious—if you let it lead your life, you will go down a path of earthly desires and fall into unobtainable temptations like greed, intoxicants, and repeatedly hitting the snooze button. The dark horse sounds good in theory, but you end up trying to catch the wind. The light horse's downfalls are a little less obvious. Since it is proud and noble, it sets unrealistic goals that no one could possibly follow through with. If you let this horse lead your chariot, you will get caught up in so many noble deeds that you might starve to death because you'll forget to eat. That's where your job comes in. As the charioteer, you represent reason and logic, and with this, you control your horses.

According to the analogy, you should let one lead for a while and when the time is right, switch positions and let the other one lead. In the end, you will find your right path, and according to Socrates, that path will lead you to the procession gods, which I take to mean that you will achieve your personal or career goals. •

Let me break it down so you can see each player's role. According to Socrates, we are made up of the following:

A LIGHT HORSE: This is the part of us who wants to do good in the world. Every morning, your light horse wakes up next to a soapbox and says: "Today I will save the world."

A DARK HORSE: This is the part of us who is concerned about

earthly pleasure. Every morning, your dark horse wakes up and says: "Today is for me…and I am going to enjoy myself."

A CHARIOTEER: This is our reasonable and logical self who chooses which impulses to listen to. It is in charge of motivating the horses so they work together. Every morning, your charioteer wakes up and listens to each of your horses. Then, it has to decide how to motivate them so they work together and you are able to achieve your daily goals. For example: If I go for a run this morning and get everything checked off my daily to-do list at work (the light horse), I am coming home and watching Netflix in my sweatpants (the dark horse).

In terms of shear strength, the charioteer is no match for the horses. Not only are they horses, but they also have wings. And they're huge! And so are our emotions. As a charioteer, you might get an idea that you want to make a change in your life, like starting a new routine, a new diet, waking up earlier, or applying for a new job. The first week is great: our light horse is leading the way and the dark horse can get on board because it's thinking about how good it's going to look and how much money it's going to make. And then the second week hits and the dark horse gets out of sync and starts pulling the chariot off course. The dark horse starts complaining, saying it's too hard and it would be much easier for everyone if we went back to what was comfortable. That's when you as the charioteer need to lean on the light horse and try to inspire the dark horse. You can fall into the same trap with the light horse. If you spend all your time and energy on trying to make a lot of positive change in the world, your head will be in the clouds all day and you will lose track of your life down on earth. While you are saving the world, you may ignore important relationships and your health. The key, as a charioteer, is learning how to balance your horses. The goal is to have everyone working together so you can get on the right path and join the gods in their procession to heaven.

How Does Change Work?

Most people think change happens after a lot of thinking and research. Generally, we think we are in control of the choices we make, which is only slightly true. Our horses have a way of tugging at the reigns, pulling us one way, and we have a bad habit of saying, "Oh, I wanted to go this way anyway." What actually happens is we encounter something with our *senses*, have an *emotional* response to it, and then are *motivated* to do something. Here it is in three words: Sense, Feel, and Act. When someone says they have a gut feeling, they are responding to the stimuli at a low-conscious level. They are perceiving something in their environment, emotionally responding to it, and then acting on the feeling. Being aware of this process allows you to stop and ask yourself if you are acting in your best interest or if you are reacting to a feeling.

Here are some areas where Sense, Feel, and Act can be manipulated to make change work.

1. Reframe How You Get There

Even if you know you need to make a change, it might feel too big and intimidating to start working on. The trick is making change feel easy and worthwhile, so you can motivate your dark horse to action. To do this, you can break your goals down into smaller achievable tasks.

*When you **sense** a task can be completed, you **feel** like it is worthwhile to complete, and you will be inspired to **act** on your goal.*

2. Change Your Environment

Sometimes our environment is holding us back from making a change. When this happens, we need to tweak the environment, so the charioteer and horses can be more successful. In the book *Mindless Eating*, Brian Wansink suggests to people on a diet to use smaller plates and glasses when they eat a meal. These people will still be eating a full plate of food (it will feel like a full plate), but they will be eating less because the plate is smaller.

Another way to change your environment is to put post-it notes in your office or around your home to remind you of the behavior you are trying to change. It could be something as simple as putting a post-it note at your desk, so every time you sit down, you are reminded to take a breath, compose yourself, and be mindful as you begin your work.

*When you change your environment, you change what you **sense**. When your environment reinforces your new behavior, the change **feels** easier, and **action** will come naturally.*

3. Acknowledge When You Are Strong

We have more willpower in the beginning of the day than at night. At the beginning of the day, you may have your sights set on making a change. As the day wears on, you have to make a lot of other choices and this is a drain on your self-control. When you want to make a change, you will have more success if you do it in the morning than in the evening.

*When you **sense** a change, you are more likely to **feel** like it is achievable when it is one of your first choices in the day, motivating you to **action**.*

Key Takeaways

o The only thing that stays the same is change.

o We choose to do something because we sense, have a feeling, and then act on the feeling. If you change what you sense, your feelings will lead you to an action that supports your goal.

o When you encounter change, you need to get your noble light horse and self-interested dark horse working together. If one is working too hard or not enough, it will throw you off course.

GOAL FOR TODAY: Think about a change you have wanted to make or a time when you started to make a change but fell short. What specific setback stopped you and lead your horses astray? Think about some ways you can motivate the distracted horse, so it doesn't throw you off course.

TALENT

We like to think of our champions and idols as superheroes who were born different from us. We don't like to think of them as relatively ordinary people who made themselves extraordinary.
— CAROL S. DWECK

On a scale from 1-10, 1 being unlikely and 10 being very likely, how much basketball talent would you give someone growing up with their father in prison and living in the East Baltimore housing projects? How much would this change if I told you they were shot in the arm when they were five years old? And finally, how much would it change if I told you their adult height would only be five feet three inches, nearly two feet shorter than Shaquille O'Neal? Do you have a number? Write it down, because we'll come back to this later.

What is responsible for our individual success? To answer this question, we find ourselves in the middle of the nurture versus nature debate. Those who argue for **nature** believe that skills are inherited through genetics. For example, someone's height is genetic, or, if your parents are smart and have college degrees, you too must be naturally smart. Those who argue for **nurture** believe that skills come from circumstance, such as where we grew up or the role models we had. For example, having good teachers and parents that read to you and make you do your homework provides a nurturing environment that leads to success.

Who's right? Both play an important role in individual success, but scholars disagree on how much. Researchers like Carol S. Dweck are finding that talent is less about the physical advantages you genetically inherit from your parents and has more to do with how you view your skills.

In her book, *Mindset*, Dweck discusses two types of outlooks people have, and according to her research, how you view your skills can have a significant impact on your performance. Someone with a fixed mindset believes their ability comes from the roll of the dice at birth and it's fixed in stone, so there is little (or nothing) they can do to improve. This kind of mindset believes only in the **nature** side of the nurture-vs.-nature debate. Someone with a growth mindset believes they can learn from their experiences and improve on their natural talent. The growth mindset acknowledges that people have a diversity of strengths and weaknesses at birth, and argues that if someone is willing to practice, they can grow their talent, regardless of the dice they are thrown.

Regardless of your natural talent, you will be more successful if you adopt a growth mindset and improve on what you are given by nature. Below are characteristics of people who have each mindset.

The Fixed Mindset
Why this will slow you down

People with a fixed mindset tend to:

- Feel like they have to prove themselves over and over.

- Not be able to gauge their abilities, either believing they cannot do something or believing they are significantly more talented than they really are.

- Have a hard time recovering from failure, because they think failure means they are flawed.

- Run away from problems or situations when they get tough.

- See life as a competition and avoid engaging with others for fear of meeting people who are more talented than they are.

- Have a hard time forgiving others because they don't think people are capable of change.

- Get caught up in others' flaws instead of looking at what they are doing right.

- Be quick to assign blame and usually blame a character flaw.

- Give up on things if they are not better than average the first time around.

The Growth Mindset
Why this will speed you up

People with a growth mindset tend to:

- Thrive during challenging times in their lives, because they view the challenge as something they can overcome (like a quest in a video game).

- Find value in what they are doing, regardless of the outcome, because they are doing it for themselves, not to impress anyone.

- Be more open to change, because they know that nothing is constant except for change itself.

- Not get beat up by someone's negative comments, because they are confident in their skills and know it's all about getting more experience.

- Believe that everyone has value, regardless of their current skill level.

- Rise above blame by trying to understand a situation.

- Be honest with their opinions and open with their communication.

- Accept their mistakes and failures, and view them as learning opportunities.

- Accept that the world is not perfect.

Potential
Do you remember your number from the beginning of the chapter?

The person I described is Tyrone "Muggsy" Bogues, the 12th pick in the 1987 NBA draft. You may recognize him as the short guy in the 1996 movie, *Space Jam*. Bogues became one of the greatest players in the history of the Charlotte Hornets franchise and his college, Wake Forest, retired his jersey number. In an interview with the Charlotte Observer in 2016, Bogues said: "My mindset became so fearless that I just didn't care about what people said or thought. After that, what else can happen? What more do I have to be fearful of?"

If you approach the world with the mindset that you were born great, the whole world is judging you rather than supporting you. In a fixed mindset, Muggsy Bogues seems somehow more naturally talented at basketball than the thousands of basketball players who were taller, stronger, healthier, and came from more supportive home life environments—and owed nothing to his dedication and worth ethic. Remember, in a fixed mindset you are not doing the work, your genetics are. Just think, every time you did something honorable you would have to lower your head and say, "Well, it's not really anything I had to work for. I owe it all to a strong family bloodline."

The truth is our talent is only as fixed as our mindset. Young or old, naturally strong or weak, short or tall, you have a lot of potential. Grandma Moses, one of the most prolific American folk artists, didn't tap into her potential until she was 78.

My Story

"Whenever you feel like criticizing anyone," he told me, "just remember that all the people in this world haven't had the advantages that you've had."

— F. SCOTT FITZGERALD, *The Great Gatsby*

The above quote is underlined in my grandparent's copy of *The Great Gatsby*. I borrowed the book (and never gave it back) so every time I read the book, the passage sticks out. It began to resonate with me the more I saw it ring true in my own life. As a white male, I have unearned (and un-asked for) advantages in our culture **(nature)**. I also know that thanks to my middle-class family, I grew up with better teachers, coaches, and role models than most. If it wasn't for their support in my early childhood development, I wouldn't be writing this book, or writing at all for that matter **(nurture)**. Here's why: I inherited dyslexia-like symptoms from my father (I was never formally diagnosed) and have struggled with language my entire life **(nature)**.

Since my dad knew what I was up against, he made a point of creating a family culture of reading, and my mother, a voracious reader herself, supported the idea wholeheartedly. From an early age, I was read to, encouraged to practice reading out loud, and had conversations with my family about what I read. This gave me a stronger base in language than I would have had, had I been treated as a child without a learning disability. But that only went so far.

In high school, I swore off reading because it was too difficult (fixed mindset). I would look at a page and not know where to begin. I finished tests last, not because I didn't know the answer, but because I was slow to read the questions. Because I couldn't keep up with the reading in my English classes, I felt like I was naturally stupid, and learning came easy to everyone but me. I hated school. That's when I turned to music. I played in heavy metal bands the last few years of high school and continued playing into my third year in college. I loved the technicality of music, the scales, the movement, and the unconventional rhythm in the sub-genre mathcore. With music came lyrics. Even if people had a hard time understanding them (they were screamed or growled), I liked the idea of using music and words together to tell a story. This lead me down a path of writing a short story for every song I wrote and eventually the stories became more fun to write than playing music. With writing came reading, and a lot of it. I knew that if I wanted to write, I had to put in a lot of work. I discovered audiobooks and trained myself to sit down with a book and follow along with the narrator. I was six years old again, sitting for hours with books.

It hasn't been easy, but it also hasn't been miserable. I found my passion in the very thing I struggle with the most. I have accepted my dyslexia and instead of using my disadvantage as an excuse, I use it to motivate my practice (growth mindset). Each day I move forward in growing my talent and I am going to do what it takes to be the best writer I can be. And I know you can do the same, whatever your challenges are.

Key Takeaways

o   You should develop a growth mindset because a fixed mindset will hold you back from improving upon or learning new skills.

o   If something doesn't naturally come to you, it doesn't mean you will never be good at it.

GOAL FOR TODAY: I'm sure you've heard this career counseling question before, the one that goes, *if you had millions of dollars in the bank and money wasn't important, what career path or occupation would you choose?* Here's the spin: If talent were not an obstacle, what would you like to do for a career?

If you want to learn more about practice, mindset, and growing your skills, I recommend reading *Mindset* by Carol S. Dweck and *The Talent Code* by Daniel Coyle. Reading these books together will give you a full picture of how mindset and practice work together to grow talent.

FAILURE

Experience is simply the name we give our mistakes.
— OSCAR WILDE

By the time I was fourteen the nail in my wall would no longer support the weight of the rejection slips impaled upon it. I replaced the nail with a spike and went on writing.
— STEPHEN KING

Rejection. Failure. Sadness. Despair. Apathy. These are probably the most uncomfortable feelings anyone can have, and yet, they frequently appear in our lives. Almost daily, I open my email and find a message in my inbox that prompts those feelings.

> *At the present time, there are other candidates whose qualifications more closely match the requirements for this position and we will be moving forward with them in the recruiting process.*

Or this:

> *Although we will not be publishing [name of the piece I submitted] at this time and are sorry to disappoint you, please be assured that your manuscript was read carefully by editors and trained screeners.*

It might be applying for a job, a school, an internship, submitting your writing or research to a journal, or asking someone out on a date—wherever you fell short this week, know that you are not alone. And if you're like me, your failure rate will always be higher than your acceptance rate.

Failure teaches us where our skills are, where they need to be, and what areas we need to work on. With a growth mindset, mistakes and failure are nothing to get down about, they are lessons that teach us how to become better. Without failure, we wouldn't grow, and that's why failure is necessary for success.

This is important so I am going to repeat it—failure is not defeat. Failure is a teacher and necessary for success.

One more time—failure is not defeat. Failure is a teacher and necessary for success.

Here's the secret no one tells you: The act of failing isn't important. It is how you respond to failure that makes all the difference. If you view each experience as feedback to grow your skills, you will never truly fail. Whatever was lost in the process of making a mistake is merely the cost of learning a valuable lesson. In this chapter, I will describe ways you can use failure to propel you forward.

Your Network is a Safety Net
Be who you are and say what you feel, because those who mind don't matter and those who matter don't mind.
— DR. SEUSS

In the 1937 best-selling business book, *Think and Grow Rich*, Napoleon Hill writes about an uncle he calls R.U. Darby who struck gold out West. Darby went home to invite friends and family to invest in mining equipment and share in his (soon to be) fortune. Shortly after, a team was assembled and they started excavating the gold. Times were good, but only briefly. The mine immediately dried up because the site was not nearly as lucrative as he believed. The gold recovered from the mine didn't even cover the cost of labor and equipment. Defeated, Darby sold the land to a junk man and went home. The junk man, hearing that it was a former gold mine, called in a local engineer to take a second look. The engineer told the new owner that because Darby was not familiar with the area, he didn't realize that the mine stopped at a fault line. If they start digging three feet from where Darby stopped, the junk man would certainly hit gold again.

What's the moral of the story? The junk man made millions

because he sought out expert counsel before giving up. A lot of times, success is right in front of us. If you are persistent, have the right mentors, and ask the right questions, you will eventually hit *your* gold. And this is why your network is so important.

Emotional Resilience

It is tempting, when we are hurt, to believe that the thing which hurt us *intended* to do so. ... to move from thinking that 'The pencil fell off the table *and* now I am annoyed' to the view that 'The pencil fell off the table *in order to* annoy me.'
— ALAIN DE BOTTON

Emotional resilience can be defined as how agile someone is when they encounter stress. When the rules of the game change, (when something breaks down, is late, or becomes obsolete) someone who is emotionally resilient will be able to find a new way to achieve their goal. Those with lower levels of emotional resilience have a harder time bouncing back from a setback and are often the subject of tech news headlines, kicking, screaming, and demanding we do things the old way.

Roadblocks are, at their most basic level, as big or small as your imagination. According to the ancient Roman rhetorician, Marcus Annaeus Seneca, each of us has a set of beliefs about how the world *should* work. When you encounter a setback, your beliefs are being challenged. One of your beliefs about the world is preventing you from moving forward. If you are able to change your belief, your actions will change naturally. For example, if I believe a project should be done one way and the client rejects it, I respond by listening to their needs and developing a new solution. You respond to a tough situation instead of reacting to it. This is what it means to be emotionally resilient.

The good news is emotional resilience can be learned and grown like a muscle. If you focus on the thoughts and feelings behind a goal, you will be able to identify the mental roadblocks that are shutting you down. The more you practice this, the stronger your emotional resilience will grow.

Emotional resilience is one of the most important factors in predicting how well someone will perform in their career. It's more important than IQ or advanced degrees in higher education. According to a study conducted by Vielife,

[Emotional resilience] has been found to be the strongest

predictor of job and career satisfaction, and higher levels of resilience can decrease employee turnover whilst maintaining high levels of motivation and commitment in workers.

As a worker in the Age of Agility, emotional resilience is a necessary skill to manage your response to change and failure in a world that is on the move.

Practice Failing

Ever tried. Ever failed. No matter. Try again. Fail again. Fail better.
— SAMUEL BECKETT

Failing early and often is part of every success story. If you have any fear of failure, now is the time to confront it. Now is the time to get comfortable with the uncomfortable feelings of rejection and embarrassment. The best way to do this is to practice. That's right. Practice failing. Here's the logic: you might get more bruises falling off 10 five-foot ladders, but a few bruises sure beats falling off one 50-foot rooftop. The longer you wait to fail, the more it's going to hurt and the longer it will take to recover.

An easy way to practice failing is by taking the Noah Kagan Coffee Challenge. All you do is ask for 10% off your beverage at your local coffee shop. Weird? Yes, and it will catch the cashier off-guard. They will tell you to repeat yourself because who in their right mind would be asking for 10% off? More than likely they will eventually tell you no (they may have to ask a manager). And that's the point! You just faced fear in the face and got rejected! You got outside of your comfort zone and grew your confidence. Want to take it to the next level? Kagan suggests sitting in the wrong seat the next time you board an airplane.

Training for failure grows your confidence so when you do make a mistake you can bounce back quickly. For more information, look in the back of the book at the references page to find a link to an article and video about the Kagan Coffee challenge. Good luck!

Key Takeaways

o   Work with an expert in a topic area to grow your skills. When you fail, they will guide you, so you bounce back faster and stronger.

o   Failure is a necessary part of success.

o How you respond to failure is critical.

o Use failure or rejection as a learning tool, rather than a reason to quit trying to achieve your goal.

o Don't fail the same way twice and always reflect on what you learned and need to change to achieve your desired outcome.

GOAL FOR TODAY: Take a reasonable risk where you put yourself in a position to fail. Make it something simple. When you fail, do so in a way that builds your emotional resilience. Respond instead of reacting. Then share your experience with a mentor or friend and ask them what they would have done.

1.2 LEARNING HOW YOU LEARN

The next cornerstone in your foundation is understanding how you learn. In the next two chapters, you will discover what types of learners there are, how you learn, and what you can do to encourage growth through learning.

THE LEARNING ZONE

If you dare nothing, then when the day is over, nothing is all you will have gained.
— NEIL GAIMAN, *The Graveyard Book*

In Hugh MacLeod's book, *The Art of Not Sucking*, he argues that the biggest fear college seniors have about graduating is not about failure or success in their first job, their biggest fear is looking like an amateur. It's not just college grads—for most us, our careers present opportunities to learn new techniques and technologies in order to stay current with the industry as it changes. Comfort, complacency, and laziness that sometimes comes with experience (a false sense of mastery), can get in the way of learning something that will add value to our lives or careers. If you are not willing to be a beginner again, you will never be able to start the learning process. In other words, you have to be willing to suck at something for a while before you learn how to be good at it.

I started running in early 2014 when my partner, Megan, told me she thought "we" should start working out because it wouldn't hurt to lose a couple pounds. Meaning, the by-the-slice pizza shop next to where I worked was having a field day with my waistline, and she wanted to nip it in the bud before my weight got out of hand.

The last time I had seriously exercised was in 2007 when I was on my high school's crew team—unless you count rolling around on stage with a guitar as exercise.

A little embarrassed (did I mention I hated even the idea of running?), I suggested we meet early in the morning, so we would be the only people on the streets.

A few minutes before 5 a.m., I showed up at Megan's apartment wearing my Chuck Taylor high tops, baggy basketball shorts from 8th grade, and an oversized cotton Marilyn Manson T-shirt. "How far are we going?" I asked. Megan, who looked like she had just popped out of a Nike billboard for urban cross-training, replied, "Probably two, two-and-a-half and then we can see how we are feeling." (Again, meaning, see how *I* am feeling). Half a mile in, my feet were feeling like they were origami, someone was trying to take out a kidney, and I'm pretty sure I was foaming at the mouth. As much as I didn't want to, I had to stop and walk. Running sucked and I sucked. I put my hands on my head, trying to control my breathing. A couple people came up behind us, power walking, to catch a bus. "It's alright," Megan said, "We'll go at our own pace. Slow is fine, we'll get faster. It's not a race. I think the first goal should be going the whole way without walking."

The problem was, I wanted to run as fast as I could because I didn't want to look weak and out of shape. In doing so, I burned myself out early, and would end up having to walk. The trick was starting slow, so I would have enough energy to finish the whole run. We took it slow and I eventually became comfortable with the pace, my pace, but it wasn't that easy. I've always had a problem with balance, my limbs are clunky, and it took a while for my legs and arms to get used to each other moving at the same time. Twice in the first month, I tripped and had to tuck and role on the sidewalk in front of a small audience of pedestrians in the Capitol Hill neighborhood of Seattle. I remember thinking, *learning something new is a lot harder than it used to be*, and I think it's because we rarely get a chance to be a beginner again. After our early 20's, we have forgotten how to be a beginner, so we avoid anything we don't already know how to do.

A year later, in 2015, Megan and I ran the Seattle half-marathon, something I never thought I would physically be capable of doing. We are still keeping at it, and we are running longer and faster each year. Hopefully, in the next year or two, we will work our way up to a full marathon—but we're taking it slow and at our own pace.

In a nutshell, learning begins when you leave what you know and start exploring new territory. Your starting point each day begins with the things you are familiar with: the knowledge you have already acquired and the tasks you can do without risk. This is called your comfort zone. In order to learn something new, you have to push beyond your comfort zone into a place where you are vulnerable, and the future is unknown.

Remember your lovely flying horses from the chapter on change? When you are learning something new, you are going through a transition, and along with transitions come your light and dark horse. Hello, old friends.

Your dark horse spends a lot of time in your comfort zone. Here, the dark horse is familiar, cozy, safe, and best of all, it doesn't need to take any risks. Problems arise when the dark horse uses your comfort zone against you, when your inner voice tugs towards comfort when you are faced with something new: "If life wasn't so difficult maybe I would try harder. I don't have time to try anything new." "Cake? You don't ask me twice. I never pass on dessert." "You should sleep in today. Everyone knows sleep is good for you." "Why are you applying for *that* job? They wouldn't hire you. I have a list of all your skills right here and that job is not on the list." "Can I just sit here and make money? Why don't you find a job where people just pay you for doing nothing?" Your comfort zone isn't all bad. In moderation, it is a safe place you can return to, and it allows you to reflect on your skills and make sense of recent events.

Your light horse, on the other hand, is always standing at the gate exiting your comfort zone, saying, "Coach, put me in coach. Coach? Put me in the game, coach." Your light horse is excited and wants to move you forward and start learning. Just outside of the security of your comfort zone is the learning zone where you can follow your curiosity. Here, you are exploring the edge of your limits, testing how far you can stretch your abilities, and, as a result, growing your comfort zone. It works only if you don't stray too far away from your comfort zone. Your light horse can be overconfident and might want to bite off more than it can chew. What might sound like a good idea in the planning stage may end up being unrealistic. You may be overconfident in your skills or the deadline could be too short. When this happens, you will stop making progress. Energy spent on learning will instead be used to cope with stress and anxiety.

Welcome to the panic zone. The panic zone is a little like overworking your muscles when you exercise. Sure, you might want to run 10 miles this weekend, but if this is your first day running in years and you aren't wearing the proper clothing or shoes, you are likely going to damage your body. In the panic zone, you bite off more than you can chew. You are so overwhelmed, learning ceases and you're stuck walking in circles, wondering where to begin.

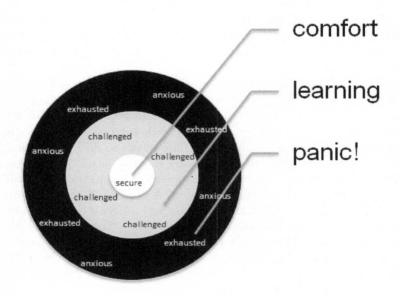

Successful learning happens just beyond your comfort zone. To get into the sweet spot, you need to motivate your dark horse to get out of the gate and pull back on your light horse so you don't go too far. The more you are in the learning zone, the wider your comfort zone will grow. Over time, your old panic zone will turn into your new learning zone and you will be able to take on more responsibilities and work on shorter deadlines.

Key Takeaways

o   Staying in your comfort zone will not allow you to grow, so you need to push yourself to do things you are not comfortable doing.

o   Pushing too hard will put you into your panic zone and you will likely stress and worry, limiting your ability to learn.

o   Working to stay out of your comfort zone while not extending so far you cannot grow is an important key to learning.

GOAL FOR TODAY: Think about a time when you spent a lot of time in the learning zone. What got you there and what kept you there? Next, think of a time when your light horse pulled you into the panic zone. What put you over the edge? Being aware of your comfort zone, learning zone, and panic zone will help you manage your horses and set achievable goals.

LEARNING STYLES

Everyone is a genius. But if you judge a fish by its ability to climb a tree, it will live its whole life believing that it is stupid.
— ALBERT EINSTEIN

Right now, your brain is learning. The question is, what is your brain paying attention to? The noises around you? The pattern on the wall or floor? The way you are holding this book or the position of your body? How much attention are you giving to the words on the page? As you are reading, how often are you stopping to clarify the concepts to yourself? How much of this will you remember tomorrow morning? If you don't already know how you learn, there are some tools I'll share with you so you can discover how you best take in information from the world. Knowing how people learn will give you many advantages including developing approaches to achieving goals and working with others.

Learning styles and cognitive approaches are huge topic areas and there are countless books written on the aspects of human learning behavior. Since this is only one chapter in one book, I am going to distillate and synthesize the basics. At a fundamental level, each person prefers one of the following learning methods:

Visual: Someone who learns best when information is depicted in maps, diagrams, charts, graphs, flow charts, and graphics. This kind of learning includes patterns, shapes, and whitespace. Enjoy drawing diagrams on a whiteboard? You might be a visual learner. Keep in mind visual learning does not include video. This would simulate kinesthetic learning (see below) and it also does not include slide presentations because slides are generally text-based.

Auditory: Someone who prefers information that is heard or spoken. This is a preference for lectures, group discussion, radio, phones, and web-chatting (like messenger). It also includes texting and email— wait, what? Doesn't that go in the next section? Yes and no, and here's why. In email and texting, we are often using a chat style of writing that mirrors talking. We use abbreviations, slang, and colloquial terms. And that's why auditory learning also includes talking. If you learn by talking about ideas (to yourself or others), you may be an auditory learner.

Reading/writing: Someone who prefers using text-based media. This type of learner prefers reading and writing manuals, reports, essays, and assignments, using PowerPoints, self-directed research on the internet, and reading and writing blog posts. When it comes to tackling a project, they enjoy making lists, using quotations, and anything to do with words.

Kinesthetic: Someone whose learning process includes touching, holding, tasting, or feeling. Kinesthetic learning also includes videos, as mentioned earlier, because videos simulate reality. When you go on YouTube and watch a video about how to take a screenshot of your desktop, it's similar enough to someone standing over your shoulder giving you directions. If you learn how to do something by digging in and doing the task, you may be a kinesthetic learner.

Multimodal: This is a fancy way of describing someone who doesn't have a preferred learning method or they are split between two of the above. This is uncommon because although we use all of these methods to take in information, there is usually a slight bias towards one style.

If you take the first letter of each learning method, you get the made-up word "vark". The VARK model was developed by Neil D. Fleming at Lincoln University in New Zealand. The model has been turned into a free online questionnaire that helps you discover your preferred learning style. If you're interested in taking the survey, go to **vark-learn.com/the-vark-questionnaire** and follow the instructions.

If you decide to take the VARK questionnaire, feel free to check more than one box if you feel like more than one describes you, or you can choose to not check any boxes if none of them sound like you.

Keep in mind that all questionnaires are based on self-reporting. You are plugging information into an equation that contextualizes it so you can understand yourself better. Basically, they put people into boxes. Boxes are good some of the time, however, the results should never be taken to mean all of the time. Use the results as a guide, never as an exact map. You may find that you are a different type of learner depending on the situation or topic. If I need to learn how to change my spark plugs, I'm better off learning it hands-on (kinesthetic) than reading or listening about it. However, if I'm learning how to change something in my settings on my laptop, I learn faster reading about it than asking someone to guide me, even though it's hands on. Learning how you learn will ensure quick and effective learning in every situation.

Key Takeaways

o   There are four primary ways we describe preferred learning methods: visual, auditory, reading/writing, and kinesthetic.

o   Knowing how you learn best will allow you to learn faster, and with greater recall.

o   Your preferred method of learning may change by activity.

GOAL FOR TODAY: Take the VARK questionnaire and share your results with one person you trust. To guide your discussion, think about the following questions: What type of learner are you? Did the results surprise you? Can you think of a time when you preferred to use a different learning method than the one you use the most?

1.3 WHAT DO YOU WANT OUT OF LIFE?

We've covered the basics: the benefits of carrying a notebook; how change, talent, motivation, and failure works; and lastly, how we learn. The next four chapters are going to be more personal. They cover topics ranging from leadership to career goals. They ask questions you may not know the answer to, and that's okay. The questions are exercises to get you thinking about the choices you will make in the future.

By the end of the next four chapters, you will have a better idea of what your career goals might be, how to talk about your goals, and what steps to take so they become obtainable. Before we begin, I want to start this section with a quote from Alan Watts' book, *The Book*.

...[Y]ou have been hypnotized or conditioned by an educational processing-system arranged in grades or steps, supposedly leading to some ultimate Success. First nursery school or kindergarten, then the grades or forms of elementary school, preparing you for the great moment of secondary school! But then more steps, up and up to the coveted goal of the university. Here, if you are clever, you can stay on indefinitely by getting into graduate school and becoming a permanent student. Otherwise, you are headed step by step for the great Outside World of family-raising, business, and profession. Yet graduation day is a very temporary fulfillment, for with your first sales promotion meeting you are back in the same old system, being urged to make that quota (and if you do, they'll give you a higher quota) and so progress up the ladder to sales manager, vice-president, and, at last, president of your own show (about forty to forty-five years old). In the meantime, the insurance and investment people have been interesting you in plans for Retirement—that really ultimate goal of being able to sit back and enjoy the fruits of all your labors. But when that day comes, your anxieties and exertions will have left you with a weak heart, false teeth, prostate trouble, sexual impotence, fuzzy eyesight, and a vile digestion.

—ALAN WATTS, *The Book*

LEAD OR FOLLOW

If everyone is thinking alike, then somebody isn't thinking.
— GEORGE S. PATTON

I grew up with a lot of traditional old-time-y sayings that encouraged hard work. Expressions like: "There are two kinds of people in the world, leaders and followers. Leaders push the world and followers sit back and enjoy the ride. Which one do you want to be?"

From resumes to internal employee reviews, business rewards workers who can sell their leadership qualities. In our culture, there is little acceptance for those who do not want to change the world. Those who want to enjoy their work and be good at it, but also have a family life or hobbies outside of their work are looked down upon. Popular business books ask, "If you aren't reinventing yourself, your image, your brand, then what are you doing?"

When did being "good" become not enough?

Most of us were raised in communities that rewarded leadership, extroversion, and Type-A personalities. Not only does having too many leaders create dysfunction, not everyone is looking to be a CEO or a leader on a team. So where does that leave those people who want to be a contributing member of a team, enjoy their work, but at the end of the day be able to go home and put their work on the back burner?

The Fisherman Fable

The fisherman fable is a business story that has been told so many times, its origin is unknown. Paulo Coelho, the famous Brazilian novelist, claims that it is a classic Brazilian story, though different versions appear in other cultures. Many scholars cite the German author Heinrich Böll. Still, others make the argument that Böll merely popularized the spoken word story by putting it down on paper and its roots are in a Buddhist or Russian fable. Regardless of origin, I am going to share the version of the story I remember being told.

A wealthy businessman was vacationing on a small island in the Pacific. From his hotel room, he saw a fisherman walk to the beach every morning and row out to sea. A few hours later, the fisherman would return with his boat filled with his morning catch.

One morning, the businessman left his hotel room and met the fisherman on the beach. He said, "Your skills are very impressive. You can catch an entire boatload of fish in one morning."

The fisherman nodded and accepted the praise.

The businessman continued, "Why do you only fish in the morning? Why not drop off your catch and go out a second or third time?"

The fisherman shrugged his shoulders and replied, "I don't need any more fish. What I catch is enough for my family to eat and sell at the market."

The businessman thought for a moment and asked, "What do you do the rest of the day?"

The fisherman replied, "Well, I wake up in the morning and go fish. And then I go home and have lunch with my partner. In the afternoon, my children come home from school and we play before dinner. In the evening, we join our friends and neighbors in town for a drink. We sing, dance, tell jokes, and catch up on the village gossip."

The businessman smiled and said, "You are a lucky man. But, you see you could be luckier. I am a business development manager at a very impressive company and I'm going to give you some advice to be more successful."

The fisherman stood and listened.

"You should spend more time fishing," the businessman started, "You should be going out two or three times instead of just once so you can catch as many fish as you can, so you can make a bigger profit. When you have enough saved up, you can buy a bigger boat and with a bigger boat comes more fish per trip. With those profits you can buy more boats, so you have a fleet of fishing boats. With that, you can set up your own processing facility."

The fisherman scratched his head, "Why would I do that?"

"So you can clean the fish, process the meat, and sell abroad," the businessman replied. "You are living on a gold mine here; don't you get it? The company will get so big you can sell it or go public. You'll make millions!"

"Why would I want to do that?" the fisherman asked.

"So you can retire and never need to work again! You can move into a big house, wake up in the morning and go fishing, and have enough time to play with your kids and spend time with your wife. And then at night you can watch the sunset, go into town with your buddies and drink, sing, and dance."

The fisherman looked down at the net in his hands and then over to the small rowboat filled with all his fishing gear. His eyes met the businessman. Puzzled, the fisherman said, "Isn't that what I am doing now?"

You Don't Need to be a Leader to be Successful or Happy

Like the fisherman fable, there is something to be said for enjoying the work you do. I believe everyone has the potential to be a leader, however, many choose not to act on their potential because their goals do not include leadership. Not everyone wants to be a manager of people, some would rather focus on growing a skill or working on tasks independently. It takes all kinds of people to make this world turn, not just leaders.

Some vocations are as good as a vacation because each morning you wake up excited for the day ahead. Too often, we work hard so we can enjoy a few hours of peace, but those few hours of relaxation are often interrupted by thoughts of work to do the next day, so you never get a break from the stress.

As you are discovering where you fit in your organization or career, ask yourself these three questions:

Why do you do what you do? If you take a leadership role you don't want, you probably won't be effective. Instead, you will be a burden on the company and you will be taking an opportunity from someone who could use it to excel in their career. More importantly, you won't be utilizing your own potential.

Is this a career or a job? Are you a leader out of the pride you have for the project you are working on, or, is this job a paycheck J-O-B? There is no shame in working a "paycheck" job, but make sure you are putting in the hours and/or energy expected for that position.

What is the time commitment? If you are working on moving up at your company or in the industry, you need to increase your time and effort. It's easy to talk about making progress, but to move ahead, you need to buckle down and do the work. Make sure you are putting in the right amount of time to achieve the goals you have set for yourself.

If your goal is to become a VP or CEO, keep in mind that every career has pluses and minuses, and the minuses should be tolerable. If you can accept the challenges that come along with a leadership position, by all means, go for it! What's important is finding a career where you can grow and follow your passion.

Key Takeaways

o   Becoming a leader and being viewed by others as a success may not be satisfying to you.

o   Being good at something, enjoying your craft, and having a balance between your work and personal life is a fine goal.

o   Work at what makes you happy, not what makes others happy.

GOAL FOR TODAY: Take a moment to think about your life and reflect on the following questions: 1) What are your priorities? 2) How involved do you want to be in your career? Deciding how much time and energy you want to invest in your career will prepare you for the next few chapters when you decide which direction you want to head towards.

CAREER GOALS

I wanted only to live in accord with the promptings which came from my true self. Why was that so very difficult?
— HERMANN HESSE, *Demian*

A popular tactic in mainstream business development books (and now, podcasts) is to tell stories about how a CEO or entrepreneur found their life's purpose after having a supernatural experience: a vision from God during a near-death experience, a life-changing dream where a deceased relative came to them and suggested starting a company, or how one day while sitting on a park bench, the wind blew against their cheek just right and it whispered insights about a career path and suddenly they were filled with joy and purpose.

This is not one of those books.

Since most of us will never receive any divine intervention telling us if we are on the correct career track, we have to rely on other measures to validate we are on the right path. This means we are in the driver's seat. We are responsible for exploring career opportunities, taking risks, and rolling with what life gives us. We are responsible for calling it quits when something isn't working, and we decide when to value our happiness over a paycheck. We are also responsible for gathering our courage and applying to positions in uncharted territories. My experience navigating these rough waters brought me to three harsh truths.

Three Harsh Truths
1. If you are unhappy, you are the only one who can change it.
2. You are responsible for the choices you make.
3. Finding your fit in the world is tough. At times, you might feel like you have a lot of skills but not know where or how they align with a career.

As I began making some progress on my goals, I started seeing the world differently. With a growth mindset, my harsh truths turned into enlightening truths.

Three Enlightening Truths
1. You have the power, energy, and skills inside you to achieve great things.
2. You have opportunities all around you that will lead to happiness in a career you love.
3. If you are persistent in your search, you will find it.

These harsh and enlightening truths are important to remember when thinking about your future. Thinking about tomorrow is a challenging and daunting task. Honestly, it can be downright discouraging. If you keep these truths in mind, you will find the will to push through.

Finding Your Passion
Finding a career you are passionate about is one of the hardest questions to answer. Most people know what they like spending their time on, but have a hard time putting it into the context of a vocation or how to make money doing it. To start, ask yourself the following questions:

- What tasks do you get caught up in where you lose track of time?
- Do you have something you are always thinking about in the back of your mind? When you see something or get an idea, your first thought is how it applies to... (some examples) politics, writing, film, music, food, business, education, teaching, helping your community, games or puzzles, your family.

- Do you have a hobby you can turn a profit with? (A side gig).
- What types of articles are you drawn to? What movies or TV shows do you choose to watch? What types of books do you like to read? Does your life have a theme you might be unaware of?
- What kinds of compliments have you gotten throughout your life? Do any specific compliments stand out? Since childhood, have people always told you that you were... (examples) Creative? Good with money? Good at talking with people when they're sad?

The activities, places, or people you are naturally drawn to might be hidden areas of passion. As you think through the above questions, try to find a common thread or identify why you excelled at something. When you find a "why", as in, "why do I like this", the next step is finding a "how", as in, "how can I add value to a company or make a living at this?"

Make Two Lists

Most of the time, people already have the basic skills to excel in a career, but they are unsure how to organize their strengths and focus on a single goal or career. This exercise will help you find your focus.

On the left side of a piece of paper, make a list of your preferred method(s) of learning and skills. Some examples may be: coding /writing programs, teaching, following written instruction, verbal communication, working with my hands, listening to people, developing strategies, working by myself. On the right side of the same piece of paper, make a list of causes or topics you care about. Some examples are: homelessness, food quality/nutrition, swimming, education, the elderly, research, writing, the arts, investing.

Skills	Interests
Coding/writing programs	Homelessness
Teaching	Food quality/nutrition
Following written instructions	Swimming
Verbal communication	Education
Working with my hands	The elderly population
Listening to people	Research and writing
Developing strategies	The arts
Working by myself	Investing

Your "sweet spot" is where your interests intersect with your skills. In other words, it's where what you like to do connects with the things you care about. This intersection is where your dream job is hiding.

Using the list above, try making connections between this person's skills and interests. The more connections, the better. Here's what I came up with:

> **Two Connections:** Coding + Swimming = App designer specializing in athletic wearable technology

> **Eight Connections:** Working Hands On + Teaching + Developing Strategies + Verbal Communication + Food Quality/ Nutrition + Education + Homeless Population + The Elderly Population = Building a Community Food Forest

Here are some more examples:

> **BEN:** Ben loves playing video games, so he writes *video games* on the right side of the page. He doesn't want to write code or develop any techie stuff that requires 1's and 0's (geek talk for binary code, meaning, computer programing), the very things his parents keep urging him to do. What he's good at is telling stories, editing written language, and working together with others on a team (he plays a lot of co-op games). Ben writes *story-telling, editing written language,* and *team collaboration* on the left side of the paper. Putting it all together and looking for connections, one of Ben's sweet spots would include video games and story design. A possible career option would be working with a team of writers creating story lines for video games. Other areas Ben could explore are marketing and copywriting.

> **SARAH:** Sarah graduated with a bachelor's degree in communications. Although she identifies more with introverts, she enjoys working with others on a team, but it doesn't come naturally. She takes pride in her interpersonal communication skills because it is something she has spent a lot of time working on. She writes *working with others* and *interpersonal communication* in the skills section on the left side of the paper. Since Sarah naturally works best alone, she writes *working independently* on the

left side of the paper as one of her traits.

In college, Sarah worked as a server at a nice restaurant downtown, and remembers enjoying the strategy of negotiating reservations and planning events, days or weeks in advance. She writes *planning* and *time management* on the right side of her piece of paper. One of Sarah's sweet spots would include working with people and having the ability to work independently. Sarah's sweet spot would also involve strategies in planning for events in the future. A career area Sarah might look into would be product development, working with a team where she could work a majority of the time alone on a product before a deadline, but still be on a team to talk strategy.

This exercise might be tough, so you may need to talk about it with a friend or colleague in your network. It may not seem like it now, but there is a career for everyone, and if you can't find it, create it. Don't underestimate how big the world is.

Visualize Your Future
When you start thinking about career choices, visualize where you want your career to take you. To begin thinking about your future, reflect on the scenarios below. This exercise will push you to think abstractly and creatively. Even if it sounds silly, try it out. If one of the scenarios makes you feel uncomfortable, ask: why does thinking about the future or past make me feel (name the exact feelings here)?

- Pretend you are hovering above your body so you have a bird's eye view looking down at yourself. With your mind, you can rewind back through time all the way back your birth. If you were to watch the last few weeks of your life and keep on going into the future, what do you think happens next? In other words, if your life was a movie and you were the main character, what would you do next?

- If someone were to take a picture of you six months from now, what would you be doing in the picture? What mood are you in? What or who is in that photo with you?

- Imagine if before you were born you were able to choose your life. This includes all its hardships, stress, joys, and wonder. In this thought experiment, you were able to choose this life from the billions of others you could have chosen. You chose this life for a reason—why did you choose this life? Why did you choose your family? Friends? Why did you decide to pick up this book? If you chose the people and events in your life, what clues did you leave for yourself to remind you of your meaningful and fulfilling life in the future?

- Imagine it is many years in the future and you have less than a week to live. On your deathbed, you are reflecting on your life. What in your life are you proud of? How do you want people to remember you? Is there anything you wished you could have done differently? This is the question Leo Tolstoy asks his readers to consider in his novella *The Death of Ivan Ilyich*. I know it's macabre, but questions like this prompt us to take an inventory of our lives, often enlightening a passion that has been hidden behind the bustle of daily life.

- You might need your notebook for this one. Imagine a door partway open with every possible career you desire behind it. If you have a lot of experience in a particular field or you have management experience, your door opens a little wider. If you have a bachelor's degree, it opens a little wider. If you have a degree or certifications beyond that, it opens wider still. The more education or experience you have, the wider the door opens to potential careers. Next, start making a list of things you want in your life that you are not willing to give up. Examples might be location, standard of living, or not working on weekends. With each addition you make, the door is going to close a little. Now make a list of things you want in a career. How much time do you want to spend behind a desk? With people? Traveling? The door closes a little more, narrowing your career choices. With your three lists: experience (door opening), deal breakers (door closing), and desires (door closing), what career options do you have left?

The Light/Heavy Test

When you're faced with a lot of choices and don't know what to do, close your eyes and take a breath. Ask yourself: does doing [career choice X] make me feel light or heavy? Does not doing X make me feel light or heavy?

Next, ask yourself why it makes you feel that way. Do you feel heavy because you are taking a risk you know you need to take but the road ahead will be difficult, or do you feel heaviness because your choice contracts one of your values? If you feel light, is it because it's too easy and it will not be a challenge? Or do you feel light because the choice will move you closer to your goals?

After taking some time to think about the causes of the feelings, ask yourself the first question again: does doing X make me feel light or heavy? Does not doing X make me feel light or heavy?

Do what feels light, and move forward with confidence.

Any Questions?

Finding your passion and developing career goals is no easy feat, and a lot of people run into challenges along the way. If you are struggling, you are not alone. The following are the most frequently asked questions I have received about taking chances and moving forward with a new career.

Q: I hate my job. I don't love doing what I do, the pay sucks, and my managers are a—holes. Can I quit on the spot right now?

A: Between the ages of 18 and 67 (retirement), you have 2,548 weekly paychecks. If you leave your job feeling drained and miserable, take a personal day and ask yourself if it's worth the paycheck. If you know that you mentally cannot handle the job, or you can't find a new job while working, quit. Easy as that. Spending time doing something you despise hurts you and the company. If it feels like you have a boat anchor around your neck, untie it and swim! (the light/heavy test). In Part 3, there is a chapter about managing your finances. There, you will learn about saving for an emergency fund. Before quitting your job, make sure you have enough saved to manage this transition. Now that you're unemployed, let's get you back to work, and quick! Your new full-time job is to find a job. Plant yourself down at your laptop or a computer at the library for eight hours a day to get started. If you qualify for unemployment, it's there to be used as a tool to get by while you are out of work. Use it, but don't rely on it as a long-term solution.

Q: My current job isn't my dream job, but I need it to pay the bills. Should I quit?

A: Great! You've identified that this is a J-O-B. Not a career. Continue building your skills while you work on finding a job that better meets your career goals (even if it's management or communication styles you want to avoid in the future). Make an exit plan and when you have the next stepping stone in place, leap! It's okay to tell yourself that this isn't where you want to be, especially if you know there is a better place you're going. Admitting that this job is temporary will make you feel less tied down to your current position.

Q: I'm working at a good company, but I'm not doing what I love. I can't decide if I should start looking for a new position or wait until there's a chance to move up in the company. I'm good at what I do, but I don't know if it's my true calling. I sometimes wonder if I would be happier somewhere else. Things are good here, so I don't want to leave what I know is stable. What if I take a new job and I regret making the transition?

A: Sounds comfortable, but moving towards claustrophobic. Here's the best advice I have at the moment. Sustainable Evolution Inc. (the publisher of this book) encourages all their employees to interview with at least one other company every six months. The main reason is to practice your interviewing skills. Being able to talk confidently about where you are now and where you want to be provides an often-overlooked insight to your current state and desired future state. Sometimes you don't know the answer until you are in the situation. You don't need to take the job, going through the motions is the exercise. The act of interviewing may confirm the position you have or it may push you in another direction.

It's true, some jobs lead to your dream job. If you stick around, you may eventually move up in the company to a position that better fits your career goals. That's a big IF. Put a time limit on how long you're willing to wait and always (always) be interviewing.

Key Takeaways

o   You control your future and your career choices.

o   Work first to discover your passion. Your passion will lead to your career goals.

o   Visualize yourself in 6 months, a few years, several years, and at retirement, and what you want your personal and work life to help you accomplish.

o   Make a list with two columns; on the left list your skills and on the right list what you care about. Then, identify where the two lists intersect or complement each other.

o   Reflect on the areas of intersection and think about how you feel about each—excited and light in spirit, or unexcited and heavier in spirit.

GOAL FOR TODAY: Try at least one of the strategies I mentioned in this chapter. Write about your experience or talk about it with a friend. Does seeing it written out in front of you change anything? Does talking about it with a friend confirm your thoughts?

WHAT WE TALK ABOUT WHEN WE TALK ABOUT GOALS

Language disguises thought.
— LUDWIG WITTGENSTEIN, *Tractatus Logico-Philosophicus*

Two data points.

1. A 2016 article in Forbes put a price tag of 10 billion dollars per year on the self-improvement industry. That's business in the U.S. alone.

2. In 2017, Business Insider reported 80% of New Year's resolutions fail by February.

Interpretation: A lot of money is invested in setting goals and a majority of people in the U.S. have a hard time following through.

While billions of dollars are spent each year fixing symptoms and contributing factors, the root cause continues to be overlooked. Goals, at their most basic level, are language. If language is at the foundation of setting a successful goal, *how* someone talks about their goals affects the outcome. The untapped billion-dollar answer could be in something called Neuro-Linguistic Programming, or NLP for short.

Neuro-Linguistic Programming

NLP is a communication approach that focuses on how language affects the nervous system. The theory is, we have an emotional response to signs and symbols, the most popular being language. How and why we respond is a combination of our past experiences and our present sensory interpretation. Before I get too far ahead of myself, let's look at the definition of each word that makes up NLP:

Neuro: indicating a nerve or the nervous system.

Linguistic(s): the science of language, including phonetics, phonology, morphology, syntax, semantics, pragmatics, and historical linguistics.

Programming: to train; predispose by rigorous teaching, condition.

So, what does this mean? At its most basic level, it means that word choice can be strategically used to affect how we think. Since there is a direct link between language to our nervous system, language has the power to shape our sensory impressions, making what we say very important. NLP has been successful in helping people work towards their goals, fight phobias, change habits, and emulate patterns of success.

Here's an example of how it works:

Each word and symbol we encounter has an associated trigger. If you hear or read the word "cat", your brain sends signals to your body based on your associations. Right now, you are probably thinking about the furry domesticated pet that says "meow". Along with the description of "cat" comes your personal feelings, positive or negative. If you were attacked by a cat as a child or can't stand them for another reason, your associations with the word are negative. If you own a cat or two (or three or four or…) or enjoy petting and playing with them, your associations are probably positive. That means when someone uses this word, depending on your association, you have a slight positive or negative feeling.

Here's an example of how language affects your nervous system:

Imagine you are sitting at your kitchen table with a bowl of freshly cut lemon slices in front of you. Using your dominant hand, take a lemon slice and raise it so it is just below your nose. Not too far, you don't want to get any juice on your upper lip. Take a breath. Can you smell it? Can you feel the moist yellow skin in your hand? Bring the lemon closer and place it in your mouth. Bite down and slowly begin to chew, making sure to grind your molars on its soft oily skin.

What did your face do? What happened in your mouth? Did your face pucker? Did your mouth start producing saliva? Besides the lemon, did any words stick out? I planted a few, did you catch any of them? The one that sticks out to me is the word "moist". Some people have an immediate aversion to words like "moist" and using it here causes most people to pucker more, even before they bite down and start chewing on the metaphorical lemon. (If you are looking for another example, I wrote a more descriptive paragraph about a tart cherry pie in the Notes & References section in the back of this book.)

When you're reading in a book about a spider crawling on a character's neck, do you feel a tingling sensation on your neck as well? When you hear someone talking about mosquito bites or a sunburn, how does your skin feel? The interplay between mind and body occurs millions of times throughout the day and most of the time we are unaware of it. Someone who is self-aware and knows their NLP triggers can manipulate their environment to affect a desired outcome. What does this have to do with goal setting? People who use NLP can engineer positive associations around a goal, making it easier to achieve.

The Positive Outcome Strategy

The Positive Outcome Strategy (POS) is a goal-setting approach that uses NLP to positively reinforce the desired outcome of a goal. That's a mouthful, so let's work through an example.

Anne is choosing to eat healthier and exercise, with the end goal of losing some weight. When she talks to her friends about her new lifestyle change, what does she say? If she tells herself and her friends that she is trying to lose weight, she may be unconsciously making it harder for herself.

Here's why.

Every time Anne says she is trying to lose weight (or thinks it), she is saying that she is currently not at her ideal weight. This triggers an earthquake of negative feelings associated with body image. Instead of focusing on the healthier person she is becoming (something positive), the words are triggering the non-ideal image she has of herself (something negative).

Let's break Anne's goal down so we can identify what she is working to achieve. Anne is choosing to eat right and exercise so she can tone her body and feel more energized. Instead of telling her friends (and herself) that she is trying to lose weight, she can say that she is achieving her ideal weight.

Here are a few more examples:

I am becoming more present earlier in the morning. Revised from: I want to wake up earlier in the morning.

I am learning to enjoy each breath as it comes. Revised from: I want to quit smoking.

I am taking an interest in how my actions can inspire others to use their time more efficiently. Revised from: I want to be an effective manager so I can get a promotion at the company I am working for.

When you are creating your own POS, focus on the positive aspects you are trying to accomplish. Ask yourself: what are you really changing and how can you use words that encourage a positive change? The more specific you can be, the better. In addition, it's helpful to use a progressive verb (verb + -ing) when constructing your POS: becoming, learning, taking. These words signal that you are always making progress, so when you talk about your goal it feels more obtainable. On a final note, I want to be clear that these are not positive aphorisms; your POS is an honest goal reframed so you can push with, not against, the emotional side of change.

Key Takeaways

o   Goals are made of words, and words matter because they

have power.

o Rather than describing the negative behavior you want to stop, reword your goal so it highlights the positive aspects.

o When you focus on the positives of your goal, you will be inspired by the things you can do instead of the things you can't.

GOAL FOR TODAY: Think of a goal you recently made and reframe it using the Positive Outcome Strategy.

ACCOMPLISHING YOUR GOALS

...that's why they're in such a bad place. It's not that they're cramming for some project. It's that long-term procrastination has made them feel like a spectator, at times, in their own lives. The frustration is not that they couldn't achieve their dreams; it's that they weren't even able to start chasing them.

— TIM URBAN, from his TED Talk: *Inside the mind of a master procrastinator*

Hopefully, the last few chapters have sparked your thinking about goals. Now that you have one or more in mind, the next step is following through. The following steps will help you construct an actionable and achievable goal.

Set a Deadline

If your dreams do not have deadline, you will never start working on them. While we diligently work to complete tasks for others at work or at school, we rarely set deadlines for our own personal goals. Whatever goal you have kicking around in the back of your head: a career change, moving into a different career or position, writing a novel, starting a company, going back to school, learning how to brew beer, or planting a garden, you need to have a deadline, so you will be motivated to start working on it today. After you figure out what your goal is, your deadline is the next step.

Setting a deadline is tough. You want to set it close enough, so you don't procrastinate, but also give yourself enough time to complete the task so you don't bump out of the learning zone and into the panic zone. When you set your deadline, ask yourself if you will be able to make progress on it every day. Parkinson's Law says that work expands to fit a deadline, so this means that if you give yourself three months to complete a project, the work will be enough to take three months to complete. If you set a deadline for the same project at six months, the work will expand into six months of work. The more time given to complete a project, the longer it will take to finish. We rarely finish anything early. If you are able to make progress on your goal each day, challenge yourself until you feel like you are in the middle of your learning zone. If other projects slow you down or if you need to accomplish more one week, you can ramp up your daily progress. If another project needs your attention, you can cut down on your time as long as you are still making daily progress.

Another law dealing with deadlines is Hofstadter's Law, which states: "It always takes longer than you expect, even when you take into account Hofstadter's Law." This means that people generally have a hard time meeting their deadline on time (even with Parkinson's Law, work expands past the deadline). If there is even a sliver of doubt that you will not be able to meet your deadline, make two. The first is the deadline you would *like* to hit and the second is the deadline you *need* to hit. As you are plotting out your strategy, make the timetable according to your first goal, knowing the second deadline is to account for Hofstadter's Law. Each week check your progress against your *like* deadline. If you are making daily progress but not at the rate you expected, revise your strategy and deadline accordingly.

Set a Strategy

Once you have a goal and a deadline, the next step is setting a strategy. The easiest way to work on a project is to outline the entire process, from start to finish. Even if you end up changing your plans, it will give you a big picture for what the whole journey might look like. Doing this will provide you with the necessary information to get the first steps in motion.

When you start your outline, think of the five or six major events or milestones you want to achieve. Once you have the major milestones identified, break each one down into smaller steps. From here, you can break your milestones down into weekly or bi-weekly sprints. When you are planning your sprint, you should identify all the tasks that need to be accomplished to achieve your sprint milestone. Capture each task and write it in a chart you can visualize. A whiteboard, notebook, or an online application like Trello are all great places to record your steps.

Next, break your chart into three columns: To Do, Doing, and Done. On Day 1 of your sprint, list everything that needs to get done during that sprint cycle in the "To Do" column. Assign yourself two or three tasks at a time. Once a task is assigned, it moves into the "Doing" column. As each task gets completed, it moves into the "Done" column.

To Do	Doing	Done!

Breaking milestones down into small achievable tasks will reduce stress and provide a reasonable plan to achieve your goal. Before you start your day, spend 15 minutes each morning reflecting on what you accomplished yesterday, what you are going to work on today, and how you are progressing towards your milestone.

If you are working with others, there are a few important things to keep in mind for this to be successful. Every morning, your team should meet for 15 minutes to discuss progress updates, the day's tasks, and to voice any suggestions or changes to the sprint or final goal. In some circles, this is called a stand-up meeting because traditionally everyone is standing to reinforce the time constraint. Being on your feet instills a sense of urgency. During and after this meeting, communication is the key to success. Having regular check-ins with your team to see if the goals have changed will keep you focused on the most important tasks.

Set an Intention

The state of mind must be BELIEF, not mere hope or wish. Open-mindedness is essential for belief. Closed minds do not inspire faith, courage, and belief.
— NAPOLEON HILL

Napoleon Hill popularized intention setting in his book *Think and Grow Rich*, the same book I cited in the chapter on failure. Hill found that intention setting was used by every successful person he interviewed in his 20-year study of modern business, including notable figures of the time such as Andrew Carnegie, Thomas Edison, and Henry Ford.

Intention setting is when you state a clearly defined goal you believe you will achieve. The theory is, since we are the stories we tell ourselves, intention setting replaces our fear-based stories with success stories. If you think there is a possibility of not reaching your goal and that you may waste years of your life chasing something that may fail, you have already failed. There are no capital "F" failures in intention setting, there are only those who choose to give up and those who see failure as a stepping stone to success. Someone who sets an intention does not see failure as defeat but a necessary condition of success. Intention setting breaks the negative feedback loop of failure and looks beyond it so you can see yourself in your desired future state. Once you have a well-defined focus, you can make better use of your time and energy. Instead of making a foot of progress in every direction, you will go a mile in the one direction you are focused on.

Napoleon Hill developed a six-step process for intention setting. Since *Think and Grow Rich* was published 80 years ago, I revised the steps to meet our current language and culture.

Napoleon Hill's Six Steps (revised for the 21st century)

1. Think about the goal you want to achieve. Be exact in the outcome and make sure it is something you can visualize. (Something tangible and measurable, nothing vague.)

2. Determine what you are willing to give in return for your goal. There is a balance to the universe and you must be willing to give up something to achieve your goal. (Time, weekends, pride, ethics, responsibility…)

3. Set an exact date when you intend on achieving your goal. (This is your deadline.)

4. Create a well-defined plan for carrying out your goal and start immediately! If you don't start today, you may keep putting it off. For this to work, you must start today. (This is your strategy.)

5. Write your goal, deadline, and the steps you are going to take to achieve your goal. (This is your contract with yourself.)

6. Read your written statement out loud twice a day. Read it once before going to bed and once when you get up in the morning. As you read, SEE and FEEL and BELIEVE yourself already in possession of your goal. (Your goal is now a part of your daily routine.)

Have Your Network Hold You Accountable

Once you have a deadline, strategy, and intention for accomplishing your goal, what's left is rallying support from your network. In addition to the people you already count on, you should join a community of people who are working on similar goals. If you want to write a novel, join a writing group. If you want to start a company, join a Meetup group in your community for small business owners and entrepreneurs. Or, tell a friend or family member about your goal, plan, and deadline. Ask them to check in with you weekly to see how you are progressing. We are stronger together in the networks we form. A community holds us to our word and supports us when we encounter a setback.

Key Takeaways

o When you set a goal, set a timeframe and two due dates. The first is a soft deadline, one that you would like to make, and the second is a hard deadline, one that you need to make.

o Define the strategy and first steps to achieve your goal and take the first step.

o   Describe and document your intentions.

o   Give this information to people in your network and ask them to hold you accountable.

> **GOAL FOR TODAY:** Come up with at least one goal you want to accomplish in the next month. It can be as small or big as you feel comfortable with, so long as you set a goal. Create a strategy to accomplish this goal and an intention to help you commit.

1.4 BEATING THE CLOCK

You've done all the preparation: you have a goal, a plan, and a deadline. Now, it's time to step away from the drawing board, step back into reality, and put all the pieces in motion. The new challenge is sticking to your plan while meeting the demands of your busy life. In the next four chapters, you will learn about motivation, how to manage your time and yourself, and finally, creative strategies for when you are stuck. Onward friends, to productivity!

MOTIVATION

When I was 5 years old, my mother always told me that happiness was the key to life. When I went to school, they asked me what I wanted to be when I grew up. I wrote down 'happy'. They told me I didn't understand the assignment, and I told them they didn't understand life.
— JOHN LENNON

When people are in fear, they don't want to go to work. So many people today have that feeling. Then the fear starts turning into hate, and they begin to hate going to work. ... Instead of instilling fear, if a company offered a way for everyone in the business to dive within—to start expanding energy and intelligence—people would work overtime for free. They would be far more creative. And the company would just leap forward.
— DAVID LYNCH

In *The Prince*, published in 1532, Niccolò Machiavelli asks if it is better to motivate others by being cruel or showing mercy? Nearly 500 years later, Machiavelli's question is still being used to guide management styles, motivate employees, and promote productivity.

Employers are asking, does an employee work harder if they know they might lose their job if they don't prove their value to the company? Or does a company get better results when an employee is given the freedom to work on the projects that interest them? This question centers around two types of motivation: Do people work better when they are motivated by external forces like rewards and discipline or is it better when people follow their internal motivation, like passion or enjoyment?

Carrots & Sticks: Extrinsic Motivation

Up until 2013, working at Microsoft looked a lot like the game show Survivor. Once a year, every department would rank their team members based on how well they thought they were contributing to the group. On a scale from one to five, one being the best and five being the worst, each person would decide the fate of their peers. The better an employee's score, the higher their bonus. The lower their score and they lose their bonus. If someone is ranked in the bottom 5%-10%, they would be asked to pack up their desk and return their ID card. Here's where it gets interesting: each team member can only give out a limited amount of each number. Meaning, they couldn't go around giving everyone on their team a one or five. Their peers are their competition. The better they do, the worse they looked. Microsoft wasn't alone in doing this. In 2012, 60% of Fortune 500 companies used a similar structure to determine the effectiveness of their employees, but most are now turning away from the practice.

This process of ranking employees is called stack ranking and it's based on the Pareto Principle, better known as the 80/20 rule or "Law of the Vital Few." It works like this: About 80% of the results come from 20% of the effort. Meaning, the top 20% of employees working at an organization are doing 80% of the work. It also means that 80% of the errors in a company are caused by 20% of the employees. In stack ranking, eliminating the bottom 10% makes sense in the company's ledger because these people aren't contributing anything to the organization, or so the principle postulates. In the 20th century, the Pareto Principle became a kind of golden ratio in business. To give you an idea of how the principle works, here are a few other examples: 20% of your customer base will be responsible for 80% of your sales, 20% of people own 80% of the land in any given area, 20% of your effort will be responsible for

80% of your daily output, and 20% of the peapods in your garden will be responsible for 80% of your peas. The figures might change slightly, and if they do, the ratio is more likely to tilt upwards: 10:90, 5:95, and even 1:99.

Back at Microsoft, stack rankings created a cut-throat culture of deception, backstabbing, and bullying, such as a few individuals ganging up on a specific team member in order to save themselves. As a result, talented employees didn't want to work with each other for fear of losing out on their bonuses or their position. Microsoft lost its drive for innovation and fell behind the pack.

This kind of motivation is called extrinsic motivation and is defined as the drive to action that springs from outside influences instead of from one's own feelings. Examples of extrinsic motivators include: money, rewards, bonuses, praise, trophies, fame, and grades.

Extrinsic motivation sounds like a great idea, but it often spirals out of control and turns an activity someone initially enjoyed doing for fun into tedious or stressful work. It is a slippery slope that can unintentionally promote bad behaviors, such as overcharging customers to meet sales quotas and taking short-cuts that are risky and may cost more in the long run. As I mentioned earlier, 60% of Fortune 500 companies have tried extrinsic motivators like stack ranking and some saw short-term results, but since 2012, many have abandoned the practice because it ended up costing the company more than they initially made. On an individual level, extrinsic motivation fails in countless ways. If the compensation for the work goes away, people generally stop doing the activity, even if it was something they didn't mind doing before there was a reward. That's why at companies like 3M, the Pareto Principle is seen as a way to manage innovation, not people's jobs.

Beyond Carrots & Sticks: Intrinsic Motivation

3M is a hotbed for new ideas. They are the winner of the National Medal of Technology, one of the highest awards for innovation, and frequently appear on lists of the most admired corporations in the United States. What's their secret? Since 1948, they have encouraged every one of their employees, not just their engineers, to spend 15% of their time exploring and experimenting with any project of their choosing. 3M's philosophy is simple: people are more productive when they are motivated by their interests. If someone is following their passion, they will not only be dedicated, they will be excited.

This excitement leads to self-imposed goals and better craftsmanship, which go above and beyond those set by management.

William McKnight, chairman of 3M's board, famously said: "if you put fences around people, you get sheep." At 3M, employees are free to roam outside of the fence and for the last 70 years, it has worked. 3M has well over 22,000 patents, and most of them have come from 15% time. Other companies have borrowed 3M's philosophy with success. Notably, Google engineers are encouraged to spend one day a week on a 20% project, where they are free to work on what they think may benefit the company most. Successful projects in the past have been Gmail, Google News, and AdSense.

This kind of motivation is called intrinsic motivation. It is the drive to adopt or change behavior for someone's own internal satisfaction or fulfillment. Examples include: purpose, self-mastery, joy, personal fulfillment, connecting with others, and progress. In short, your job should not be a "job," but a hobby you happen to be compensated for. If you can't find your passion at work, you may want to rethink your career path (reread Career Goals). Identify tasks or jobs you would enjoy doing, and get started looking to those career options.

The old carrot and stick model doesn't work anymore, and perhaps, never worked. Fear-based motivation and rewards can only inspire so much before it starts to backfire. When you are working on a project or setting a goal for yourself, think about what is motivating you. Is it for money, glory, or status? Or is it something you can truly engage with?

Key Takeaways

o   Beware of companies who value short-term profit over long-term curiosity. Real productivity comes from self-motivated employees, not iron-fisted managers.

o   Working for self-satisfaction and personal curiosity (intrinsic motivation) is a bigger motivator than money or fame (extrinsic motivation).

o   A sense of urgency can get in the way of a purpose or your passion. Be mindful while working on deadlines so your focus is on the idea first, not the due date.

o   Your productivity, creativity, and life satisfaction will increase if you enjoy your work. You will be happier, AND the company you work for will be more profitable.

GOAL FOR TODAY: Think about extrinsic motivators that have worked for you the past. Now, think about what you have been intrinsically motivated by. Which has lead you to more successes and why?

If you want to learn more about motivation, I recommend reading *Drive* by Daniel H. Pink and *The Element* by Ken Robinson. These books explore motivation at work, school, and in our personal lives. Additionally, there are more suggestions on page 353 in the Suggested Reading & Listening section.

TIME MANAGEMENT

When you know what you want, you realize that all there is left then is time management. You'll manage your time to achieve your goals because you clearly know what you're trying to achieve in your life.
— PATCH ADAMS

Although we can budget time like money, we can't get more of it by working harder. We can only learn how to be smarter with the time we have.

My grandfather, like most grandfathers, has a handful of stories he works into nearly every conversation we have. In his story about working at Upjohn in the 1960s, he ends it by saying this: If you don't plan your day, someone else will. I have heard this line my entire life, but it didn't sink in until I was able to see how true it was in my own life. When I don't plan my day, the tasks I need to accomplish are slow in getting started or are put on the back burner. The same time management rules my grandfather lived by are still just as relevant today. The only thing different is the amount of people and technologies that are fighting for that time.

While I was in the SEI Business Analyst Apprenticeship program in Seattle, my mentor Andy suggested keeping an activity log of how I spend my time each day. If you have ever been on a diet or nutrition regimen, you may be familiar with food logs; this is the same idea. Ultimately, the idea is to track what you are spending your time on, so you can become more mindful of your day-to-day activities.

After tracking my actual time spent against what I thought I was spending my time on, I realized that how I saw myself was quite different from what I was really like. Deep down, I had this idea that I was a humble genius of the night, an intellectual and philosopher, perhaps deeply troubled because of a fight with evil during infancy, wearing dark robes and scaring neighborhood children... In reality, I was some mid-20s guy dressed in button-down business casual, dawdling on the computer most of the day while eating my wife's skinny popcorn (yum). I was able to complete my work, ask the right questions, and get by alright, but I wasn't seriously developing my business skills or becoming a misunderstood Dark Lord of prose.

When I became aware of how I was actually spending my time, I was motivated to align my true hour-by-hour actions with my desired goal actions. To do this, I sat down with my mentor and we discussed time management strategies. Four years and a lot of revisions later, we are ready to share our favorite time management tools.

4 Corners Time Management

I use a paper planner to keep track of my appointments and tasks I need to complete each day and week. Even though I have an online calendar, having a paper planner allows me to look at my schedule without getting distracted by technology. I can quickly look at my schedule, scribble out tasks I have completed (which feels great), and keep track of how many times I have checked my distractions that day: email, social media, stocks market, and newsfeed.

There are a lot of different kinds of planners and even more ways to use them. I created my own system I call 4 Corners. Feel free to try it on and experiment with different methods so you can find out what works for you.

4 Corners works by splitting all my work into four lists based on when a task needs to be accomplished. The top two boxes are for the current day: On the left is what I NEED to accomplish that day (sometimes I tell myself that I need to finish all these tasks by noon) and on the right, is what I WOULD LIKE TO accomplish that day. Meaning, if I have a perfect day, everything in both the top quadrants

will be completed and properly crossed off with enthusiastic scribbles. If I don't make it to all my to-do items in the upper right quadrant, that's okay. I'll move those to the left column tomorrow and they will become my NEED TO ACCOMPLISH items.

The bottom two boxes are a big picture view of what I will be accomplishing in the week or weeks to come. In the bottom left box, I write the tasks I need to accomplish this week. When I am doing my daily morning reflection (See: Goal Construction), I pull from this list, so I can plot out my top two boxes for the day.

The final box is located in the bottom right. This is where I keep a list of items I want to accomplish in the near future or within in the next month. Basically, it is my everything-else pile. As work or additional tasks come up, I add it to this list so I can start planning for the weeks to come. On Friday afternoon or Monday morning, this is the list I sit down with to plan the week ahead.

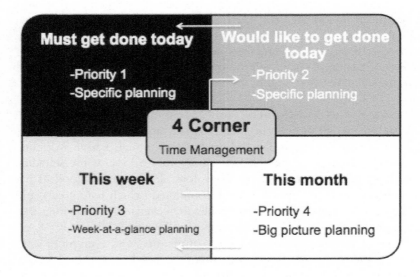

That's 4 Corners: plot out tasks based on when you want to accomplish them. Any task, meeting, or deadline flows through my boxes, so I can plan my day and week with enough forethought. I like to write my list by hand each day. My theory is, if I see a task enough times, eventually I will want to get it done. Then, I don't have to keep putting it on my list. Like any self-imposed structure you implement into your life, it only works if you play by the rules.

That means you have to be honest with yourself and hold yourself accountable for finishing your NEED TO ACCOMPLISH box every day.

Here is an example of my 4 Corners list in 2015 when I wrote a blog post about time management. This should help you visualize what yours may actually look like.

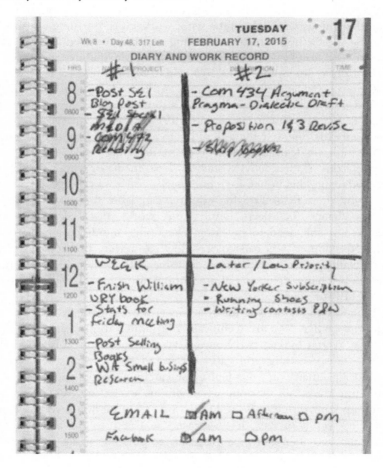

Budget Time Like Money

Another one of my grandfather's sayings is that everyone is given the same 24 hours in the day as everyone else. Nobody gets any more or less, and it is up to us to figure out how we should use it. Time (pause for dramatic effect) is the great equalizer.

Again, grandpa is right. The one thing we all share is time. Like I said before, we can't buy more of it, we can only learn how to use the time we have more efficiently. In the Budgeting Time Model, you budget hours like you do money. To start, you take your total weekly time allowance: 168 hours, and start assigning your weekly tasks an hour value. Go ahead and start crunching numbers. Don't forget to budget for downtime, like sleeping, eating, traveling to work, and all the other things we fill our time with: work, class, pursuing a hobby, relaxing, doing home repair, attending community events, going to the grocery store, exercising, spending time with family, and so on. Rich or poor, unemployed or CEO, you have 168 hours.

Once you lay out all your activities and record the hours you need to budget, you can start adding and subtracting to account for the other tasks you want to accomplish. For example, you can shave a few hours off one activity and add it to another. If I want to spend two extra hours learning a new programming skill, I will have to take it away from another activity, such as social media or reading. As you are budgeting the hours for your week, you can color code your hours by their flexibility. In red, you can label the activities that cannot change (i.e. sleep, family time, work). For tasks that can change but still need to be done, like doing laundry or meeting a friend for dinner, you can color yellow to indicate that it's flexible. And finally, you can color green anything that you would like to do but can be changed, like social media time, watching TV, or going for a walk in your neighborhood.

One way to manipulate the system is to find activities you can pair and do together. You are technically not limited to one task per unit of time. If you budget two hours a day for your daily commute on public transportation, you can also spend those same two hours composing emails on your laptop or catching up on your reading. The same thing can be done while you are exercising. When you're lacing up your running shoes, bring a pair of headphones so you can catch up on your favorite podcasts or listen to an audiobook. Doubling activities will increase your output, but make sure both tasks can be reasonably accomplished together. Since I am only productive when I focus on one thing at a time, I only combine tasks when one of them requires my attention. That's why public transportation or running are good tasks to double up on.

Here's an example of how someone might budget their hours, followed with how it would look in a calendar program. In the hour table, column A includes tasks you need to complete. Column B is hours you need to budget to accomplish the specific task. Finally, column C includes the hours from column B subtracted from the running total of remaining weekly hours.

	A	B	C
1	Task	Hours	Total
2			168
3	Sleep (8 hours x 7 days)	56	112
4	Work	40	72
5	Hobby or second job	20	52
6	Commuting	10	42
7	Exercise (1 hour daily)	7	35
8	Morning routine/shower (1 hour daily)	7	28
9	Friends & family time	14	14
10	TV and checking social media (1 hour daily)	7	7
11	Laundry/housekeeping	7	0
12			
13	Eating dinner is with friends or borrowed from TV/social media time		

When budgeting, give yourself the exact amount of time you need; don't forget Parkinson's Law and Hofstadter's Law in the chapter Accomplishing Your Goals.

Parkinson's Law: It will take you as long to accomplish a task as the time you give it.

Hofstadter's Law: It will always take you longer than you expect to complete a task.

If you know a task will take an hour to complete, budget for an hour and a half as a hard dealine, but in your mind shoot for completing it in one hour as a soft deadline.

On the next two pages is a copy of my budgeted calender. You probably won't be spending 20 hours/week on writing like I was, but I'm sure you can find something else to spend that time on.

GMT-05	Sun 4/16	Mon 4/17	Tue 4/18	Wed 4/19	Thu 4/20	Fri 4/21	Sat 4/22
12am	8p – 4 Sleep	8p – 4 Sleep	8p – 4 Sleep	8p – 4 Sleep	8p – 4 Sleep	8p – 4 Sleep	8p – 4 Sleep
1am							
2am							
3am							
4am	4 – 10 Write	4 – 5 Write	4 – 5 Write	4 – 5 Write	4 – 5 Write	4 – 5 Write	4 – 10 Write
5am		5 – 6 Get ready for work	5 – 6 Get ready for work	5 – 6 Get ready for work	5 – 6 Get ready for work	5 – 6 Get ready for work	
6am		6 – 7 Commute to work	6 – 7 Commute to work	6 – 7 Commute to work	6 – 7 Commute to work	6 – 7 Commute to work	
7am		7 – 3p WORK	7 – 3p WORK	7 – 3p WORK	7 – 3p WORK	7 – 3p WORK	
8am							
9am							
10am	10 – 11 Run						10 – 11 Run
11am	11 – 12p Get ready for the day						11 – 12p Get ready for the day

Time	Day 1	Day 2	Day 3	Day 4	Day 5	Day 6	Day 7
12pm	12p – 3p Brunch w/ friends						12p – 4:30p Houskeeping
1pm							
2pm							
3pm	3p – 5:30p Laundry/cleaning	3p – 4p Commute home	3p – 4p Commute home	3p – 4p Commute home	3p – 4p Commute home	3p – 4p Commute home	
4pm		4p – 5p Run	4p – 5p Run	4p – 5p Run	4p – 5p Run	4p – 5p Run	4:30p – 7p Family BBQ
5pm	5:30p – 7p Dinner at home with family	5p – 6p Write	5p – 6p Write	5p – 6p Write	5p – 7p Game night w/ friends	5p – 7p Dinner reservation/date night	
6pm		6p – 7p Dinner with friends/family	6p – 7p Dinner with friends/family	6p – 7p Dinner with friends/family			
7pm	7p – 8p Wind down. TV/Social media.	7p – 8p Wind down. TV/Social media.	7p – 8p Wind down. TV/Social media.	7p – 8p Wind down. TV/Social media.	7p – 8p Wind down. TV/Social media.	7p – 8p Wind down. TV/Social media.	7p – 8p Wind down. TV/Social media.
8pm	8p – 4 Sleep	8p – 4 Sleep	8p – 4 Sleep	8p – 4 Sleep	8p – 4 Sleep	8p – 4 Sleep	8p – 12 Sleep
9pm							
10pm							
11pm							

Other Tips

Distractions are all around us fighting for our attention and interrupting workflow. More often than I would like to admit, I space out or switch focus without realizing it. I catch myself checking my email or clicking on a series of Wikipedia links when I'm supposed to be working on something else. That's why I wrote the first draft of this book in the unfinished second story of my house, because there is nothing up there to distract me. You don't need to sit in a camping chair in a room lit only by candles like I did, but you could consider a few tricks I picked up along my journey from teenage entrepreneur to working in Seattle's fast-paced tech industry.

- If you go to multiple locations throughout the day, identify the location of where each task needs to be completed. If some tasks are not location-dependent and can be done remotely, identify these as flexible tasks, and do these when you have downtime between your location move. Instead of running back and forth between locations, if possible, do everything in one location before moving to the next.

- Limit yourself to checking social media once in the morning and once in the evening, with a time limit of 15 minutes each session. I set a timer on my phone and when it goes off, I log off and close the window.

- Limit yourself to checking your email three times a day: in the morning, right before or just after lunch, and in the evening. This works out to about every 2-3 hours during the normal work day. (See how I keep tabs on this and social media checking in my 4 Corners table in my example from 2015 on page 103.)

- Delete all the apps on your phone that suck up time and energy.

- Change the notification setting on your phone so you don't get distracted by emails, social media updates, app updates, and text messages.

- If a task is going to take longer to write down in your to-do list than it is to complete it, do it NOW and get it over with. My personal rule: If it is going to take 2 minutes or less, do it now.

- Figure out what time of the day you are the most productive. I believe that there are morning people, after coffee but only until lunch people, after lunch people, evening people, and night people. Once you know where and when you will be productive, schedule accordingly by doing the hardest tasks in your productivity zone.

Key Takeaways

o   We all have the same 168 hours to spend each week. Knowing how you spend those hours and then controlling your time will help you achieve your goals. Your time is your most precious asset.

o   Start by writing down what you spend your time doing.

o   To stay on task and accomplish what you need to, write down what you must get done each day, what you want to get done each day, what you must get done during the week, and what you want to get done during the month.

o   Create a time budget that includes eating, sleeping, work, socializing and other tasks you spend time on.

GOAL FOR TODAY: Track how you spend your time for a 24-hour period. The goal is to get an accurate picture of where your time is really being spent compared to where you think it is being spent.

Are you really in control of your schedule or is someone (or something) planning your day for you? We all have 24 hours, spend wisely.

SELF MANAGEMENT

In a few hundred years, when the history of our time will be
written from a long-term perspective, it is likely that the most
important event historians will see is not technology, not the
Internet, not e-commerce. It is an unprecedented change in the
human condition. For the first time—literally—substantial and
rapidly growing numbers of people have choices. For the first
time, they will have to manage themselves. And society is
totally unprepared for it.
— PETER DRUCKER

In 1894, William Porter lost his job at the First National Bank of
Austin, Texas for accusations of embezzlement. Two years later,
when a federal case opened against him, he changed trains on his way
to the courthouse and fled the country. Porter returned to Austin a
year later when his wife was too sick to meet him in Honduras, where
they were supposed to start their new life together. Upon his return,
he surrendered to the court and began serving his five-year sentence.
As a licensed pharmacist, Porter took on the duty as the night
druggist at the prison hospital where he had a lot of down time to
pursue another passion in his life: writing. While still in prison, he
began publishing short stories under a pen name—the household
name we all know him by today: O. Henry.

Prison gave Porter a structure that forced him to become disciplined and work against time restraints. He was notorious for making last minute deadlines, which is possibly the reason for his staple plot twists and surprising endings. The Gift of the Magi, O. Henry's most popular story and one of the most widely read short stories in the world, was written in just two or three hours, finishing minutes before his deadline.

When Porter was released from prison, his work ethic stayed with him. During one productive year, he wrote one story per week for New York World Sunday Magazine.

For the rest of us who are not currently serving time in an early 20th century prison, we have to create our own time structures with self-imposed deadlines. For a long time, I told myself that all I needed was one more hour in the day and then I could meet all my deadlines. I thought about it like this: Imagine you are packing a suitcase and you are trying to fit as much as you can in a limited space. If I only had a slightly bigger suitcase, I could fit all my deadlines. The truth is, if I had a 25-hour day, I would find a reason to need a 26-hour day, and once I had a 26-hour day, well, you get the picture (remember Parkinson's Law in Accomplishing Your Goals: workload expands to fill a deadline). My suitcase would always be too small. And Parkinson's Law agrees.

There is good news. The problem looks different when you flip Parkinson's Law. What if you only had 23 hours in a day to work with? Timothy Ferriss asks a similar question in his book, *The Four-Hour Workweek*. He poses the question: what if you were recovering from a surgery and for the next six months, you could only work for two hours a day? Given the limitations, how would you plan your time?

I think most people are asking the wrong question when it comes to managing their time. Instead of asking how can I fit all my tasks into one day, the question you should be asking is what can I do today given the amount of time I have? Instead of cramming all our favorite tasks into a suitcase and trying to close the zipper, we should instead be asking ourselves if we need to pack half the things in the first place.

Here are some ideas to help you reframe how you use your time.

Cut your priorities. When everything is a priority, nothing is a priority. Start by asking: what is the one thing I need to finish today?

This is likely the first thing you think about in the morning. A task you carry around with you day after day and never accomplish is a drain on your mental energy. Take inventory of what you are packing in your 24-hour suitcase and be mindful not to overpack. Start by asking: "What is the best use of my time right now?"

Cut your wants and leave your needs. Strip away anything that is not necessary and use only what you need to complete a task. Knowing the difference between a "need" and a "want" will streamline your workflow by getting rid of unnecessary security blankets.

Cut your lists. Too often, people make a to-do list that fills up the entire page and carries on to the back. This is overwhelming and cripples your motivation (that's why the 4 Corners Model breaks down the list and focuses only on the most important tasks). As an exercise, schedule your daily to-do list as if you only have two productive hours in the day. This will cut any unnecessary fat from your list and help you focus on what is really important.

Cut your quality. Find your lowest passable limit. When you don't have time to spare, do the minimum for all the things you absolutely need to get done. This is hard to stomach if you are a perfectionist like I am, but "good enough" is sometimes all that is expected and needed. Here is an example: Does your co-worker deserve a 10-minute email, or will a brief point-by-point 5-minute email be just as effective? Multiply by 10 emails and you've saved nearly an hour.

Cut the fluff. Do you need to write a long document or give a long presentation, or do you need to give the right information? Sometimes length can hide your message. Keep it short. When writing a story or essay, most professional writers ask: "Does this sentence pay its rent?" Meaning, if the sentence is not providing anything to the reader, it is taking up space and not offering anything in return. By cutting the words or sentence, you are leaving more space for the important ideas to shine through. If you keep it brief, you will save time and your audience will have an easier time recalling your main points.

Cut the distractions. Eliminate distractions from work time. If you know you get caught up in social media or texting, turn off your phone and silence email and social media notifications. The idea is to create a physical and mental workspace where you can be productive and creative. My vice is hobby research, specifically, Wikipedia. I catch myself falling into the black hole of related links and snazzy trivia facts (did you know O. Henry coined the term "Banana Republic"?). My remedy is turning off the Wi-Fi on my laptop. By turning off the possibility of distraction, I am able to focus on the tasks on my list.

Do not take anyone's monkey. William Oncken, Jr. and Donald L. Wass wrote one of the most popular articles in the history of the Harvard Business Review. In this article, Oncken and Wass propose the following scenario: You are walking down the hall at work and a co-worker comes up to you and says, "I've got a problem." You say, "Sure, what's going on?" The problem ends up being something more complicated than a quick fix in the hallway, so you tell your colleague that you will think about it and get back to them.

What just happened? Your co-worker's problem just became your problem. Now, instead of thinking about your own project, you are thinking about your co-worker's problem. The monkey hopped off their back and landed on yours.

Instead of saying "I'll get back to you", say, "Send me an email about it." The monkey stays on their back and you are free to deal with your own monkeys. Your co-worker will only send an email if the problem is important enough to sit down and write to you about it. In the meantime, they may figure out a solution on their own and not follow-up with you. If they do send you an email, you can deal with it on your time, not theirs.

DO NOT cut what matters most. While we are on the topic of priorities and making good use of our time, don't cut something you may regret later. Never do anything you wouldn't want to watch if Hollywood made a movie of your life. Every choice is a tradeoff for something else. Make sure it is a good trade every time. We only have one chance at this life, so make sure you are doing what is most important to you, always.

Key Takeaways

o   Manage your time like you have less of it than you do—don't ask for another hour, plan like you have an hour less.

o   When planning your day, prioritize the most important things.

o   Don't borrow other people's priorities.

o   Plan your day according to what you value most.

GOAL FOR TODAY: Imagine you can only work for two hours a day. Hey! You've moved into semi-retirement early. The catch is, you're not retired. You have gotten so good at managing your time, you are still able to put in a full day's work in those two hours. What do those two hours look like? How would you prioritize your tasks, write your emails, and complete your deliverables on time?

GETTING STARTED

I don't know how to get things started... It's like there's this great big wheel I've got to start rolling only I don't seem to have the muscles to get it going.

— CAROL SHIELDS, *The Stone Diaries*

I want to end this section on time management and productivity with a list of my favorite remedies for getting started when you are stuck—when you have a hard time finding the motivation to finish. When your light horse bites off too much work or your dark horse wants to lay in bed all day (see Change, page 39), you need to motivate both of them, so they can work together and stay on track. The following list of strategies will get you moving so you're not stuck revving your engine.

1. Try a Different Format
Your idea or project might be limited by the medium you are using. If you are using language, try drawing a picture on a whiteboard to see it visually before writing it with words. You might find that you are more comfortable sketching the idea, verbally explaining it, or writing it out by hand first before sitting down to type it out. The book *The Sketchnote Handbook* by Mike Rohde popularized visual note-taking and it is a great resource for getting started. On the other

side of the fence, if you are creating something visual, try using words by writing a short description of the project you are working on.

2. Play a Game

Play a short game that takes no less than five minutes but no more than 20 minutes to complete (in the gaming industry, these are called casual games). Focusing on a quick problem-solving activity, like the game Cranium Brain Breaks, may be enough to warm up your mental muscles. For more information about the benefits of gaming, start with the Jane McGonigal books I listed in the suggested reading section at the end of the book.

3. Invent a Better Drinking Fountain

Think about how you can improve upon a tool we take for granted. For example, think of ten new improvements for a drinking fountain. Where does the water come out? How is it designed? Can you design one that doesn't waste water? Abstract thinking, even if it's not on a topic related to the one you are stuck on, can help you approach your problem in a creative way. If you already came up with a better drinking fountain years ago and can't do any better, try improving a refrigerator, a lamp, or a teapot.

4. Ordinary to Extraordinary

Reframe your brain by writing a product description for an unconventional use of a tennis ball (i.e. cut the ball in half and now you have over-the-ear hearing protection). Make sure your description is written simply and flows from one idea to the next.

5. The Egg Timer

Set small, achievable goals to build momentum. If you can't identify a small goal to complete, you can use a timer. Set the timer for 10 or 20 minutes and take a short break when the time is up. When I need to write something and I don't know where to start, I open Word and format the document. I put my name where it needs to be, the title, the margins, the spacing, all the technical stuff. (Ding! Ding! Ding! Break time). A couple minutes later, I start on the research and I get an idea of how I want to frame what I am writing about. (Break) I create a rough outline with three to five big points I want to hit on. (Break) Then I take apart each big point and break it down into small ones. (Break) I write an intro paragraph that I may use in the final, revising it heavily after I am finished with the body. (Break) I start writing each of the big bullet points, using the smaller bullet points as guide. Before I know it, I've written my first draft.

6. Try Something New
Listen to a new kind of music. Go to an exhibit you would never think of going to. Order something you have never eaten before. Anything to break you out of your normal routine and experience something new.

7. Get Physical
Exercise will wake up your body and you will be rewarded with healthy endorphins. Go outside, breath in some fresh air, and walk around the block. Or, if your building is large enough, walk up and down some stairs.

8. Get Interviewed
Sometimes you are too close to the project to see it fully. Ask a friend or colleague to question you about what you are working on. Being put on the spot and having to explain what you are working on from the ground up will pull you back to the big picture. Their questions will, even at a non-technical level, open up potential blind spots you have overlooked.

9. Healthy Energy
You might need a snack. Eat some healthy sugars from berries or an apple. For vitamins and minerals, snack on vegetables and nuts. For an energy boost, I make a smoothie with one or more of the following: cacao, maca, matcha, moringa, barley grass, wheat grass, and/or alfalfa.

10. Write a Haiku
Send it to a friend. If you've forgotten, a Haiku is a 17-syllable verse form consisting of three metrical units of 5, 7, and 5 syllables. Five for the first line, seven for the second, and five for the third. Creativity with boundaries promotes focused creative thinking and it may be what you need to get your brain warmed up.

11. Mix It Up
Don't drive or walk home the same way you usually do. Take a new route. New surroundings can help you think differently.

12. Let Your Lower Conscious Take Care of It
The jury is still out when it comes to sleep learning, but your brain does process information that was gathered while you were awake.

Before bed, think about the project you are working on and focus on the parts you are having trouble with. Many great thinkers credit their dreams for inspiration or simply waking up with a solution to a problem they were stuck on during the day. Keep a notebook within an arm's reach so you can write down your ideas. If you don't write the idea down, chances are you will forget it.

13. Shower Shock
Take a shower and alternate between hot water and cold water. Try switching every 30 seconds. Some people hypothesize that this increases the circulation of your blood, thus promoting brain activity, however, research is mixed.

14. Look at Books
Being surrounded by knowledge and ideas is inspiring. Go to a bookstore or library and read the first page of every book on a shelf. Open an art book and flip through the images. Unfold a map and try to put it back together.

15. Wake Up Earlier
Start your day earlier or mix up your schedule. Briefly pulling yourself out of your routine will give you a new perspective and help you think differently

16. Get a Stress Object
This could be a stress ball, a worry stone, or a small toy you buy at the grocery store quarter machine. Letting your hands fidget with something may be enough to get a creative spark.

17. TED
If you like TED talks, try watching one every day. Watching inspiring people talk about exciting ideas inspires us to do the same.

18. Do a SFD
Having something is better than nothing. Whatever your project is, keep moving forward even if you know it's not your best work. Put your pride aside, because you can always go back and revise. No one will see your SFD (sh*tty first draft) and getting something down will help you put the gears in motion.

19. Become Your Alter Ego
How would someone you look up to (Arianna Huffington, Steve Jobs, Batman, etc.) approach your project? Close your eyes and

imagine you are in their skin. What would they do next?

20. Smile

Bite down on a pencil. This causes the muscles in your face to mimic a smile. In doing so, you relieve stress and the result is an increase in focus. It really works!

21. One Sentence

Describe your project in one sentence and try to keep that sentence under twenty words. Difficult? Yup, that's the point. You are pulling out the most important thing or things that summarize your project. This is a strategy some of my writing friends use when they are working on a novel, and if a novelist can condense a 300-page book down to one sentence, I'm sure you can fit your project into one sentence as well.

22. Map It Out!

Using a whiteboard or a piece of notebook paper, write FIRST on the top left corner and LAST in the bottom right corner. Fill in the steps in between the first task you need to accomplish today and the last goal for the day. I find it easiest to plot out the big steps first and then break each big step down into smaller hour-by-hour goals.

23. Get a Little Zen

Mindfulness and meditation is becoming more and more popular in the workplace. Short mindfulness exercises help clear your mind, unwind, and reduce your stress level. When I get tired, I shut off my lights and set a timer for five minutes. Sitting in my chair or on the ground, I count my breaths up to four: one as I breath in, two as I breath out, three breathing in, four breathing out, and then I start back at one. After a minute or two, my mind drifts off and I stop focusing on counting. If I am still too restless, I count to five breathing in and 10 breathing out (about 4-6 breaths per minute). Slowing the breath down and extending the exhale lowers your pulse and blood pressure. Five minutes of breathing/meditation leaves me with a rested mind and I am able to start work immediately, something a quick nap can't do.

24. Pick Your Posture

It might be as simple as standing at your desk or sitting on the ground. Ernest Hemingway famously wrote standing up, while Truman Capote and Marcel Proust got their best ideas lying down. Throughout the day, I stand, sit, and pace around my desk. For me, movement is directly associated with thinking. The more I'm moving, the more I'm thinking.

25. Dress Up
Even if I am working from home and no one, besides the cats, are going to see me, I dress up when I need to make progress on a difficult project. I put on a tie and jacket, even some nice shoes. Dressing up sends a signal to my brain that what I'm doing is important. I am distracted less and achieve more.

26. Talk and Transcribe
Talking about your project, even to yourself, gets your ideas out of you and into the room. To capture what you talk about, record and transcribe your conversation or monologue. Programs like Nuance's Dragon NaturallySpeaking transcribe your ideas as you speak, and seeing the text may be enough to get you started.

27. Look for the Essence
Details, procedures, and technical jargon can clutter our thinking, and the very basic essence of what we are stuck on is hidden. When you get stuck, think about the issue at its most basic level and then think about the traits of what your project is solving.

Key Takeaways

o   At times, you will be overwhelmed or in other ways not able to start, and the first step will be the hardest step.

o   Find one or several go-to ways to get started.

o   Vary the approach you use to get started to keep things fresh and exciting.

GOAL FOR TODAY: What are some tactics you use when you are stuck? Tweet me your strategies @andrewjwilt or email me at andrew.wilt@sustainableevolution.com and I'll put together a list in a future blog post (giving **you** credit, of course).

1.5 BUILDING RELATIONSHIPS

Have you ever felt like you could trust someone within the first few minutes of meeting them? If you have, it's because they did a good job at building rapport. Rapport is the ability to establish mutual understanding and trust with another person or group of people over the course of an interaction. The quicker you do this with someone, the easier and more productive your encounter will be. In the next few chapters, you will learn about emotional intelligence, how to remember names (a critical skill in forming relationships), and learn ways to become more confident in your communication through word choice, listening, and body language.

EMOTIONAL INTELLIGENCE

And if they could master these emotions [love, pleasure, pain, fear, spiritedness] their lives would be just, whereas if they were mastered by them, they would be unjust.
— PLATO, *Timaeus*

I've learned that people will forget what you said, people will forget what you did, but people will never forget how you made them feel.
— MAYA ANGELOU

Joel Pumper is one of the many successful small business owners who has achieved what many would call The American Dream. Growing up as one of nine kids in a small town in rural Minnesota, Joel was not earmarked for success. He was an average student in high school and never thought twice about going to a four-year university. At 20, he became a husband, and a father a year later. After four years of service in the Air Force, Joel settled down working with his father in a trade job welding and fitting industrial piping. It was strenuous, both physically and mentally, and with four children at home, the Pumper family lived paycheck to paycheck.

It wasn't all work. Welding and working on industrial pipe was where Joel's skills met his passion. After working in the industry for 15 years, he started thinking about starting his own mechanical contracting company. In 2001, company headquarters were open for business. The location? In his garage. His wife, Jeanne, chose to stay inside the house where she managed their paperwork. When the company won a job, Joel packed up his gear and hit the road in his used Dodge pickup truck that he had modified to hold a welding machine mounted on the back.

Today, Mechanical Systems Inc. employs over 200 welders, fitters, and laborers across offices in Minnesota, Wisconsin, North Dakota, and Louisiana. How did someone from a small town in the Midwest without an advanced degree create such a thriving business? And why did the odds fall in Joel's favor when 50% of businesses don't make it past the four-year mark?

I'm sure you know someone who is incredibly smart who will never score in the top percentile on a standardized test. Likewise, you probably know someone who can test high, but can't hold a job for very long. This means we need to have a new definition for intelligence.

What Is Intelligence?

Traditionally, we think of a smart person as having a high IQ, but looking back at the history of the IQ test, it has nothing to do with someone's intelligence. The first practical IQ test was invented by Alfred Binet in 1904. Binet was commissioned by the French Ministry of Education to develop testing that would identify children with special needs so they could receive alternative education. It was never meant to determine mental worth as we think of it today.

In 1916, shortly after the IQ test reached the U.S., Lewis Terman of Stanford University published a revision of Binet's IQ test. This revision turned into the modern test we grew up with and is still being used today. As a eugenicist, Terman believed that intelligence is fixed and someone's IQ would remain the same throughout their life. Back in France, Binet was outraged. He responded to Terman (and other scholars) by saying:

[Some] assert that an individual's intelligence is a fixed quantity which cannot be increased. We must protest and react against this brutal pessimism...With practice, training, and above all method, we manage to increase our attention, our memory, our judgment, and literally to become more intelligent than we were before.

We now know Binet was right and intellectual traits are only fixed if we think of them as fixed (fixed mindset vs. growth mindset). If intelligence isn't only IQ, what else is it?

In casual conversation, we talk in terms of street smarts and book smarts. We call people book smart if they test high on IQ tests and go to college. Street-smart people, on the other hand, are taken less seriously. They are stereotyped as people who can wheel and deal; they are the ones who can negotiate and talk themselves out of anything. Sure, these people might be smart, but they are often charged with not playing by the books (no pun intended).

Over the last 20 years, research in personality psychology coined a name for many of the qualities we consider street smarts: Emotional Intelligence/Emotional Quotient (sometimes EI or EQ for short). These are the people who are able to understand and recognize their own emotional state and the emotions of others so they know what to say at the right time and to the right person. John D. Mayer and Peter Salovey are the pioneers of emotional intelligence and they define it as being:

> ...[T]he ability to perceive emotions, to access and generate emotions so as to assist thought, to understand emotions and emotional knowledge, and to reflectively regulate emotions so as to promote emotional and intellectual growth.

I asked Joel what he thought about emotional intelligence. He smiled and shook his head: "Can't tell ya I know what that is." When I told him about the basics of EI, his eyes lit up, and his thoughts came to fruition. "Reading a lot of books doesn't make you smart, it only means that you are good at reading books. ...Just because you have an education doesn't mean you are smart. Well..." he started, and then paused to clarify, "you might be smart, but it doesn't mean you are going to be successful."

Success is connected to how well we are able to build relationships through emotional awareness and communication. Daniel Goleman popularized emotional intelligence and broke it down into the following components.

1. Self-awareness

The first component of emotional intelligence is self-awareness. This is the ability to honestly assess your emotions. It is the ability to recognize and understand what drives you to action and what types of behavioral triggers get under your skin. It is also the ability to understand how people perceive you.

Someone who is self-aware knows what their strengths are, is open to feedback from others, and sees failure as a form of feedback.

2. Self-management

Strong emotions can overwhelm your thinking and memory. Once you are aware of your moods and emotional triggers, you can start learning how to manage them. Self-management is the ability to control, regulate, and redirect impulses long enough so you can think before acting. Too often, anxiety and fear lead to self-fulfilling prophecies. When you are aware of your emotions, you can choose to act on them or decide to ride them out until they pass. Having the option to act on an emotional impulse puts you in control of your emotions instead of letting them control you.

I'm not saying that you should turn into an emotionless robot. This is only for controlling impulses you want to act on but may regret doing so later. Thomas Jefferson said, "When angry count to ten before you speak; if very angry, count to one hundred." That is emotional self-management.

If you are interested in learning more about self-management in the context of emotional intelligence, look up the Stanford marshmallow experiment.

3. Intrinsic Motivation
(Remember carrots and sticks? See page 96.)
When you are intrinsically motivated, you are doing something because you want to do it, not because of an extrinsic reward. Remember your learning zone (comfort zone, learning zone, panic zone)? Intrinsic motivation is when you are working on something that is hard enough to be challenging, but not so hard that you become distracted or overstimulated. This is when you are excited to meet a challenge and time flies by. When you are intrinsically motivated, you enter what Mihay Csikszentmihalyi calls *flow*.

People who are intrinsically motivated are not afraid to roll up their sleeves and get dirty because they enjoy what they are doing. As a result, good work ethic and working in their learning zone comes naturally.

4. Social Awareness (Empathy)
Social awareness is being able to understand what other people are feeling and then having the capability to respond appropriately.

If someone cuts you off on your way to work, instead of reacting with anger, frustration, or rage, take a moment to think about why that person might be in a rush. They might have an ill family member in the hospital or their dog might have just died, and they are so distraught that they didn't even realize they cut you off. Or they may not know how to handle their emotions and are acting out the only way they know how: as they did when they were a child. Regardless of what it is, everyone you meet has something else on their mind. Whatever that thing is, it might be distracting them from being in the present moment. When they yell at you or cut you off in traffic, they might be channeling frustration from a completely different situation, and you just happen to be the closest living thing to observe it. Social awareness is recognizing that people are not perfect. And because we would want people to be patient when we are having a bad day, we too should be patient with others. And sometimes being patient is letting someone calm down.

5. Relationship Management

Knowing what to say to the right person at the right time is relationship management. This is done by figuring out what is important to another person (what they are intrinsically motivated by and respond to emotionally) and using that to motivate them to a mutual advantage. Networking and identifying social connections play a big role in managing relationships.

Since people are more than their jobs, one thing I like to do when I meet someone new or see an old friend I haven't talked with in a while is ask: what are you working on these days? Instead of asking "what do you do?" or "where are you working?", which can pigeonhole a person into defining themselves as their career, asking what they have been working on opens the conversation up to skills that they might not associate with their job. When I do this, I get to know the whole person, and this guides the relationship as it is forming.

Emotional Intelligence is the missing human factor that is more important than IQ when measuring personal success. It is the reason why someone like Joel Pumper, who never went to school for business, learned an even more important skillset outside of the classroom. Joel's education in navigating relationships started at an early age at home with a house full of brothers and sisters. Early in his life, he learned **self-awareness** while negotiating chores with his siblings on their family-sized farm. These skills continued to grow into **social-awareness** while he was in the Air Force, where he met a diverse group of people from all over the U.S. While training to be a pilot, Joel was pushed to his physical and mental limits, teaching him discipline and **self-management**. When he moved back to Minnesota and started working for his father, he learned skills like craftsmanship that could only be perfected through **intrinsic motivation**. When Joel started his company, he relied on the **relationships** he made when he was working for his father and used his network to expand a one-truck company into a multi-state operation. Mechanical Systems Inc. has the same one core value it did since its inception: integrity, which also happens to be a trait of someone with a high emotional intelligence—pretty good for someone who had never heard of emotional intelligence or soft skills.

Key Takeaways

o   Emotional Intelligence is less about what you know and more about how you interact with others.

o   In order to grow your Emotional Intelligence, you must be aware of and in control of your own emotions.

o   You must also be aware of what motivates you and what motivates others.

o   Emotional Intelligence is being able to say or do the right thing at the right time with the right person.

GOAL FOR TODAY: If you can, identify all the emotions you are feeling right now. Ask yourself again in a few hours and compare the lists. Any differences? Can you identify why you are feeling the same or different? Today or tomorrow, take a moment to reflect on your emotions when you are talking with someone. How is this conversation making you feel? Why do you think you are feeling the way you are feeling? How do you think the person you are talking to feels? The more you understand your emotions, the easier you will pick up on the emotions of others.

REMEMBERING NAMES

As soon as His Royal Highness [Napoleon the Third, Emperor of France] was alone, he wrote the name down on a piece of paper, looked at it, concentrated on it, fixed it securely in his mind, and then tore up the paper. In this way, he gained an eye impression of the name as well as an ear impression.

— DALE CARNEGIE, *How to Win Friends and Influence People*

You're standing in a modestly decorated conference hall, holding a drink of some sort, and as you're talking you begin to realize how sweaty your palms are. You put your right hand by your side and move your fingers back and forth, air-drying the perspiration before the closing handshake. Josh? You think. Or, is it…John? The person you've been speaking to for over 20 minutes—someone you realize could add significant value to your work—suddenly doesn't have a name anymore. And worse, you can tell the conversation is winding down to an exit. He sees the conversational exit and takes it, saying that he'd better return to his colleagues. What do you say? You decide to go with Josh, because he kind of looks like a Josh. It's a stretch, but he's more of a Josh than a John, that's for sure. You say, "Thanks, Josh, for the wonderful conversation. We'll have to connect over coffee or a drink sometime soon." He extends a card, says thanks and says your name again, as if to rub it in. After you're out the door and on your way home, you pull out the card he gave you. The name Stephen shines back at you in black glossy letters. Stephen? Really? You weren't even close. Now, as you are on your way back home, you don't know if you should email and apologize for the name mix up, ignore it and send an email using his correct name to show that you are aware of his actual name, or do nothing because you would rather not have the embarrassment hanging over your future conversations.

We hate it when someone calls us by the wrong name, and yet, when the tables are turned, we can empathize with forgetting someone's name because we have so many things, let alone names, to remember. In this section, you will learn some tricks that will help you commit a name to memory so you can successfully recall it later. To begin, why are names so important?

Your Favorite Word: (Your Name Here)

When you remember someone's name, it shows the person that you are listening to them and are taking an interest in what they have to say. At a party, we can hear our name rise up amidst the background of conversation, even if it is spoken across the room. Many times when we hear our name being spoken, it sounds louder than other words—even if it was in a hushed whisper. Why is this? Most of us have associated our "self" with one name since we were young, so when someone new remembers it, our entire life, birth to now, is being validated. It's really that important.

If you have a hard time remembering names, don't beat yourself up. There's a reason why it is tough to remember names.

We Remember in Details

If you struggle to remember someone's name, but can remember details about the person, you're not alone. In one study published in British Journal of Developmental Psychology, participants were introduced to fake names and biographies. Later on, the participants were tested to see what they could recall. Here is what they remembered:

1. Jobs: 69%
2. Hobbies: 68%
3. Hometowns: 62%
4. First names: 31%

5.   Last names: 30%

Hobbies, where someone lives, and personal details are stickier in our memory than names. This is because details we can relate to in our own personal stories create quicker (automatic) associations. It would be easier if we all had names that were descriptions of our characteristics (a practice that was common in past civilizations). This why nicknames are stickier than real names.

If you are someone who remembers details better than names, don't fret, you can harness your strength through associations.

Making Room for Associations

Below are some tips to increase word associations and remember names.

- Repeat the person's name as soon as you are introduced:
  Megan: "Hello, I'm Megan."
  Andrew: "Hi, Megan. My name is Andrew."
  Megan: "Nice to meet you, Andrew."
      –Switched–
  Andrew: "Hi, I'm Andrew."
  Megan: "Andrew, it's nice to meet you. I'm Megan."
  Andrew: "It's nice to meet you too, Megan."

- Use the person's name (again) as soon as you can in the conversation. This sounds hard, but with practice, you will discover spaces in normal conversation where you can slip in their name. Try this: work an example of a concept you are explaining into the conversation with using the person's name you just met. Make the person a character in the example. This will help you learn the name by association and engage them in the concept you are talking about. It's a win-win. Create an association with a detail you will remember about the person. For example: Megan from Minnesota. Two M's.

- You can create an image association with the person you are talking to. If you forget the person's name, the image will jog your memory and the name will pop up with the association. For example: Jason is talking about organic food. I am going to create a mental image of Jason in a kitchen surrounded by organic greens. He is cutting up veggies and putting them in a bowl for a salad. He pours a dressing on the mix and on the side of the bottle is his name: Jason's dressing. Jason sure likes pouring Jason's dressing on Jason's organic salad. Come on Jason, that's enough Jason dressing on Jason's salad.

- You can form a new association by playing off one you already have. If you meet someone who has the same name as someone else you are familiar with, you can make an association with a name replacement. The easiest way to do this is to pull out similar features of the new person and the person you already know. For example: both Megans like volleyball.

- Think about how the name is spelled. An easy way to slip the name back into the conversation right away is to ask for clarification of the spelling. This is best used for names with multiple spellings so it doesn't seem forced. For example: "Megan, nice to meet you. Is that M-E-G-A-N or M-E-G-H-A-N?"

- Have a genuine interest in the person. Too often it is "in one ear and out the other"—especially when you're at an event where you're meeting a lot of new people. If you can calm yourself down and be present with each individual you talk to, their ideas will stick with you and you will be more likely to recall what you talked about and with whom. If you are really taking an interest in what they are saying, the listening part will come naturally.

- If you do forget someone's name, it's not the end of the world. If you want to continue the conversation, a sly way to get their name is to ask for the New-Friend's email address or open up a new contact in your phone and have them fill it out. If asking for an email address or phone number is not appropriate in the context of the conversation, it's better to be honest than call someone the wrong name. You can say: I'm really enjoying our conversation. I had a whirlwind of a day and my brain is a little foggy. Can you remind me of your name? Chances are, they may need a second introduction to your name as well.

- Finally, end the encounter using their name. For example: "It was really nice meeting you, Megan. Have a great night."

Key Takeaways

o   Remembering other people's names is an important skill to building rapport.

o   Use various approaches to remembering other peoples' names. A first step is to repeat their name when they tell it to you.

o   Use association, such as a fact about them, and in your mind (or aloud) say the association.

GOAL FOR TODAY: Go to one of your social media sites and look through your recently added contacts. Practice creating memory associations with their names. Know all your contacts already? Try creating memory tricks for the roster of a sports team or the cast of a TV show.

If you are interested in learning more about memory, check out the book *Moonwalking with Einstein* by Joshua Foer. In the book, the author recounts his visit to the 2005 U.S.A. Memory competition as a journalist for Slate, and after training for less than a year with a few international memory gurus, he becomes the 2006 U.S.A. Memory Champion.

HOW TO AVOID MISS COMMUNICATION

Most people do not listen with the intent to understand; they listen with the intent to reply.
— STEPHEN R. COVEY

We have two ears and one mouth so that we can listen twice as much as we speak.
— EPICTETUS

Whether it's a barista not spelling your name right on the side of your morning coffee drink, or a retail company sending you the wrong product, miscommunication is common and occurs in every industry. According to Mark W. Sheffert of Manchester Companies, miscommunication can cost an organization between a quarter or more of its annual budget. Miscommunication is more than making costly business mistakes, it's also about being able to clearly express what's in your head so the person you are speaking to can understand you. You might be brilliant and have an idea that could change the world, but you are only as smart as your ability to communicate that idea.

Listening & Being Heard

Relationships, both at work and at home, hinge on being able to listen and speak clearly. However, this is a lot easier said than done.

According to Boaz Keysar and Anne S. Henly at the University of Chicago, speakers have a hard time gauging if a listener understands them. In their study published in *Psychological Science*, a speaker was asked to tell a listener a series of ambiguous statements and rate how well they thought the listener understood them. The listeners also recorded their level of understanding. The results showed that when the speaker thought the listener understood their intended meaning, they were really being misunderstood 46% of the time. Additionally, over 80% of the speakers showed a tendency to overestimate the listeners' understanding. The results signal a huge problem in communication: speakers overestimate their effectiveness and misunderstandings go undetected.

Language Patterns

How someone communicates with others starts with how they perceive and take in information about the world around them. That's why each of us responds differently to the same communication style. In order to clearly communicate, you need to be able to express your ideas and ask questions using the same communication style as the person you are talking to. Likewise, if you are talking with more than one person, you may have to diversify your communication.

It's common for someone's preferred communication style to also be their learning style. (If you need a refresher, look back at the chapter Learning Styles on page 62.) If you know how someone learns, you can change your verbal and written style to match theirs. Using clever word choice and phrasing, you can switch to their communication channel.

Visual language

- It was the **brightest** thing I've ever **seen**.
- It just **looked** wrong.
- What does it **look** like to you?
- Can you **imagine**…
- It **appears** to me
- It's **clear** to me that…

Auditory language

- Do you **hear** what I'm **saying**?
- It fell a little **flat**.
- The two are **harmonious**.
- It was as **quiet** as...
- To **echo** what you're **saying**...
- It **sounds** a little **off-pitch**...

Kinesthetic (emotional) language

- I'm **following** you.
- That **makes** sense.
- It's about to **crash**.
- I **feel** like...
- It's **funny** that...
- I want to **explore**...

Here's an example of language patterns in practice:

> *Andrew (emotional communicator)*: "How do you **feel** about Rob's decision to switch teams?"

> *Megan (visual communicator)*: "What do you mean how do I feel? What do I **look** like, his mother?"

What if instead Andrew took Megan's communication style into account and placed an emphasis on visual language?

> *Andrew*: "How do you **envision** Rob's transition to a new team working out?"

> *Megan*: "**Looking** at all the projects he's on right now, I don't **see** it going very smoothly. Can you **imagine** switching groups every six months and having to drop all your projects and relearn everything from scratch? **See** what I mean?"

Next, let's explore a few small, but important, communication tricks. As cliché as it sounds, it is the small things that make a big difference.

Large group communication. Communicating in large groups is a part of daily life for many of us. When presenting in a meeting, it's important to remember that no matter what, you will have a room full of people who prefer different communication styles. Knowing this, you should try to connect with a variety of preferences so you can reach as many people as you can.

"and" & "but". As you saw with language patterns, word choice is important. Two additional words that have an incredible effect on recall are the words "and" and "but". When a speaker uses the word "but," listeners typically do not remember what the speaker said before the word. However, when a speaker uses the word "and," listeners tend to remember what the speaker said before and after.

"Yes, and…" never "Yes, but". John Gottman and his researchers at the University of Washington Love Lab got so good at picking up on communication patterns, they were able to predict (with 90% accuracy) if a marriage would last or end in divorce within the first 15 minutes of a conversational exchange. Gottman called the patterns he found in destructive relationships, "The Four Horsemen of the Apocalypse", the most popular being the yes-but. The yes-but is when a speaker starts a sentence agreeing but ends disagreeing. These messages are confusing because they seem to say one thing but really say something else. It is sometimes hard to pick up on unless you are listening carefully. To the listener, the yes-but negates any positive comments and they only focus on the second half of the speaker's comment, which is negative.

<u>What not to do:</u>

You are at home with a good friend and getting ready to go out for dinner.
Your friend changes into a new outfit and says, "I'm all ready to go. Do you like my outfit? I just bought it last weekend." You look at your friend and say, "Yes. Wow. That is a great outfit. But are you sure you want to wear it tonight?" Your friend only really listens to the last half of the sentence and thinks you are implying that you don't want to go out with them as they are dressed.

At work, a co-worker is shot down with a yes-but after suggesting an idea.
The room goes quiet and someone at the table speaks up. "I hear you. It's an excellent idea, but I don't think it is going to work here." To the co-worker who just shared the idea, the yes-but sounds like this: "I know you think you have come up with a great idea, but it really isn't worth much."

Instead of using a yes-but statement, the speaker should try using a yes-and statement. Using a yes-and statement is clearer because it doesn't negate itself and the listener will hear both halves of the sentence instead of only the last half. Here is an example with a "Yes, and…" version.

<u>What to do:</u>

You are at home with a good friend and getting ready to go out for dinner. Your friend changes into a new outfit and says, "I'm all ready to go. Do you like my outfit? I just bought it last weekend." You look at your friend and say, "Wow, you look great! Honestly, I wasn't expecting you to dress up so much. Would you like me to wear something that better matches you?" Your friend hears your concern and realizes that it's not because you don't like the outfit, it's because it makes you feel underdressed.

At work, a co-worker is shot down with a yes-but after suggesting an idea. The room goes quiet and someone at the table speaks up. "I here you, it is an excellent idea and I like the direction you are going in. Can you tell me how your idea addresses the gap in my thinking? I am having a hard time connecting the two." The co-worker who shared the idea is validated and asked to clarify. If they already know the answer, they will share it. If they don't, this politely signals that they have more work to do.

Here's one final example to drive the point home:

A co-worker comes to you with a new vendor and says, "Do you think it would be a good idea if we tried using this new company?"

(Not empowering) Yes, bringing on new vendors is always a good idea, but do some research first before you approve them.

(Empowering) Yes, bringing on new vendors is always a good idea and I'm curious to learn more about the company. Honestly, I haven't heard of them before. Do you know if they are competitive and pre-qualify to our vendor specs? (There are multiple "ands" in this statement. Did you catch the silent ones between sentences?)

Yes-and statements force us to be clearer with our communication. Instead of assuming a listener understands what we are negating, we direct them with additional information.

Listen First, And Maybe Only Listen

Using words is a small part of communication. On the receiving end, being a good listener means making sure the speaker feels like they are being heard. For example, being given advice when it is not asked for can make the listener feel talked down to. Even if this is not your intention—and for many, it is out of concern and friendship that they are giving advice—the speaker only wants to be heard and have their emotions validated.

Talking is not only exchanging information, it's also how we work through stress, joy, fear, and the array of emotions we feel every day. We talk to be understood, first. If a speaker wants advice, let them specifically ask for it. Give the speaker your full attention by moving other thoughts to the back of your mind. While listening, don't think about what you're going to say next. Spend that energy trying to understand what the person is saying now. If you do speak, only do so to validate the speaker so they can continue. Let them finish their piece and wait for them to ask you to respond (verbally or with their body language). If it takes you a moment to respond, it's okay to say, "Give me a moment. I was listening to what you were saying, and I want to make sure I heard you."

Instead of responding with your own story, respond by asking a question. You can let the speaker know you are listening by paraphrasing and using opening statements that invite the speaker to say more, like: "tell me more". Avoid using statements that close off the listener like: "the same thing happened to me".

Giving your own me-too example without validating the person's feelings first will shift the focus of the conversation from attending to their problem to yours. This is often unintentional. Instead, you should ask them to open up about what they are feeling. For example, if someone says, "I hate my manager", instead of you saying: "me too!", ask what the manager does that makes the speaker feel that way. Asking to elaborate will give the speaker time to be heard and process their feelings, when this is all they wanted to do in the first place.

We Are Still Children...Kind of...

Most of us manage to survive childhood, but not all of us outgrow it.
— MICHAEL P. NICHOLS, PhD

It's not just children who are childlike. Adults, too, are—beneath the bluster—intermittently playful, silly, fanciful, vulnerable, hysterical, terrified, and pitiful and in search of consolation and forgiveness.
— ALAIN DE BOTTON

Under stress, how someone copes with their emotions resembles how they processed them when they were growing up. That's why when someone is angry or frustrated, they do not always understand the weight their words carry. Instead of being offended, as emotionally intelligent listeners we should recognize that inside of the grown adult we are talking to lives a stubborn, shy, or strong-willed child. We wouldn't talk back to a child or give into their games, so why do we entertain the child inside of our co-workers and loved ones? Instead, this behavior should alert us to becoming a more compassionate and understanding listener. We should be as kind and patient with them as we are with children, while giving them the same respect we give adults. Instead of getting angry, giving advice, or sharing personal anecdotes, we should remember to listen first, and maybe only listen.

Communicating effectively is a challenging and worthwhile skill we will be working on our whole lives. It involves both listening and being heard. The more we understand about the diversity of communication styles, the better we will be able to tailor our communication.

Key Takeaways

o   When a person hears something, they overestimate what they think they understand, and when someone speaks, they overestimate how well they are understood.

o   When speaking to someone, try to match your com-munication style to their style.

o   When speaking with a large group or several people, use a variety of communication styles so you are able to reach everyone.

o   When speaking with someone, give them your full attention and consider what they are saying, rather than how you want to respond.

GOAL FOR TODAY: The next time someone comes to you and tells you something that is on their mind, practice being a good listener. Focus only on what they are talking about and see if you can listen to what they are saying (which may be different from the words they are using—language is a limited tool we use to express and understand feelings). Afterwards, think about what went well and what you can improve on. Look back at this section for tips on how to improve your listening and communication and flip to the suggested reading section for additional resources.

BODY LANGUAGE

Your body communicates as well as your mouth. Don't
contradict yourself.
— ALAN RUDDOCK

Body language is everything we communicate without the words we
speak. It is how we say words, the way we position our body, and the
speed of our breathing. Studies have found body language to be 60 to
90 percent of person-to-person communication, making it the most
powerful methods of communication. In this chapter, you will learn
how to use body language to help enhance your relationships.

Thinking with Your Body
In a study of Neuro-Linguistic Programming (NLP), thinking is
believed to be done with the whole body, and our thoughts leak out
into body language. Generally, we think in three ways: seeing (visual),
listening (auditory), and touching (kinesthetic). Yes, this is similar to
the learning styles we talked about earlier. Just as learning styles affect
our word choice, our body language depicts the type of thinking we
are using. For example, if you notice someone pointing or talking
with their hands (visual body language), they are likely a visual
thinker. Does the person use a lot of inflection? Do they hum a tune
or use sound effects when explaining a point? It's likely this person is
an auditory thinker. Is the person you're speaking to touching the

142

objects they're talking about and using them to demonstrate what they're saying to you? It is likely they are a kinesthetic thinker. If you pick up on a thinking style, you can tailor your language so they understand you more clearly. You can ask: "How do you see it?", "how does it sound to you?" or "Can you show me what you mean?"

Eye Movement

Researchers in NLP claim that where someone is looking (up, level/straightforward, or downward) is an indicator of what part of the brain they are accessing. Combine this with the direction they are looking (left or right) and it tells the observer if the person they are talking to is recalling a memory or creatively constructing an idea.

Here's how it breaks down.

Visual: Ask someone to spell the word "estuary". E-S-T-U... where are they looking? When people spell words they often look up and straight ahead as if the word was written on the ceiling or just above their left shoulder. Remembering how a word is spelled is visual thinking. In school, when a teacher would say, *you're not going to find the answer looking at the ceiling*—well, if you are a visual thinker, you probably did find the answer on the ceiling or on the upper left half of the classroom wall. This is because a person thinking visually is trying to get a clear view of the image in their mind's eye.

If you are talking with someone who is a visual thinker, they will tend to speak quickly and in a higher tone of voice. When doing this, they are trying to describe the images they see in their mind's eye before they flicker away or turn into something else. You will be able to tell by their rapid shallow breathing, and their body positioned with their shoulders high in the air.

When talking with a person who thinks visually, you should use visual language such as: *What do you imagine this would look like?*

Auditory: Next, there's auditory thinking. When a person is accessing the auditory part of their brain, their eyes move to their left or right (toward the ears).

When someone looks to the left, they are *remembering* a sound or a conversation. When someone looks to the right, they are *imagining* a conversation or what someone or something might sound like.

When talking with someone who prefers auditory thinking, you should use auditory language such as: *How does this sound?*

Kinesthetic: Finally, we have kinesthetic thinking. When a person is accessing the kinesthetic part of the brain, their eyes look downward, either to the right or left.

When someone looks down to the right, they are checking their feelings. They may also be thinking of remembered smells, tastes, and feelings. When someone looks down to the left, they are having an inner dialogue and asking themselves questions—this is called *self-talk*.

When talking with this person, you should use kinesthetic language such as: *How do you feel about this?*

To review, if someone is looking up, they are thinking visually. If their eyes are looking from side to side in the middle, they are utilizing auditory thinking. If a person is looking down, they are using kinesthetic thinking.

If the person you are observing is looking to their right, they are using their imagination or creativity. If the person is looking to their left, they are recalling information. See below a visual summary.

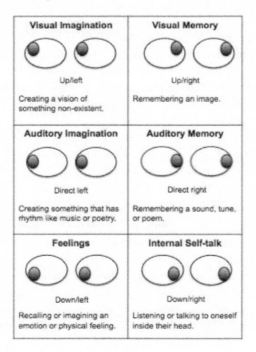

In some cases, the left and right may be switched (more common if the person is left-handed), but more often than not, the diagram on the previous page will be true.

There are people who make the claim that if a person looks to their right while answering a question, it is an indicator that they are lying, and if they look to their left, they are telling the truth. There are too many factors involved in most casual conversations to accurately identify if someone is lying. Instead use the information to foster better conversations, not to expose a liar.

Mirroring

Finally, using mirroring techniques is a great way to build rapport. The field of NLP describes mirroring as listening with your whole body. One way to do this is by identifying the keywords the person you are communicating with is using (including favorite phrases and mannerisms) and subtly building these into your side of the conversation. You can deliberately do this to build rapport until it becomes natural; however, it should be done genuinely. People can pick up behavior that is forced and may interpret it as mockery. To negate this, pace yourself. Be aware of the signals you send out and receive back, and be mindful of what is effective and what you need to change. If you are doing it right, it should feel natural—like dancing. You won't even notice that you have fallen into the same step while walking, or are sitting up in your chair at the same time, or taking a drink of water when they lift their cup, or breathing at the same rate.

If you are interested in how this works, check out the Meta-Mirror technique developed by Robert Dilts or do some fieldwork yourself and watch how people do it naturally in coffee shops or bars. If you are a recreational "people watcher" you can probably think of a time when you have observed two people engaged in a conversation. What did their rapport look like? First dates are great to watch. As an observer, what does a good first date look like? A bad one? What kind of body language do they use? What are they doing with their hands? Follow their eyes—what are they doing?

Learn from what you are observing and use what you see, but remember things that worked well with one person may not work for another. With body language, it is especially important to remember everyone is different, so treat each relationship as its own. And remember, be confident and don't be afraid to practice these methods. It is the only way you will build skill in this area.

Key Takeaways

o   Where a person looks when listening and speaking may give clues to whether they are a visual, auditory, or kinesthetic thinker.

o   Most likely, if someone is looking up, they are thinking visually. If their eyes are looking from side to side in the middle, they are thinking auditory. If a person is looking down, they are using kinesthetic thinking.

o   Try to match your responses to the type of thinking the person you are speaking with is using.

o   Use mirroring techniques to build rapport with someone quicker, but only if you are genuine.

GOAL FOR TODAY: Go to a public water hole like a coffee shop, bar, or food court. Bring your computer and a pair of headphones, but don't turn on the music. Open your laptop to a new text document. Now watch. Write down what you see and hear. How are people building relationships? What's working? What's not? Are there any noticeable changes in body language from the time they sit down to the time they stand up and leave?

Part 2:
Building Structure

Welcome to Part 2. You've worked your way through the foundational skills in Part 1 and probably have a good idea of a few goals you want to work towards. Now, it's time to build some structure so you can reach those goals. As you learned in the previous section, it's hard getting started. Change is tough. Often, we set out with the best of intentions only to find ourselves weeks or months later in the same place we started.

This section covers the Dock Model, something I created to keep myself mentally and physically fit during a time when every part of my life was incredibly busy. The model worked so well, I continued using it after my life returned to its normal pace, and I still use it to this day. The Dock Model is based on the four areas I believe to be directly correlated with living a meaningful and successful life: health, practice, play, and reflection. Whenever I feel like my life is unmanageable, one or more of these areas is off balance. The model confronts the myth that was popularized in the 20th century: work-life balance. Life is a balancing act, but it's not between work and life, it's between what we say we value and our actions. When our actions are misaligned with what we value, it causes an imbalance.

To integrate the Dock Model into your life, Part 2 ends with building models, routines, and rituals. Following these patterns of success, your goals become a part of your daily lifestyle.

INTRODUCTION TO THE DOCK

I moved through the days like a severed head that finishes a sentence. I waited for the moment that would snap me out of my seeming life.
— AMY HEMPEL, *The Harvest*

You wake up to the soothing songs of a humpback whale that are "scientifically proven" to naturally ease you out of your lightest phase of sleep. You reach for your phone and open your sleep tracking app. Sitting up in bed, you scan through the text messages you received during the night. You get an email and slide it aside for later. In your kitchen, you pour some green juice, what you like to call "swamp water," and do a web search for "reconstituted concentrate" to see if it is really 100% juice. You track the swamp water along with the rest of breakfast in a nutrition app that's linked to your watch that triples as a step counter and quadruples as a heart rate monitor. You check the weather app and decide to bring an umbrella. On the bus, you read the news using an app that selects stories based on the stories you have clicked on in the past. You listen to that new song you like on your streaming music app and share it with a friend. You take a picture of the sunrise, and share it with your followers. On your walk from the bus stop to the office, a local coffee shop sends you a message using a location-based restaurant app promoting their seasonal drink that happens to be on special. You buy a coffee and pay for it by scanning your phone. In the elevator, you post a review. Good morning.

We are, for better or worse, connected (and distracted), making it challenging to keep our priorities straight. As our lives become more fluid, the line between our work life and personal life has started to disappear. The nine-to-five job has become a thing of the past, as most employers expect us to answer emails and reply to work-related text messages outside of working hours. This becomes a problem when your career is not your passion or when your work tries to make itself a priority over something you value higher outside of working hours. It's no wonder why so many people get confused about work-life balance. You can't partition your life between eight hours of work, eight hours of free time, and eight hours of sleep. They all influence each other: If you have a rough night and don't get much sleep, you will be tired at work. If work is stressful, you will come home stressed. If your home life is fulfilling, you will sleep more soundly and be happier at work. Everything is connected.

Balancing Priorities

Shortly after moving to Seattle, WA, one of my new friends asked me if I had looked up something we had been talking about the previous week. Shocked that he still remembered (I had completely forgotten) I offhandedly said: "No. I didn't have time." Without missing a beat, he responded with: "You did have time, but you chose not to make it a priority." I told him that I honestly didn't even think about it. He was inspecting my book collection and didn't look up when he spoke next. He said: "I'm not offended. Don't say you didn't have time, say you didn't make it a priority. You have all the time in the world to do whatever you want. If it was a priority, you would have done it. It wasn't. So, you didn't do it."

My friend's offhanded comment changed how I saw time. Up until this point, I had chosen to do things not because I valued it over something else, but for other reasons I didn't quite understand. Although I had goals, I was without a plan. To identify my priorities, I examined what I had completed in the past. If I finished something, it must have been important to me. If I didn't finish something, it meant that wasn't as high of a priority as I thought it was—even if I had been telling myself for years that it was. It was hard to admit, but these were the tasks that were pulling me away from the things I truly loved.

This is what people talk about when they talk about work-life balance. You can't balance work and life, there is only your life. The hard part is prioritizing what you value when so many responsibilities, people, projects, and opportunities are calling your name.

Path Priorities

In my late teens and early 20's, I wore a lot of hats. Under each was the same troubled head. At the time, I was pursuing a career in music. As a backup, I was in school and taking a lot of science classes with the intention of going into the medical field. But I wasn't 100% sure. There was also the study of law, something I liked because of its attention to detail and crafting arguments. And then there was Philosophy, the one class I took my sophomore year as a Gen. Ed. that soon became my favorite subject and a minor. Not to mention a brief fling with sociology and later, its cousin, anthropology. Most of my time outside of the classroom, I spent reading and writing. I also liked the idea of owning my own business and was always starting small side projects that were incredibly exciting for a couple of weeks, but usually fizzled out and were replaced by a new grand idea the next month.

My problem was, everything felt important and I was moving an inch in every direction instead of focusing on making progress in one direction. Everything was important, which made nothing a priority. There was nothing leading my way besides a general curiosity for life. When I decided to move out West, I accepted that I needed to pool my efforts and focus on only a few things. The first week, I monitored where I spent my time and realized that I enjoyed music, but couldn't stand working with other musicians. There were several other roads I could have gone down with music, but none of them were calling my name. I crossed music off my priority list, but kept my bass by my desk so I could play it when I needed to de-stress (inspired by Einstein, who would play his violin to destress).

Over the next few weeks, I realized that I was clicking on more news stories dealing with philosophy and politics than healthcare. When I went to the library, I found myself scanning the works of John Locke and Jean-Paul Sartre instead of seeking out scientific journals. I crossed healthcare off my list and put a check mark next to philosophy. The next week, I crossed anthropology off my list because I chose writing a satirical story (a story I showed to no one and wrote for the shear enjoyment of putting one word in front of the other) over doing my reading for my Cultural Anthropology class. This mindful monitoring continued over the years. Some priorities have shifted, but I have always stopped at about three or four because that's all I can really work on at one time. Each priority has steadily fallen into one of the following categories. The first is my job (something I enjoy that will pay the bills), the second, a hobby (with the hope that it will one day replace my job), and third, close friends and family (because the connections I make with others are more valuable to me than anything I can buy). And finally, an optional fourth priority is a spiritual practice or volunteering to help a cause I feel a strong connection to.

After I identified my three-to-four priorities, I kept them in mind when making my daily and weekly to-do lists. To this day, I make sure to prioritize activities that will further my work, my hobby, and still leave time to spend with the people I love. I call these my path priorities, because each one plays a role in shaping my path.

Core Priorities
In addition to path priorities, there are core priorities, like a healthy lifestyle, that support your goals. In Maslow's hierarchy of needs, core priorities represent the bottom two layers in the pyramid: physiological and safety.

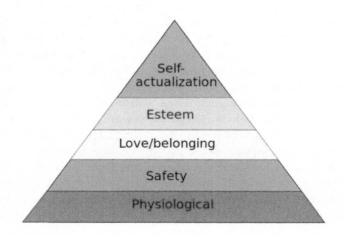

Even though core priorities don't directly correlate with a specific skill, they are necessary to have before you can start growing a skill. Some examples of core priorities are: eating well, exercising, paying bills, doing laundry, maintaining personal hygiene, and taking out the trash. It's life maintenance, and if you don't make them a priority, it will bleed over into the rest of your life.

Core priorities provide the structure for my path priorities. When I take care of my health, practice my skills, allow for unstructured time at work and home, and spend time reflecting on my actions and goals, the balance shows in my work and in my relationships.

Your Dock

To maintain the balance of both core and path priorities, I created a model I call the Dock Model. The idea is that we all have a dock to maintain, and if we keep it in good shape, opportunities will come and drop anchor.

The dock rests on four pillars that start at your core and move out to your path. The two closest to the shore are Health (sleep, eat, move, breathe) and Practice (skills you are growing). These are the pillars you need stable before you extend your dock and reach the other pillars. Once you are ready to diversify your skill set, you can venture away from the shore by taking healthy risks and exploring what's in the open sea. The two pillars supporting the dock out in open water are Play (active discovery) and Reflection (time alone for meditation or journaling).

We often only think of one or two of these pillars, but according to the model, we need all four to keep our dock level. When one of the pillars is built up too much, it creates an uneven environment where it's easy to fall into the water. Similarly, if you neglect one of the pillars, your dock will start to sink and flood.

Planks

The wood connecting the foundation pillars, forming the dock's walkway, are the planks. The planks symbolize the routines, rituals, and models to keep the dock stable and free from cracks and rot. They are also a symbol of the interconnectedness of each pillar. If a plank breaks, it affects the structural integrity of the whole dock. Daily rituals and routines provide your dock with regular and structured maintenance to keep your whole dock above water. You will find more information on building and strengthening these planks at the end of Part 2.

Water, Waves, and Weather

The water, waves, and unpredictable weather represent the stress and unexpected tasks life throws at us. The only way to keep from sinking into the unforeseen storms of deadline and self-doubt is to have a sturdy dock with a solid foundation and well-maintained planks. If you keep a solid dock, there's no telling what opportunities may anchor there.

There are no crash diets or one-times fixes for balancing your life. Sustainable change comes from lifestyle change. The model is a full life approach instead of focusing on the details or separating one priority exclusively from another. My hope is that the Dock Model will encourage you to think differently about how you structure your day. I also hope it provides a framework you can use to start incorporating the skills you are currently learning about in this book.

HEALTH:
THE FIRST PILLAR

Health is not valued till sickness comes.
— THOMAS FULLER

Let's face it, when life gets busy, health is the first thing to go. I know I've caught myself bragging about how little sleep I have gotten, as if sleep deprivation is a testament to my willpower or dedication. During busy times, I have regretfully eaten food from a drive-thru because I was too tired to make something healthy at home. I have justified skipping exercising with spending more time on work projects, only to have a hard time concentrating for the rest of the day. My choices have led to stress, and instead of calming myself down through breathing, I have said things I later regretted. Other times, stress has turned into anxiety, and I have forgotten words at critical moments. All of these choices lead to poor health, and due to poor health, I have lost and gained weight, missed opportunities, unintentionally hurt others, and worst of all, felt detached from my own body, as if I was watching myself react to life instead of living it.

The first pillar, Health—sleeping, eating food, moving, and breathing—is arguably the most important factor in living a happy and successful life. If you take care of your body, you will have more energy, be more focused, and work quickly with precision.

Just a couple of reminders before we get started: This is a book about how to be agile in your work and at home so you can live a fulfilling life in our new paradigm of technology and education. Part of being agile is building routines around your health so you can operate at your peak. Please, don't confuse this for a health book. That said, although I am citing information from peer-reviewed journals, you should always talk to your doctor before making any big lifestyle changes. Knowing your health history, your doctor can provide you with the unique support you need, even if they are only supporting you from the sidelines. Also, this book is meant be a guide to introduce you to the basics. Since this is only an introduction to how health affects your life, work, and productivity, I encourage you to research any ideas that pique your interest. A good place to start is with the books I have listed on the Suggested Reading & Listening page. For now, let's keep it simple and only go over the basics. As long as you sleep, eat food, move, and breathe, you will keep the first pillar of your dock above water.

Sleep

Moderate sleep deprivation produces impairments in cognitive and motor performance equivalent to legally prescribed levels of alcohol intoxication.

— A.M. WILLIAMSON and ANNE-MARIE-FEYER, in *Occupational & Environmental Medicine*

The myth of working harder is being replaced by the science of working smarter. In the old paradigm, sleep was an obstacle to overcome, something one could power through if they had enough determination. In the new paradigm, sleep is a tool we can use to become the high-functioning version of ourselves our sleep deprived selves haven't allowed us to be. Recently, there has been a movement to change our cultural view on sleep. Super-humans, i.e. the Dalai Lama, Arianna Huffington, Ellen DeGeneres, Bill Gates, and Warren Buffett, have all spoken about the importance of getting a full night's sleep. So, what is a full night's sleep? According to the *Journal of Clinical Sleep Medicine*, an adult needs seven or more hours of sleep each night. Young adults and people recovering from sleep debt need somewhere around nine hours per night. If you are regularly sleeping less, there's a good chance that you haven't been operating at your peak in a while. Productivity goes down if you are not consistently getting a full night's sleep. This means that your energy level and work output could be much higher than it is now. Even though you may not see it, if you are getting a full night of sleep, you are less productive and making mistakes.

Here's what's going on when you're not getting a full night's sleep…

You're not tired, you're drunk. After staying up all night, your attention to detail and decision-making may *feel* better than ever, but scientific literature tells a different story. Multiple studies suggest that sleep deprivation affects neurobiological function in a way that is similar to alcohol intoxication. According to Harvard Medical School Professor Charles A. Czeisler,

> We now know that 24 hours without sleep or a week of sleeping four or five hours a night induces an impairment equivalent to a blood alcohol level of 0.1%.

All U.S. states pin drunk driving at a blood alcohol level of .08%, meaning, if you pull an all-nighter, you are legally drunk. Your manager wouldn't pull up to the bar at closing time and ask all your co-workers to hop in and car pool to work, and yet, we continue to celebrate people who sacrifice sleep for their job. If you're not sleeping, you shouldn't be working…or driving.

Lots of health problems are brewing, even if you don't see it yet. I get it. It's fun to stay up late. If you're in school, you might have to pull an all-nighter before finals, or go to that super awesome concert and after-party that lasts until 4am. Will doing this occasionally, kill you? The studies I've read only show a correlation with prolonged and repeated behavior. Meaning, if you need to sacrifice sleep to pull a project together in the 11th hour, it's probably ok, just don't make a habit of it. And to make sure you don't make a habit of it, here is a small list of the health problems associated with lack of sleep: Obesity, diabetes, heart disease, heart attack, heart failure, irregular heartbeat, stroke, hypertension, anxiety, depression, substance abuse, Parkinson's disease, Alzheimer's disease, dementia, and a variety of cancers, including prostate, oral, nasal, colorectal, primary nervous system, and breast cancer. In addition, your immune system takes a hit. According to a recent study conducted at University of California-San Francisco, you are four times more likely to catch a cold if you don't regularly get a full night's sleep. Add it all together and those who don't get enough sleep have a shorter life expectancy and report having a lower quality of life.

You're sleeping, and you may be unaware of it. In his book, *The Sleep Solution*, sleep specialist W. Chris Winter writes about a research study conducted by David Dinges and Hans Van Dongen. In the study, Dinges and Dongen separated research participants into three groups: a four-hour-per-night sleep group, a six-hour group, and an eight-hour group. The researchers kept them busy with a series of psychomotor vigilance tasks (a sustained-attention reaction time task that measures the speed a subject responds to visual stimuli) and tracked their attention every day for two weeks. At the end of the study, a quarter of the participants in the six-hour group were falling asleep while they were performing tasks, and the four-hour group was much worse. The kicker is, the sleep-deprived participants didn't think they were impaired. They were literally falling asleep on the computer while they were emailing all their friends about how they just powered through some dumb sleep-deprivation experiment.

Dr. Winters ends this section in his book with the following:

...[T]o sum up the current thinking among every reputable sleep scientist in the world, here is the gospel: There is probably a very small percentage of the population that can get six hours of sleep or slightly less over a relatively prolonged period of time and can maintain their performance, but performance deterioration will occur. The idea that there are people out there getting two or three hours of sleep for long periods of time and are still able to walk, chew their own food, program their DVRs, and string together coherent sentences is simply not true.

If, however, you are the chosen one, I want to be the one who discovers you and receives all of the scientific accolades and awards. So, please...send your information to my publisher. We'll sort it all out from there.

If you think you are only sleeping a few hours per night, and have been for years, what do you think is going on when you space out for a few seconds, err, minutes, during a meeting? Or when you catch yourself staring into your computer screen? Your body is shutting down and forcing you into something called microsleep, which is a momentary and involuntary pocket of temporary unconsciousness. If this is you, please, don't get behind the wheel of a vehicle. And if you live in or around Seattle, WA, and you take the 545 bus between downtown and Redmond, I've seen you with your laptop open, head resting against the window, slack-jawed (is that drool?), taking a little cat nap. I mean, you were only catching up on your email. That's right, you are part of that new group at Microsoft developing an app that sends email directly to the back of your eyelids.

Your body needs sleep. Just like the little dog I see walking around my neighborhood that plops down in the middle of the sidewalk and refuses to move when she's tired, your body does the same. If you aren't letting it sleep, it will eventually force you to.

Now that I have thoroughly scared you with the harmful effects of not getting enough sleep (hopefully you're not so anxious about sleeping that you can't fall asleep), I put together a list of habits, some to-dos and some not-to-dos that will increase the quality and quantity of your sleep. But first, a little background on why we sleep and why environmental cues are so important.

Why we sleep at night. In the 1960's, Jürgen Aschoff, a German behavioral physiologist, conducted a groundbreaking study sponsored by the Max Planck Institute. The study asked: If there was no sunlight to trigger our biological clocks, how would the human body respond?

To answer the question, Aschoff and his team turned old World War II bunkers into comfortable living areas. Each one included a sleeping area, bathroom, and kitchen. Forbidden items included televisions, radios, clocks, watches, and anything that could indicate what time or day it was. Test participants were asked to go about their day, eating three meals per day and not taking any naps. Aschoff observed participants slowly lengthening their day. The participants perceived they were living a normal 24-hour day, when they were actually living a lengthened day, on average somewhere between 24.7 hours and 25.2 hours.

What Aschoff was measuring is something called a circadian rhythm—it's a fancy term for the internal clock our bodies use to regulate when we should sleep, work, and procreate. It's a biological function that relies on environmental triggers, like sunlight, (the very thing Aschoff denied his participants) to keep us in tune with the 24-hour Earth day. If we aren't exposed to those triggers, or we confuse our body by exposing it to sunlight at night, our circadian rhythm gets thrown off. This is why the sun is so important, because it resets our circadian rhythm. If we didn't have the sun to remind us when to go to sleep and when to wake up, everyone would be on a different clock. Since our bodies rely on the sun, we can feel it in our energy level when the seasons change and the days start getting slightly shorter or longer. Sunny 6:00AM with birds chirping is a lot easier to wake up to than 6:00AM in the December when it's dark enough to still see the stars.

To avoid your life turning into Achoff's experiment and to keep environmental cues working as they should with your circadian rhythm, here are some things you can do to get quality sleep every night.

Cut out blue light at least one hour before bed. Ever wonder why you can see your TV, laptop, tablet, phone, and other screened devices so well during the day? It's because they emit blue light. Even if the sun is shining, you can still see the cool colors on your illuminated screen. The only problem is, the brain reacts in a similar way to blue light as it does when it is exposed to sunlight. When you use your screened devices at night, it throws off your circadian rhythm by making your brain believe it's still daytime. As a result, you have a harder time falling asleep.

Starting tonight, turn off your TV, close your laptop, and leave your phone on the kitchen table.

Uhhhhh…. you still there? This is a good time to reflect on your technology usage. I am definitely tied to my phone, and reducing screen time before bed is something I am working on. In the bedroom, you should only be doing two things, and watching TV isn't one of them. According to top sleep researchers, your bed is for sleeping and having sex. That's it. (Pillow talk is part of the second one…well, maybe the first one for some of us).

If you are still having a hard time breaking screen time before bed, find something you like just as much (or better). Better options I have found include talking to the real non-digital people you live with, reading something on paper like a book or news articles you printed, meditating, journaling, playing with a brain puzzle or a LEGO® toy, doing a craft like knitting, crocheting, sewing, or listening to music. If this is a struggle, you can ease into your new no-screens-evenings by using the free app f.lux (https://justgetflux.com) to reduce the blue light on your screen at night. The f.lux app adjusts the color temperature on your screen according to your location and the time of day. Many newer devices have a setting that does this automatically, all you need to do is turn it on by going into the tools or settings function. Another option is to buy glasses designed to block blue light. I have some I use at home and it's worth looking like a haggard rockstar trying to hide the last few decades behind thick yellow lenses, because they work! That said, my wife doesn't let me walk out the front door with them on.

Set a bedtime. Sleep problems occur when we try to power through Monday through Friday and hibernate Saturday and Sunday. <u>Your bedtime should be the same on the weekends as it is during the week.</u> If you are constantly changing the time you go to bed and wake up, you are exposing your body to triggers it is not used to. You will throw off your circadian rhythm and struggle to fall asleep and wake up.

Moderate caffeine, alcohol, and nicotine intake. Getting better sleep includes reevaluating some choices we have become dependent on. Second to screen use, caffeine is probably the biggest habit getting in the way of a good night's sleep. Don't worry, I've already tried taking away your phone at night, I'd be a terrible person if I also tried taking away your morning coffee. Besides, there are numerous studies that show positive links to coffee consumption. In the research, problems arise when people are drinking too much caffeine, especially before bed. A 2013 study published in the *Journal of Clinical Sleep Medicine* recommends stopping caffeine use six hours before bed. Even if you can fall asleep shortly after drinking a pot of coffee, caffeine disrupts the quality of your sleep. A good rule of thumb is: if you need caffeine to feel "normal," you should consider reducing your coffee intake.

A few years ago, I switched from drinking coffee to tea. It took about a week for my body to adjust, but it was worth it. As contradictory as it sounds, consuming less caffeine has given me more energy. When you're used to drinking gas station jet fuel every day, your body builds up a tolerance to caffeine, so when you need an extra kick, you're already maxed out. Caffeine should be a kick when you need it, not the crutch you use every day. You can still get the same benefits from coffee if you drink decaf, and it comes without all the jitters. I know plenty of people who drink one or two cups of regular coffee in the morning and switch to decaf the rest of the day. They are still able to get their coffee fix and they can sleep through the night.

If you are looking to completely remove caffeine from your lifestyle, try drinking warm lemon water. Lemon water is believed by many to provide a lot of health benefits such as aiding in digestion, skin health, and brain health. Just a reminder: before consuming your morning beverage, drink at least one large glass of room temperature water. Your body needs to rehydrate after sleeping for seven or eight hours.

One last downside about caffeine: It's a diuretic. Meaning, it increases your production of urine. If you are drinking caffeine in the afternoon or evening, it may disrupt your sleep by waking you up for a visit to the bathroom. While we're on the subject of nightly bathroom visits, drinking alcohol suppresses the production of anti-diuretic hormone (ADH), so your body starts producing more urine than it normally would. Not only does alcohol dehydrate your body, it keeps you up at night.

The bad news about alcohol is that it disrupts your sleep in other ways. Many people associate alcohol with sleep because it can make you drowsy. Among my friends, some of them casually refer to alcohol as a sleep aid. Again, quality of sleep becomes an issue. According to a study authored by researchers at The London Sleep Centre, alcohol consumed in any quantity causes sleep disruption. When moderate or high levels of alcohol are consumed, there is a reduction in the rapid eye movement phase of sleep (REM sleep), the part of sleep associated with retaining memory and dreaming. If you've ever had a hangover, you know how badly you want to sleep. This is because your body needs to recover, and you haven't had the quality sleep you need to repair your body. If you decide to let loose one weekend, give your body some time to recover.

The last chemical in the trio is nicotine. Nicotine is a stimulant. As such, it will keep you awake, and like caffeine, your quality of sleep will suffer even when you do fall asleep. If getting quality sleep is important to you, you should reduce or cease your nicotine, caffeine, and alcohol intake.

Short mid-day naps are ok. I'm going to keep this section short and sweet, just like your naps should be. Our circadian rhythm dips towards sleep in the early afternoon. William Dement, founder of the Sleep Research Center at Stanford University, told the New York Times: "It seems nature definitely intended that adults should nap in the middle of the day, perhaps to get out of the midday sun." This is one factor contributing to your drowsiness after lunch (another being postprandial somnolence, aka food coma, but we'll get into that later). If you do decide to take a nap, it should be for no longer than 20-30 minutes, because a nap should supplement, never replace, your sleep at night. The time limit is to avoid going into deep sleep so you don't wake up feeling worse than when you went to sleep. In fact, a study published in the Journal of Sleep and Research suggests taking a six-minute nap helps with remembering facts, data, and events. A great alternative to napping is meditation. More on meditation in a few pages.

Journal before bed. If you have a hard time falling asleep because you have too many thoughts racing around your brain, journaling about them is a good way to put them to rest. When I write about what's on my mind, I think about how I am catching the thoughts and tying them down to the page. If the thought is on the page, I don't need to keep it in my head. A bonus is the next day when you wake up, you will have a full to-do list to start with in the morning.

Eat food. Finally, the last suggestion I have is to eat good, quality food. Your diet plays a big role in the quality of sleep you get. As I transition to food, keep in mind that all of these sections: sleep, food, exercise, and breathing, are connected.

This first pillar is a doozy. If you are reading one chapter a day, this is a good place to break.

Eat Food

Food is medicine and medicine is food.
— AYURVEDIC PROVERB

The American paradox is we are a people who worry unreasonably about dietary health yet have the worst diet in the world.
— MICHAEL POLLAN

Before I met my wife, I was a sucker for lifehacks. If you're not familiar with the term, a lifehack is a trick or shortcut to increase productivity or speed up results in an area of one's life. Lifehacks encompass a variety of topics, including: time management, sleep, energy conservation, and nutrition, to name a few. Lifehacks offer an alternative to the traditional way of thinking, often in the form of quick and easy solutions. Although I believe some lifehack websites were created with the best of intentions, the culture around lifehacks has grown toxic. This is largely due to many of the hacks being grounded in pseudoscience, cultural myths, and the misinterpretation of scientific studies. When I first started using lifehacks, I thought of myself as an early adopter to what would eventually become the norm. In reality, most lifehackers are buying and selling modern-day snake oil.

I can summarize every lifehack I tried in two words: It. Sucked. Temporary hacks do not solve real problems. Most of the lifehacks I tried were about cutting down on mealtime. I saw eating as an inconvenience. It took too much time to sit down and eat—forget about preparing it. If I couldn't blend it or microwave it, I didn't buy it. I saw food as fuel and ate as quickly as I could. As a result of all my lifehacking, I gained weight, and felt tired and sick. The hour or more I gained from avoiding cooking and traditional eating was lost due to my slip in productivity. One of the many problems was, I was eating prepackaged laboratory food that only resembled the meals I grew up with. I thought I was being healthy—that's what killed me. The packaging on my energy bar said it was packed with nutritional benefits, so why was I feeling sick and gaining weight, and why couldn't I pronounce half of the ingredients?

Twenty pounds heavier and 20% less productive, I turned from internet lifehacks to science journalism. While browsing the nonfiction books at the Seattle Public Library, I discovered the author Michael Pollan, who had already asked (and answered) the same question I was struggling with: "What should we have for dinner?" Pollan calls this the *Omnivore's Dilemma*, which also happens to be the title of his book. And by asking what's for dinner, Pollan grapples with the cultural, ethical, and political implications of our food choices. For the first time, I was seeing what was actually going into the food I ate.

Take a moment and think about what food looks like now and what it looked like 100 years ago. Your relatives a century ago wouldn't recognize most of the products on the shelf at your local chain-grocery store, and would probably hesitate before calling it food. Walk down an aisle and pick an item at random, turn it over and look at the ingredients. You'll notice that there's little real food (naturally occurring plants or animals) in your box, bag, or wrapper. Take, for example, my cartoon-endorsed pink tube of packaged portable yogurt—what plant or animal did it come from? And, excuse my language, but what the hell is a Twinkie? I don't think they're plucked from Twinkie branches, slowly baked in the Kansas sunshine, packaged, and shipped to aisle 12 of your local grocery store. Through extensive processing: isolating compounds, heating, cooling, hydrogenating, saltwater injections, and vitamin sprays, we get food-like substances. The products inside the boxes, cans, or wrappers that resemble food, may have been food at one time, but are now nothing more than a chemistry experiment made by people with PhDs with fancy lab equipment. In these laboratories, scientists can isolate flavor, vitamins, proteins, fats, carbs, you name it, and create food-like substances that appear nutritional, but are nothing more than extensive cellular plastic surgery. The result is a taste our mouths water for, with just enough added minerals and reduced fat so someone in advertising can give it the name we have come to love and trust: healthy.

Walking down the supermarket aisle, I realized how obsessed our culture is with the idea of health, dieting, and detoxing. Brightly colored packages and boxes screamed at me with their "healthy" advertising. *Less Fat! Whole Grain! Organic! 100 Calories!* I felt like I was in the John Carpenter movie, *They Live*, and I had just put on the sunglasses that depict the world as it truly is: surrounded by subliminal commands to obey, consume, reproduce, and conform.

If I want to eat healthy, but can't trust food labels, how do I know what to eat? Great question. In his follow-up book, *In Defense of Food*, Pollan spends 256 pages unpacking these seven words: "Eat food, mostly plants, not too much." In short, we should steer clear of anything our grandmother (or great-grandmother) doesn't recognize as food, meaning: avoid all processed foods. A good rule to follow is the more advertising it has, the less healthy it is (i.e. the fruit and veggies I buy have zero packaging or health claims—the organic, NONGMO, 100 calories, made from 100% real whole grain, vitamin B12 cookies I sometimes buy are a billboard for health, when they are the furthest thing from healthy).

Food is important because it is how we fuel our bodies. If you put bad fuel into your body, your body will run slowly, produce a lot of gas, and eventually, break down. In order to think clearly and have enough energy to complete all your daily tasks, you need to eat quality food. Now that you know what real food is, this next section is about which foods to eat, when, and how much. The following are tips to help you find your starting point, and by no means is a full nutrition plan. My hope for the section is for you to reevaluate your relationship with food so you can make permanent lifestyle changes. That's it. If you eat good food, you will feel better (physically and mentally) and you will be more productive.

Cut out refined sugar and rely on complex carbohydrates, proteins, and fats as your fuel source. When you consume simple carbohydrates like refined sugar, your energy spikes and then crashes, making you jittery and tired. The result is poor performance and fatigue. If that isn't enough, the refined sugars that taste so good and make their way into a large percentage of the Western diet are just as harmful as smoking cigarettes. According to a study published in the *American Journal of Public Health*, drinking sugary drinks like soda (pop, if you're from the Midwest) are directly correlated with stress, cardiovascular disease, diabetes, and cancer. In the study, researchers found that drinking eight ounces of sugar soda a day over the course of the three-year study corresponded to 1.9 years of additional aging. Bump the dose up to a 20-ounce serving (the average single serving bottle size) and participants aged 4.6 additional years over the same three-year time period. In the discussion, the data was compared to a similar study with the average smoker who aged at the same rate (4.6 additional years over three years). If you need a pick-me-up, sugar soda will not only make you crash, but it will put you at a higher risk for disease and pre-mature aging.

In order to maintain a healthy level of natural energy throughout the day, you should eat a balanced diet of good fats, proteins, and complex carbs (sometimes called slow-burning carbs). Foods like the ones I have listed on the next page are packed with nutrition for your body and brain. They will fill you up and give you sustainable energy throughout the day.

Complex Carbohydrates

Acorn Squash	Garbanzo Beans	Rye
All-Bran Cereal	Green Peas	Split Peas
Amaranth	Kamut	Sorghum
Barley	Kidney Beans	Teff
Beets	Lentils	Tritcale
Black Beans	Lima Beans	Sorghum
Black-Eyed Peas	Millet	Spelt
Buckwheat	Navy Beans	Starchy Vegetable
Bulgur	Oats	Sweet Potatos
Butternut Squash	Oatmeal	Taro
Carrots	Parsnips	Wheat
Corn	Pinto Beans	Wheat Berries
Durum	Plantains	Whole-Grain Breads
Einkorn	Pumpkin	Whole-Grain Cereals
Emmer	Quinoa	Whole-Grain Flours
Farro	Rice (Brown/Wild)	Yams

Fat

Almonds	Edamame	Pistachios
Avocados	Flaxseed	Pumpkin Seeds
Brazil Nuts	Hazelnuts	Salmon
Canola Oil	Herring	Sardines
Cashews	Macadamia Nuts	Spirulina
Cheese	Mackerel	Sunflower Seeds
Chia Seeds	Milk	Tofu
Coconut	Olives	Trout
Dark Chocolate	Olive Oil	Tuna
(70% or higher)	Pecans	Yogurt
Eggs	Pine Nuts	Walnuts

Protein

Almonds
Anchovies
Artichokes
Beef (grass-fed)
Bison
Beans
Broccoli
Brussels Sprouts
Cashews
Chia Seeds
Chicken
Cod
Cottage Cheese
Edamame
Eggs
Gruyere Cheese

Guava
Halibut
Peas
Pumpkin Seeds
Lentils
Milk
Oats
Octopus
Ostrich
Peanuts
Peanuts Butter
Pork
Quinoa
Salmon
Sardines
Shrimp

Spinach
Soba Noodles
Sprouted Whole-Grain Bread
Sun-Dried Tomatoes
Swiss Cheese
Teff
Tilapia
Tofu
Triticale
Tuna
Turkey
Wheat Germ
Whey Protein
Yogurt (Greek)

Fruit

Açaí Berries
Apples
Bananas
Blackberries
Blueberries
Cantaloupe
Cherries
Cranberries
Dragon Fruit

Grapes
Grapefruit
Guava
Lemons
Limes
Kiwi
Mango
Oranges
Papayas

Pineapple
Plums
Pomegranate
Strawberries
Tomatoes*
Raspberries
Watermelon

* "Knowledge is knowing that a tomato is a fruit, wisdom is not putting it in a fruit salad." — Miles Kington

Vegetables

Asparagus	Cauliflower	Mushrooms
Artichoke	Celery	Okra
Arugula	Collard Greens	Onions
Beets	Cucumber	Scallions
Bell Peppers	Eggplant	Spinach
Bok Choy	Fennel	Swiss Chard
Broccoli	Green Beans	Peas
Brussel Sprouts	Kale	Peppers (hot)
Cabbage	Leeks	Watercress
Carrots	Lettuce	Zucchini

Misc.

Here are a few more food suggestions that don't always fit into a category. Many of them are spices. This is by no means a complete list, these are a few I think are most important.

Apple Cider Vinegar	Oregano
Basil (Holy Basil)	Parsley
Cilantro	Peppermint
Cinnamon	Rosemary
Garlic	Sage
Ginger	Tarragon
Ginseng	Thyme
Lavender	Turmeric (use with black
Matcha/Green Tea	pepper for cancer fighting
Mustard Seed	benefits)

Cut out processed foods. Doctors and undertakers in Germany have observed that bodies are taking a longer time to decompose than previous generations. The scientific community is skeptical and is still investigating factors causing the delayed decomposition, but the hypothesis gaining the most attention is food preservatives in processed foods. According to the theory, not only do preservatives give our food shelf life, it gives us shelf life too. Food radicals believe that when we consume preservatives, we are slowly embalming ourselves while we are still alive. Whether or not this is true, I started thinking about preservatives, specifically how the government determines if chemicals are safe to use in our food.

In the U.S., the Food and Drug Administration (FDA) approves all chemicals labeled as food preservatives, the only problem is, since this is a new field in food science, the FDA often approves chemicals for use without knowing the long-term health effects. According to an article published in the peer-reviewed journal *Reproductive Toxicology*, there are many data gaps and oversights in the FDA's approval process:

> Almost 80% of chemical additives directly—intentionally—added to food lack the relevant information needed to estimate the amount that consumers can safely eat in FDA's own database and 93% lack reproductive or developmental toxicity data, although FDA requires feeding toxicology data for these chemicals.

Until more research is done, it's safer to stay away from lab-made food preservatives, sweeteners, and fats, even if they are approved by the FDA. This includes plant-made ingredients including high-fructose corn syrup, partially hydrogenated oils, monosodium glutamate, sucralose, and aspartame. Bottom line, if your food doesn't decompose (with the exception of foods like cheese, pickling, and fermentation) it's probably no longer food.

Get your vitamins from plants, not pills. In December of 2013, the journal *Annals of Internal Medicine* published an article authored by Eliseo Guallar, MD, DrPH, at the Johns Hopkins Bloomberg School of Public Health, titled *Enough Is Enough: Stop Wasting Money on Vitamin and Mineral Supplements*. In the article, the researchers review current peer-reviewed studies and conclude that multivitamins are largely ineffective:

> With respect to multivitamins, the studies published in this issue and previous trials indicate no substantial health benefit. This evidence, combined with biological considerations, suggests that

any effect, either beneficial or harmful, is probably small.

Since the research on taking supplemental vitamins is mixed and hasn't shown to be beneficial, I suggest pocketing the money and buying more vegetables. Our bodies can easily break down vitamins and minerals that are naturally occurring in food. As long as you are eating a balanced diet of leafy green vegetables, fruits, healthy fats, protein, and complex carbohydrates, you will never need a vitamin supplement.

Avoid diets, cleanses, detoxes, and other health buzzwords. When most of us talk about going on a diet, we are typically referring to something short-term. A quick fix. An uncomfortable time when we try to drop a few pounds before gaining it all back over the next holiday. The problem is, if you want to keep the weight off and feel healthy every day, you need a lifestyle change, not a short-term fix. Diets suck for two reasons. 1) Most of the time, diets are starvation based. This means that it's uncomfortable, and because you're shocking your system by depriving it from fuel, you end up slow-walking through the day like a sad zombie. 2) If you don't change your eating habits, you will gain back all the weight you lost. In fact, even calling your lifestyle change a diet may work against you. According to neuroscientist, Sandra Aamodt, the stress of dieting leads to more weight gain, not weight loss. The only way to achieve your ideal weight is being mindful of what you are eating, exercising regularly, and making this a permanent routine.

Cleanses and detoxes have taken over the health industry, and like traditional American diets, they may do more harm than good. Despite the popularity of juice cleanses and skin detoxes, there haven't been any studies to prove their effectiveness. In 2014, the *Journal of Human Nutrition and Dietetics* published a review of detox diets, stating: "To the best of our knowledge, no randomised controlled trials have been conducted to assess the effectiveness of commercial detox diets in humans." Why is the scientific community reacting so strongly to detoxes and cleanses? Because detoxing doesn't make any sense. According to Alexandra Parker, a dietitian and co-owner of The Biting Truth in Sydney, Australia, our bodies don't need any help detoxing—they do a good job of it on their own: "These organs [liver, kidneys, colon, lungs] help remove any harmful substances that should not be in the body." In essence, the body is always in a natural state of cleansing. Detox diets can sometimes do more harm than good because you are depriving your body of necessary nutrients from other sources. If you eat well, and are eating a mostly plant-based diet, you will never have to worry about cleansing or detoxing.

Know your labels. There are a lot of labels on display at the grocery store. Here is a quick guide so you know what you're looking at.

Certified by the United States Department of Agriculture (USDA). Produce was grown without fertilizers, herbicides, pesticides, or GMO seeds. If the label is on meat, both animal and its feed were produced without fertilizers, herbicides, pesticides, or GMO seeds. Animals are not given hormones or antibiotics. All organic livestock and milking cows must graze on pasture at least four months of the year.

USDA rule that applies to ruminates, such as cattle, sheep, goats, and bison. Must be fed grass, forbs, browse, or cereal grain crops in the vegetative state. Animals must have continuous access to pasture during growing season. American Grassfed Association prohibits animals to be confined to a pen, feedlot, or other area during growing season. Prohibits antibiotics and synthetic hormones.

The Animal Welfare Approved and Certified Humane label means the animals are never housed in cages, crates, or tie stalls. Animals are given space to exhibit their natural behaviors, including perching, dustbathing, and rooting. There is adequate shelter and resting areas. The USDA has no standardized definition of "humane".

Meat, eggs, and dairy that were raised primarily or completely outdoors, either on pasture or range. No animals can be kept in cages, crates, or tie stalls. They must be allowed to exhibit natural behaviors. Breeds chosen for a farm must be well-suited to that farm's weather conditions.

The FDA has not developed a definition for use of the term natural or its derivatives. "Natural" does not refer to the way the animal was raised. This is a really confusing label and doesn't really give us a whole lot of information. I could probably label this book at 100% Natural.

"Cage Free" indicates that eggs come from chickens that were not confined in cages, but the label is not highly regulated by the Food Safety Inspection Service of the USDA. "Cage Free" does not necessarily mean that the birds were raised with adequate space or that they had access to the outdoors.

TransFair USA certifies coffee, tea, herbs, cocoa, chocolate, bananas, sugar, rice, vanilla, flowers, and honey, based on the principles of fair prices, fair labor conditions, direct trade, community development, and environmental sustainability. This label ensures that farmers receive fair prices and workers receive fair wages, and it enables more direct access to the global market.

Buy healthy organic food. If your budget can handle it, buy organic. If your lawn and hands can handle it, grow your own food in a community garden, your backyard, or front lawn. Organic food is free from pesticides, preservatives, and unnatural GMO structures—all of these are hard on your body. The more your body has to work filtering out what is nutritious and what is toxic, the less energy there is going to your brain. This is why digestive health is so important. If your gut is running smoothly, you will have more brain power.

Here's where it's tricky: buying organic doesn't mean it's healthy. The term "organic" only refers to how it was grown. Anything can be organic. Organic cookies are still a carb-heavy dessert and should be eaten sparingly. Organic corn can be turned into organic high-fructose corn syrup. Even when eating organic, continue following the food rules, and don't give in to an unhealthy choice just because it has a fancy label.

If you are a meat eater or eater of animal products, you are what your food eats. Humans are at the top of the food chain, and as such, we are the most toxic species on earth, because we eat all the crap our food eats. The only upside is if there is an alien invasion—let's say we wouldn't be good eat'n. If you eat eggs that come from free-range chickens who hang around the dumpster all day eating plastic, you too are eating plastic. If the oceans are contaminated and fish are consuming mercury, you are also consuming mercury. If strong chemical fertilizers are used to grow grass for cow feed, you are also eating chemical fertilizer. If an animal is injected with a growth hormone, you will also be consuming a growth hormone. That is why organic foods are so important. If you're a vegetarian or vegan, the only thing you have to worry about is overly processed vegan-labeled (un)healthy food. More info here: plenteousveg.com/vegan-processed-foods.

Stop grazing. Eating several small meals per day was once thought to boost your metabolism and burn more fat. Science has debunked this myth—not only will you not burn any additional fat, but eating more frequently may make you *more* hungry. A 2013 study published in *Obesity* concluded: "…increasing meal frequency from three to six per day has no significant effect on 24-h fat oxidation, but may increase hunger and the desire to eat." In fact, contrary to popular opinion, research suggests that eating fewer meals is healthier. In a 2009 study, participates in an eight-week weight loss study who ate frequent small meals fared worse than those who ate the same amount of calories, but in larger portions, less frequently. Studies in groups who fast for part of the day show positive links. Not only does it give your brain more energy in the morning and helps you shed pounds of fat, intermittent fasting also counteracts conditions like Parkinson's, Alzheimer's, and dementia. And, it makes your neurons stronger, making them and you live longer. In 2014, the journal *Diabetologia* published a study that found eating two large meals per day was more effective in reducing body weight for patients with type 2 diabetes than eating six smaller meals of the same calorie count.

Start (intermittent) fasting. I'm more of a brunch person. I can't eat anything when I first wake up, and when I do, it makes me nauseous and gives me a stomachache. In my high school health class, I pressed my teacher when she told our class that breakfast is the most important meal of the day. I told her that listening to my body was more important than structured meal times. She politely told me I was wrong, and said that I should at least drink a glass of orange juice to start my metabolism. Shortly after her class, I started reading about the history of fasting. If fasting has been part of religious practices since, well, the beginning of religion, I thought not eating breakfast was miniscule compared to a day- or week-long fast. I still wasn't eating until around 11am, and chose not to take my health teacher up on her juice advice (you shouldn't drink juice on an empty stomach, either—spiking your blood sugar is a terrible idea and can lead to type 2 diabetes if this behavior is repeated over time). Researching the history of fasting led me to current day practices and eventually to something called intermittent fasting.

Intermittent fasting sounds a little misleading. You are fasting, but you are still eating the same number of daily calories, just in a shorter timeframe. Typically, the fast is 16 hours long, which gives you eight hours to eat:

16 hours fasting + 8 hours eating.

If you deduct the seven or eight hours you should be asleep, you are really only fasting for eight hours:

8 hours sleeping + 8 hours fasting + 8 hours eating.

You can choose to eat at any time, so long as you finish eating eight hours after you start. I know some people who are starving when they wake up, so they eat from 6 a.m. until 2 p.m. Other friends are night owls, and don't start eating until around 2 p.m. or later so they can stay up late and eat until bed. Since my first meal of the day is around 11 a.m., I usually finish dinner around 7 p.m. This gives me a few hours of fasting in the morning and a couple of hours before bed.

8 hours sleeping + 5 hours fasting + 8 hours eating + 3 hours fasting

I like to leave a buffer on each end, but you don't have to. The buffer at the end of the day is a personal choice, not a health-related one. Researchers once thought that eating before bed lead to weight gain. There are now several studies showing positive benefits to nighttime eating, debunking old research. The problem is, most of the old research was done on shift workers and those with Night Eating Syndrome, so the populations they studied did not accurately reflect the general population. When the general population was studied, positive physiological outcomes were observed. If you want to fast all day and eat the last eight hours before bed, you have the current medical research's permission.

The reason why I fast longer in the morning is slightly more complicated. Your brain uses a lot of energy. In fact, it is the biggest drain on your total energy usage. When your body starts digesting food, it too requires a lot of energy. The theory is, if you don't start your digestive system in the morning, all your energy will go to your brain. For this reason and others, like decision fatigue (more on this in Building Your Dock at the end of Part 2), I try to do the most important tasks before I eat my first meal of the day.

My last advice on fasting is meal size. If you are looking for energy *after* a meal, don't eat Thanksgiving dinner-sized portions. Meals this size lead to something called postprandial somnolence, which is drowsiness associated with too much food in your gastrointestinal tract, colloquially called a "food coma". This is why vegetarians are just as tired as the turkey eaters (tryptophan) after a big Thanksgiving meal. Instead of preparing one huge meal during my eight-hour eating window, I eat three normal sized meals or two slightly larger dinner-sized portions.

Wait wait wait wait, WHAT!? Breakfast is not the most important meal of the day? Night eating is okay? You should be eating bigger meals less frequently? That goes against everything I was taught!
...I know. Me too. Now on to that eight glasses of water a day myth everyone's always been on your case about.

Drink water. Drinking water keeps your brain and body hydrated. The exact number of ounces you need per day varies from person to person because it's based on a person's weight and activity. To calculate the bare minimum, you need on a day you are not exercising, divide your body weight in half and that's how many ounces of water you need to drink per day. For example, if someone weighs 200 pounds, they need 100 ounces of water, minimum. On days you do exercise, you need to add an additional calculation to the first number. This is the number of minutes you exercised divided by 30 minutes multiplied by 12 ounces. It sounds harder than it really is.

If you work out for one hour, divide 60 minutes by 30 minutes and you get the number two. Two multiplied by 12 is 24. This means that you need an additional 24 ounces on top of your bare minimum.

Minutes of Exercise	Additional Ounces to Drink
30	12
60	24
90	36
120	48

So, if someone weighs 200 pounds and they work out for one hour a day, they should be drinking 124 ounces of water, minimum.

There are some additional factors to consider. If you are pregnant or breastfeeding, you need to increase your fluid intake by 24 to 32 ounces. Finally, if it's a hot day or you're drinking soda or caffeinated beverages, you will need to drink more water to stay hydrated.

If you wait until you are thirsty to take a drink of water, there's a good chance you are already dehydrated. This means that you should drink before you feel thirsty, and if you plan on working out, drink a couple glasses of water before you hit the gym. If you don't know if you're drinking enough, monitor how frequently you're urinating and the color of your urine. You should be going to the bathroom about once every two to four hours, and your urine should be colorless or a very pale yellow. If it's darker, you're not drinking enough fluid. If you are feeling dizzy or if you get a headache, this might be your body telling you to drink more water ASAP. I recommend finding a water bottle small enough to carry with you and noting how many times you need to refill it to reach your water goal. For example, if you weigh 200 pounds and work out for an hour each day, you should be drinking a 24-ounce water bottle at least five times per day.

If you need help keeping track of your water consumption, there's an app for that. My favorite water-tracking app is called Plant Nanny. With each cup of water you drink, you water a virtual plant. If you drink your daily water goal, your plant blooms and is happy. If you don't hit your goal, your plant gets sad and begins to wilt. Other water tracking apps include: Water Drink Reminder, Waterlogged, Hydro Coach, Waterbalance, Hydrate Daily, Water Time Pro, and Daily Water. (Who knew there were so many apps dedicated to staying hydrated!)

The Powdered Life. In the 1960's during the space race, back when scientists and engineers could be celebrities, kids like my dad dreamed about becoming an astronaut. For many kids of this generation, a perk of being an astronaut was eating space food: dehydrated, freeze-dried, and bite-sized gelatin coated tubes, stored in pop-top aluminum cans and plastic pouches that could have easily been confused with toothpaste. Sitting on their backs, looking at the stars, as David Bowie sings about protein pills in the background—this was the future they dreamed about. Fortunately for the kids of the 1960s, many of the products they dreamed about very well may be in the supplement section of most health stores.

There's a cupboard in my kitchen I refer to as my space cabinet. I have a variety of powders, pills, and supplements. This is my space food, and it's admittedly a little more experimental than some people are comfortable with. Before I adopt a new food into my diet, I ALWAYS do my research and look for peer-reviewed studies to confirm their health benefits. If a dehydrated powdered food has a proven track record of being safe and beneficial to my health, I slowly integrate it into my diet. From there, I monitor how it makes me feel for a few days in a row. When I eat something and it consistently makes me feel good an hour after consumption, I stick with it. If I eat something and an hour later I consistently get stomachaches, I usually don't try it again. Since the feeling I get might be a placebo effect, and because powdered supplements can be expensive, I only recommend using them if you have the means to do so. Otherwise, I would stick to a mostly plant diet and avoid processed foods, as discussed in the previous paragraphs. If you do want to try some dehydrated, powdered, superfoods, here are a few to get you started (citations in Notes & References).

Matcha: Matcha is finely ground green tea leaves. It has been linked to the prevention of many types of cancer, including lung, colon, esophagus, mouth, stomach, small intestine, kidney, pancreas, and mammary glands. Matcha/green tea has been associated with increased bone mineral density and liver function, a strengthened immune system, and combating Parkinson's disease, Alzheimer's disease, as well as other neurodegenerative disease, and preventing neurotoxin-induced cell injury. It has also been shown to aid in weight loss and used to manage obesity. Matcha/green tea may be effective in preventing coronary heart disease, and treating diarrhea and typhoid. Do not use if you are at risk for iron deficiency.

Maca: Maca is a Peruvian plant that has been used for centuries in the Andes for nutrition and reproductive health (male and female). Studies have shown a link to memory and learning, as well as providing a boost in energy.

Cacao: Take away the fat and sugar from chocolate (and roast at a lower temperature), and what you have left is cacao. Cacao was first used by Western physicians in the 1700s to treat cardiovascular illness, and since then, researchers have confirmed its unique properties. In addition to heart heath, studies show a positive link to mental health, including memory, attention, executive function, perception, language and psychomotor functions, as well as improving your mood. There is evidence that eating cacao supports cognitive performance, especially in aging populations, putting them at a reduced risk of Alzheimer's, dementia, and stroke.

Wheatgrass/alfalfa grass/barley grass: These are all young cereal grasses. You might already be familiar with wheatgrass (or wheatgrass shots) because of its popularity at health stores and juice bars. In powder form, wheatgrass is commonly blended together with other young grasses such as alfalfa and barley. They all have a similar structure and as such, similar health benefits, including fighting cancer. More peer-reviewed studies need to be published about the nutritional benefits of young cereal grasses, so anti-cancer properties are all I'm comfortable listing at this time. I choose to drink my grass mix because when I do, I feel energized and clear-minded. I chalk this up to it being a nutrition powerhouse. At a molecular level, wheatgrass is a source of Potassium, dietary fiber, Vitamin A, Vitamin C, Vitamin E, Vitamin K, Thiamin, Riboflavin, Niacin, Vitamin B6, Pantothenic Acid, Iron, Zinc, Copper, Manganese, and Selenium. If nothing else, it's a natural vitamin.

Chia: Sometimes called "runner's food", chia seeds have a long history of being used as a superfood. Aztec warriors ate chia seeds in battle, and the Native American Hopi tribe ate chia on their long runs from Arizona to the Pacific Ocean. Christopher McDougall writes in his book, *Born to Run*, that chia seeds build muscle, lower cholesterol, and reduce your risk of heart disease.

He writes:

> In terms of nutritional content, a tablespoon of chia is like a smoothie made from salmon, spinach, and human growth hormone. As tiny as those seeds are, they're super packed with omega-3s, omega-6s, protein, calcium, iron, zinc, fiber, and antioxidants.

Even if you're not running long distances, chia seeds can offer huge health benefits when part of a healthy diet.

Moringa: Moringa oleifera is native to the sub-Himalayan northern parts of India and has been historically used to combat malnutrition in that region, particularly in infants and nursing mothers. In addition to having antioxidants and anti-inflammatory properties, moringa also has strong cancer fighting capabilities. A 2014 study in South Korea strongly suggests that moringa could potentially be an ideal anticancer therapy.

There are other things in my space cabinet, but I'll let Dave Asprey tell you what those are in his book *Head Strong* and Timothy Ferriss in his book *The 4-Hour Body*. It's science, but bio hack science. So proceed with your researcher's cap on: be skeptical and use caution.

One final caveat. Since these are some of the best (and most potent) superfoods from all over the world, I do not advise putting them all together in a multicultural superfood cocktail, unless you want to risk having a disaster in your pants (something else I learned from Dave Asprey: "disaster pants"). Your body needs to slowly become accustomed to processing nutrient-dense foods, so start small and slowly increase week by week. And please, check with your doctor before using if you are on any medications or have any pre-existing medical conditions.

Change food culture. We have a food problem in the United States. The best food for us (organic vegetables, free-range meat, and cage-free eggs) is expensive. To be completely honest, it's a little outrageous. I have a hard time paying the high prices and my family has had to make sacrifices (i.e. going out to eat less so we can allocate more money to our grocery budget). The good news is, as consumers we get to vote where business invests their resources. Business follows money and if there is money to be made, business will find a way to make a profit. If more people are buying organic food and humanely raised meat, the business model will shift as the culture shifts, and lower prices will be the result.

Eat like Nassim Nicholas Taleb...or don't. Nicholas Taleb is a blunt and opinionated statistician and essayist. He is the author of New York Times bestselling books *Black Swan* (not to be confused with the film starring Natalie Portman) and *Anti-Fragile*—and has an answer (right or wrong) for just about everything. I like Taleb. I have truly enjoyed reading his books and often check his Facebook page to see what he's ranting about—and to scroll through the comments on his posts where he aggressively argues with his followers. According to Taleb (who doesn't cite any research and doesn't work in the health field), you should eat like your ancestors and only consume foods and liquids your genetics have been processing for thousands of years. For example, if you are of Eastern Mediterranean descent (like Taleb), you should eat only foods that naturally grow in that region and avoid "any fruit that does not have an ancient Greek or Hebrew name, such as mangoes, papayas, even oranges. Oranges seem to be the postmedieval equivalent of candy...". The reason behind this ideology is that our bodies have adapted to process those specific foods. That means if you're thirsty, the only options are to drink wine, water, and/or coffee (juice is too new of an invention). The reason why I'm including Taleb's diet is because it shows just how complex food is. I do value Taleb's opinion, and his books have expanded my perspective on a lot of things, but asking a statistician for a meal plan is like asking a political philosopher when the best part of the day is to have a bowel movement.

Which, unfortunately, really did happen.

John Locke (1632-1704), the philosopher whose writings strongly influenced the Founding Fathers and the Declaration of Independence, wrote about more than political philosophy. He also wrote that one should have a bowel movement every day after breakfast. This, of course, is ridiculous.

> Then I guessed, that if a man, after his first eating in the morning, would presently solicit nature, and try whether he could strain himself so as to obtain a stool, he might in time, by a constant application, bring it to be habitual. (From *Some Thoughts Concerning Education*, Section 24, Line 4).

The point is, nearly everyone you ask has an opinion about...well, just about everything. Before jumping into a new dietary lifestyle, ask questions, even if the information is coming from a well-known celebrity or someone who has unrelated specialized knowledge. Food is incredibly personal, and our opinions often include how we were raised, culture, and for some of us, how we cope with stress. At the end of the day, it's up to you to do research and form your own opinions. You are responsible for the food at the end of your fork.

> **That was a lot of information. If you are reading one chapter a day, this is a good place to break.**

Move

All truly great thoughts are conceived while walking.

— FRIEDRICH NIETZSCHE, *Twilight of the Idols, Or, How to Philosophize With the Hammer*

Human beings were not meant to sit in little cubicles staring at computer screens all day, filling out useless forms and listening to eight different bosses drone on about mission statements.

— PETER GIBBONS, character in *Office Space* (20th Century Fox)

I've struggled with my image since high school. Growing up with a congenital heart defect, my doctors didn't allow me to do isometric workouts (strength training, like lifting heavy weights). As a result, I have tiny muscles on an already tall and lanky body. I tried going to the gym, but there was something about doing 15-pound curls that made me feel naked and insecure. Every time I heard someone whisper or laugh, I thought it was about me—even though I knew I was probably just being paranoid. Next, I tried running, but I've always been a slow runner. I was too hard on myself and didn't want to run unless I could keep an eight-minute mile for more than three miles. (I could make it about one at that pace.) Afraid of looking stupid or weak, I stopped exercising. From 2007-2014, my only exercise was swinging a bass around when I played with my band and the occasional sporadic late-night adventure with a group of friends. I was too self-conscious to be comfortable in my own skin and too self-conscious to do anything about it.

In Part 1 (The Learning Zone), I wrote about how my girlfriend (now wife) encouraged me to start running again. Since I was too embarrassed to run slowly, she asked me to keep her company on her runs. Since I was doing her a favor, I was able to overcome my self-consciousness and begin a regular exercise routine (clever girl). Running at a pace we could both hold a conversation at, we were able to increase our distance each week. Sure, we were running 11 or 12-minute miles, but we were able to keep this pace over a long distance.

Distance running is a perfect workout for me, but it may not be for you. That's why I've included other types of movement that may better fit your body, goals, and lifestyle. Before we get into the various types of movement and their benefits, I want to give you some background on why moving around is important and why sitting all day can harm your health and productivity.

Just Move

Researchers are finding that sitting for too long is a health hazard. This is a real problem as many jobs are becoming more sedentary. Even though many of us are spending a lot of time staring at a screen, it doesn't mean that we have to be tied to our desks. There are a lot of ways to stay active at work while maintaining our productivity.

Research tells us that any movement is beneficial. You don't need to leave the office, all you need to do is move from a sitting position and change your posture. A 2014 study published in *Occupational & Environmental Medicine* found that moving from a sitting position to a standing position every 30 minutes during the workday led to a significant reduction in fatigue levels. Not only is it a benefit to your health, moving gives you more energy.

Moving every 30 minutes is a good guideline to follow. In a 2017 study, participants who sat for less than 30 minutes at a time had the lowest risk of early death. To achieve this goal, some people are choosing to work at a standing desk. A standing desk is just like a normal desk with one important key difference: it can rise to the level of your standing height. This way, you can work as you normally do only from a standing position. If you decide a standing desk is right for you, I recommend having the option to sit. I have a tall chair (like a barstool) next to my desk, but others prefer to use a normal chair and to lower the desk. Depending on the desk, this can be done electronically or with a hand crank. Standing all day, especially in the first week, is tiring and may lead to bad posture. I recommend starting with 20 minutes every hour and gradually increasing your time.

If a standing desk isn't for you, you might want to consider taking a short brisk walk every hour. A 2016 study found that participants who went for a five-minute walk (at moderate-intensity) every hour of a six-hour work shift (totaling 30 minutes), had positive health benefits, like more energy, and reported an increase in mood.

If you are still struggling to stay active at work, here are a few more suggestions to keep you moving:

- Take the stairs. If your floor is too many flights up, get off two floors early and take the stairs from there. Another option is to use the restroom on the floor above or below, so you get in an extra set of stairs.
- Park in the back of the parking lot when you arrive at work, so you get a few more extra steps.
- Have small weights at your desk to do curls with or use a water bottle.
- Walk in place at your standing desk or do squats. Take a break by walking around the building.
- Eat lunch away from your desk. This is important for a few reasons. First, you should only associate work with your desk so when you sit down your brain is triggered to get work done, not eat (or browse the news headlines or text your friends, etc.). Second, it gives you a break from your work so when you come back to your desk, you have a fresh perspective. Finally, it gets you moving and this is important if this is the only time you can realistically move away from your workstation.

In addition to staying active at work, having a regular exercise routine provides enormous benefits to your physical and mental health. The 30 minutes you spend on daily exercise is an investment in your mindset, health, and ultimately, your productivity.

Types of Movement
Aerobic
Aerobic activities work your cardiovascular system. They increase your heart rate by continuously working large muscle groups (legs, abdominals, chest, and arms). Within the aerobic umbrella, there are many different types of workouts—all of them are beneficial to your health. There is lower intensity movement like walking, and higher intensity activities like running. Some people who regularly participate in aerobic activities focus on hitting a target heart rate or keeping their heart rate within a certain range for a period of time.

Their target heart rate depends on what they want out of their movement (growing endurance, building strength, burning fat, gaining muscle, etc.) and their preferred activity.

Examples: Walking, running, swimming, cycling, rowing, boxing, dancing, playing tennis, jumping rope, hiking, cross-country skiing, ice-skating, and kickboxing.

How Often: The Department of Health and Human Services' recommendation to adults is 150 minutes of moderate aerobic activity or 75 minutes of vigorous aerobic activity every week. This can be broken into 30 minutes a day, five days a week.

Strength Training
Strength training is a type of movement that uses strong resistance to induce muscular contractions. As a result, it increases your muscle mass, tone, and bone density. Strength training exercises are typically done in a series of 8 to 12 reps and repeated in a total of two or three sets. When you can do more than 12 reps of the same movement, more resistance is typically added.

Examples: Weight lifting using free weights, machines, or resistance bands.

How Often: Be careful not to over train. Your body needs time to recover so it can rebuild. The Department of Health and Human Services' recommendation to adults is to work each major muscle group twice a week. You can break it up so you are going to the gym four days in a row, but only working half your muscle groups at a time.

Anaerobic Cardio
Anaerobic cardio activities have the same movements as aerobic exercise (like running), but it turns into an anaerobic exercise when you push your body to its limits for a short amount of time (like sprinting, but only in short bursts no longer than two minutes). Instead of your body making energy aerobically using oxygen, it uses a different process called anaerobic respiration. The benefit of turning a cardio exercise into an anaerobic one is the extra calories you burn after your workout. When recovering from anaerobic respiration, your body burns calories for up to 38 hours after a workout in something called post-exercise oxygen consumption.

Examples: High Intensity Interval Training (HIIT), sprints, and plyometrics.

How Often: No more than three times per week. Like strength training, you need to allow your body to rest, recover, and rebuild.

Balance

Balance movements improve your flexibility, posture, and coordination. It is the invisible force that keeps us centered in our bodies. Unlike previous movements, balance exercise is slow, with a lot of attention on technique. The better you become at balance, the better your posture will be in other activities. No matter how big your muscles are, they're no use if you're easily thrown off-balance.

Examples: Pilates, dance, tai chi, yoga, qigong, kung fu, karate, capoeira, and judo.

How Often: Daily. Stretching and balance activities like yoga have been shown to aid in recovery after exercise. You can make it part of your daily mindfulness or breathing routine.

How Movement Increases Health & Productivity

Now that you know the types of movements, here is a list of benefits regular exercise has to offer.

Exercise improves brain function. In a study of older adults funded by the National Institute on Aging and the National Institutes of Health, researchers found that regular physical activity increases cell production in the hippocampus, the area of the brain responsible for memory and learning. In the one-year study, participants who were in an aerobic exercise program, on average, grew their left hippocampus by 2.12% and their right hippocampus by 1.97%. The control group, who was not part of an exercise program, showed a decline in hippocampus size. In one year, the average decline in the left hippocampus was 1.40% and 1.43% in the right.

It's not only older adults who benefit from exercise. Children who regularly participate in aerobic exercise show an increase in academic achievement, behavior, social skills, and mental wellness. For the rest of us, exercise does a lot for our brains. Physical exercise is linked to neurogenesis (the creation of new neurons) in the brain, which improves memory and learning, reduces stress and anxiety, and helps fight depression. What's exciting are the new studies about the positive link between the brain and exercise that are consistently being published. While researching this chapter, I found a study that links new stem cell growth to exercise (the study was conducted on rats, so it's inconclusive about what this means for humans). We know exercise is good for the brain, but honestly, we don't know just how good it is yet.

Sweating removes toxins. Sweating removes toxins from the body, including arsenic, cadmium, lead, and mercury. These toxins can cause serious damage to our brain, muscles, immune system, and cardiovascular system. The good news is, studies have found that sweating removes toxins at the same rate, and in some cases, at a higher rate, than urinary excretion. This means that sweating regularly is an important part of the body's natural detoxification process. In other words, the more you exercise, the more you sweat, and the more you sweat, the more toxins you release.

Exercise is great for your blood. Your blood is responsible for transporting nutrients and oxygen to your brain, skin, and other vital organs. Regular exercise regulates blood sugar, lowers high blood pressure, and promotes good circulation.

Exercise increases productivity. There is evidence that exercise increases productivity and decreases the amount of sick days someone takes. In one study, dental healthcare workplaces replaced 2.5 hours per week of work time with time for physical exercise. The result was an increase in number of patients treated, a self-reported increase in productivity, and an overall reduction in time taken off for illness. The study suggests that working less and moving more increases overall productivity.

Exercise is an energy boost. It sounds backwards, but if you're tired, light to moderate exercise will give you an energy boost. According to Patrick O'Connor, co-director of the University of Georgia Exercise Psychology Laboratory, exercise can significantly improve energy levels and decrease fatigue:

> A lot of people are overworked and not sleeping enough... exercise is a way for people to feel more energetic. There's a scientific basis for it, and there are advantages to it compared to things like caffeine and energy drinks.

In his research, O'Connor found that those who exercised at low and moderate intensities when they were tired had a 20-percent increase in energy levels compared to the control group who did not exercise. Forty-nine percent of the participants who exercised moderately reported feeling less fatigued, and 65% of those in the low-intensity group reported felting less fatigued. If you're tired, going for a walk is a great alternative to reaching for another cup of coffee.

Better, deeper sleep. People who exercise regularly have deeper, more restful sleep, and report waking up feeling more refreshed in the morning. These benefits are more significant in the adult and elderly populations. In addition, an early evening activity may encourage sleep quality, especially for those with a mood disorder.

Exercise is a natural high. Aerobic activity, like running, increases blood levels of both β-endorphin (an opioid) and anandamide (an endocannabinoid). No, you didn't misread that. Opioid and endocannabinoid. β-endorphin is 18 to 33 times more potent than morphine—even though you're not being pumped full of the opioid like you would be if you were going into surgery, it's still enough for runners to report a mild buzz. The second molecule is anandamide, a molecule that binds to THC receptors in the brain and produces the feeling of euphoria. It's named after the Sanskrit word *ananda*, which means, joy, bliss, or happiness. When coupled with β-endorphin, it's no wonder so many people run marathons.

Some books and doctors claim that exercise is as good as an antidepressant, and this is partially true. Dr. Michael Craig Miller, assistant professor of psychiatry at Harvard Medical School said: "For some people it works as well as antidepressants, although exercise alone isn't enough for someone with severe depression." Exercise is a good way to improve your mood, but don't stop treatment of any medication without the approval of your primary care physician.

Movement is a form of meditation. Scheduling time for daily exercise gives you time to distance yourself from your life. It is your time to think (or not think) about what you spend the rest of the day on. After exercising, I always have a new perspective on life and all the feel-good chemicals to go along with it. Movement doubles as reflection (Pillar Four) and is also a good form of meditation (the last part of Pillar One you'll read about in the next section). When I'm frustrated about a project I'm working on or need to release some stress, I run faster than I normally do. I can always tell because my breathing is out of sync and I'm gasping for air. Eventually, I slow down and fall into a rhythm, but only after I have worked out whatever is on my mind. With arms pumping and legs catching and springing, I can finally breathe.

Making Movement More Enjoyable

When I exercise alone, I need some extra motivation. I catch myself thinking about how tired I am and asking how long until it's over. That's why I take something I like doing (like listening to an audiobook) and pair it with a new habit (like running). In Part 1, I suggested combining tasks, so you can get more done in less time. Grouping tasks is not only good for productivity, it can also be a source of motivation. When I pair a fun activity with a new "less fun" task, it makes the experience more enjoyable and I am more likely to follow through and achieve my goal. Here's a tip: I have an audiobook I only listen to while exercising. If I want to find out what happens next, I put on my jogging shorts and shoes, and hit the streets.

Move isn't as big as Sleep or Eat Food, but if you are reading one chapter a day, this is a good place to pause and reflect.

Breathe

You can't calm the storm, so stop trying. What you can do is calm yourself. The storm will pass.
— TIMBER HAWKEYE

Your mental health is just as important as your physical health, and often the two go hand in hand. When we encounter stress or powerful emotions like fear or anger, our bodies suffer with us. Prolonged stress can lead to heart disease, cancer (studies show a strong relation to breast and prostate), ulcers, a weakened immune system, and mental illness. Naturally, we respond to stress by trying to stop it. This is done by fighting or running away from it, and when this happens, we are in a high state of arousal where we cannot access the parts of our brains that help us make rational decisions.

192

Since stress at work can be constant, our natural approach to handling stress can lead to burn out. Instead of always being in a Fight-or-Flight response mode, being aware of our breath gives us the power to observe our stressful emotions as they pass through us and act once they have passed. Not only will this reduce the amount of time we are stressed, but the decisions we make will be rational.

The first thing you can do when you start feeling stressed or angry is take control of your breathing. If you are holding your breath, let it out. If you realize that you are taking rapid shallow breaths, take a long deep breath. Remembering to breathe may sound silly or oversimplified (like, "have you tried turning it on and off again?" when you have a tech problem), but it is the first step in bringing you back to your body.

In this section, I'm writing broadly about mindfulness—specifically, how breathing reduces stress and can make you happier and more productive. Consistent with the rest of this book, I cite everything I write about with peer-reviewed studies or literature written by subject matter experts. I have listed several books in the suggested reading section on mindfulness, including one for those who are turned off by the topic's affiliation with organized religion. If mindfulness or meditation are words you don't like, think of it simply as breathing, because the benefits are too great to ignore in protest.

Mindfulness: What Is It Exactly?

People who practice mindfulness believe that life unfolds in moments. When someone practices mindfulness, they are paying attention to each moment as it passes, on purpose and without judgment. Doing this will reset your awareness and increase clarity. What you once thought was a catastrophe may be easier to manage than previously thought. Mindfulness isn't religious, though many religions have included it in their practice (prayer is a form of mindfulness). Mindfulness is conscious living. When you are fully conscious of your life, you respond to life events with clarity.

You can practice mindfulness in all areas of your life. In the food section, I mentioned how I got into lifehacks in my late teens/early 20s. I blended up fruits, vegetables, protein powder, and choked down some pills with the sludge. I called that a meal. I was all about results—doing things fast because we live in a fast-paced world, and the less time I spent on eating, the more time I'd have for work. And then I met my wife. My wife is a really great cook and the first time I ate her cooking, I asked her why we were spending so much money going out when she could cook better than most of the restaurants we had been going to.

Needless to say, for the first time in my life, I enjoyed eating food. It wasn't just a numbers game anymore about balancing fats, proteins, and carbs. It was art. Instead of spending 30 seconds guzzling down a blended mixture ("what's that?", "I don't know, but I think we can juice it."), I took longer than I ever did savoring each bite of food. Thinking back, when I ate a meal, I would remember the first bite and the last two or three bites—everything in the middle was a blur. When I started eating the great food my wife prepared (I'm not trying to reinforce any stereotypes, I think all people should help preparing meals, men and children included), I was practicing mindfulness and didn't know it. I was savoring each bite, tasting each flavor as it made its impression on my taste buds. That's what mindfulness is: sensing each detail in the moment as it makes itself known to your senses.

You can practice mindfulness just by sitting at your desk or looking out a window. All you need to do is take in each moment as it unfolds before you. I like practicing mindfulness when I walk, and it doesn't even have to be a long walk. You can set a reminder by thinking, "Each time I walk to the restroom today, I am going to do it mindfully. I am going to feel the air on my face. I am going to feel my legs moving and feet hitting the floor. My hands, touching the metal door. My breath, my chest, slowly rising and falling."

That's it. You don't need to be constantly paying attention to every moment. Spending five minutes a day will change your perspective, and in a good way. You will see the world as it is, from its smaller parts to the bigger picture. Instead of reacting with anger or fear, you will let the moment sink in before responding in a way you will regret later.

Benefits of Mindfulness Meditation

In a 2015 article published in the Harvard Business Review, the authors provide evidence that mindfulness can literally change the structure of your brain. Participants in an eight-week mindfulness program had an increased amount of gray matter in the hippocampus, a region of the brain associated with emotions and memory. An increase in gray area makes the hippocampus more resilient to stress, and increases its ability to handle emotions and recall memories. After reviewing the brain scans of the research participants, the authors of the study wrote:

Mindfulness should no longer be considered a 'nice-to-have' for executives. It's a 'must-have': a way to keep our brains healthy, to support self-regulation and effective decision-making capabilities, and to protect ourselves from toxic stress.

Other studies have shown that practicing mindfulness affects the brain in areas relating to perception, body awareness, pain tolerance, emotion regulation, introspection, complex thinking, and sense of self. One Harvard article boasts that when comparing stress levels and mood, practicing mindfulness has more long-term restorative qualities than going on vacation.

Meditative Breathing Exercise

Here's a five-minute exercise to get you started:

1. To begin, find a place where you can spend a few minutes without being interrupted. This could be at home in your bedroom, on a park bench, or a quiet place at work—the person who taught me this exercise would turn off the lights in his office and sit under his desk.

2. Next, find a place to sit and make sure it is comfortable enough to maintain with ease, but not so comfortable that you fall asleep.

3. Before you start, set a timer so you know when you are finished. Five minutes may feel like a long time if this is your first time with this exercise—that's normal—in a few weeks it will go by very quickly and you can extend if you would like.

4. Now that you are sitting, close your eyes so you can focus your attention on your other senses. Breathe in, and feel each part of your breath moving through your body. Take your time on the exhale, breathing all the air out of your lungs. Long exhales naturally lower your anxiety and blood pressure.

5. Take another breath and start counting the inhales and exhales up to the number four. Breathe in, one, breathe out, two, inhale— feel it fill up your body, three, exhale—slowly let it all out, four, and then start back at one. After some time, you will realize that you have stopped counting—your focus is not on the numbers, but on the moment. Then, you will be completely at one with your breath.

6. Instead of counting breaths, you can count the length of your inhales and exhales. Count to five on the inhale and to 10 on the

exhale. Doing this will drop you to about four to six breaths per minute. Trust me, doing this for five minutes is as good or better than a smoke break.

At the same time every day, spend five minutes doing this breathing exercise. Don't force any thoughts, you should observe any thoughts that come into your mind, but don't act on them until the five minutes are up. This exercise is about observing, not thinking.

If the first week is hard or if you don't know if you're doing it right, that's normal and it will get easier. There are two apps I've used that are helpful for beginners, and both have free versions.

- calm.com/meditate
- headspace.com

Good luck! And don't be too hard on yourself if you feel like you're not getting it. With practice, you will, and you'll discover what postures and time of day work best for you.

Breathe Better Air

After you find your breath, the next task is finding quality air to breath. In every building, new or old, there are volatile organic compounds (VOCs) in the air, usually at low enough levels we don't realize they are there. VOCs are chemical compounds like acetone, benzene, and formaldehyde that can come from paints, furniture, printers, cleaning supplies, dry-cleaned clothes, and even cosmetics like nail polish. In low doses, VOCs can lead to headaches, fatigue, sleep disorders, personality changes, and emotional instability. In larger doses, VOCs can lead to something called sick building syndrome, which reduces productivity and can cause dizziness, asthma, or allergies. Office buildings have ventilation systems that keep VOCs low, but the levels remain high enough to irritate some people. At home, depending on the age of the house or building, ventilation may not be enough.

Plants (the green stuff you see outside) naturally clean the air by absorbing pollution in the air and producing oxygen. Vadoud Niri, from the State University of New York at Oswego, found that some houseplants are better at absorbing VOCs than others. In his studies, he found the Dracaena and the Bromeliad to be the most effective. Other plants Niri found to be good absorbers of VOCs include: the Caribbean Tree Cactus, Spider Plant, and Jade Plant.

Since each plant is better at absorbing one type of pollutant over another, Niri suggests having a variety of plants for maximum effectiveness.

Breathing clean air will improve your overall health with higher quality sleep and recovery after a workout. If you want your very own 100% natural and organic air purifier, you should add plants to your workspace, the place you relax, and to your bedroom. They don't even require an outlet! Additionally, plants are great for creating a welcoming environment for mindfulness. Greenery has a natural calming effect and inspires creativity. Studies have shown that bringing in elements of nature reduces workplace stress and increases mood.

Here are some plant recommendations to keep you breathing easy.

Recommendations from The NASA Clean Air Study:

Dwarf Date Palm	Lilyturf
Boston Fern *	Broadleaf Lady Palm
Kimberley Queen Fern	Barberton Daisy
Spider Plant *	Cornstalk Dracaena
Chinese Evergreen	English Ivy
Bamboo Palm *	Variegated Snake Plant
Weeping Fig	Red-Edged Dracaena
Devil's Ivy	Peace Lily
Flamingo Lily	Florists Chrysanthemum

* Indicates pet-friendly (I knew you'd ask)

Additional oxygen producing plants that are cat and dog safe:

Areca Palm	Dwarf Date Palm
Money Plant	Moth Orchids
Variegated Wax Plant	Barberton Daisy
Lilyturf	

Vadoud Niri's VOC Absorbing Plants:

Dracaena	Spider Plant
Bromeliad	Jade Plant
Caribbean Tree Cactus	

How Health Works in the Model

Health is the first of the four pillars in the Dock Model. Located closest to the shore, it sets the stage for the remaining three pillars. Productivity starts with a healthy mind and body. Your path to success begins with getting enough rest, eating clean and nutritious fuel, getting enough movement, and remembering to breathe when life becomes stressful.

GOAL FOR TODAY: How are you sleeping these days? What's your diet look like? Are you moving enough throughout the day? How about stress: are you using effective calming strategies like mindfulness or meditation? This is a huge pillar and it might be a little intimidating. If you need to make a few changes, what are they? Right now, only think about the first step. Maybe it's cutting out screen time before bed, or maybe it's taking 10 minutes after lunch to sit in silence and meditate. Whatever it is, the first step is the most important one, and it will help strengthen this pillar. Write the first step or first thing you want to work on changing down in your notebook.

PRACTICE:
THE SECOND PILLAR

If I don't practice one day, I know it; two days, the critics know it; three days, the public knows it.
— JASCHA HEIFETZ, Lithuanian-born American violinist

Growing up, I hung around a lot of radicals: musicians, artists, crusty punks, and some very (very, very) creative misfits. The media we consumed was post-modern, most of it dealing with how The System or The Man was screwing all of us. Anyone with a real job was a goody-goody and an unconscious product of the evil corporate world.

When we were kids, our teachers told us that we could become anything we wanted. We believed them. They were kind people who would never intentionally lie to us. And then somewhere around middle school we started hitting roadblocks. If we wanted to be a pilot for NASA, it meant we had to know math, and Algebra was hard. Like, really hard. Being a doctor meant passing Anatomy and Physiology in high school, and that meant memorizing all the bones and muscles in the body—who wants to do that? Instead of pushing through the difficult times, we took a seat on the bench. Life wasn't supposed to be this hard. And if it was, why didn't anyone warn us?

Sure, we could be anything we wanted to be, but it wasn't going to be easy. We felt lied to. Disenchanted.

Our lives became a downward spiral. Anyone who got ahead in life was a sucker, a scam, or a fraud. We didn't take advantage of the opportunities that were given to us because we believed that The System wanted to turn us all into slaves. As young adults, the reason we were poor wasn't because we could have done something different in our lives, it was because The System punishes those who see the truth.

Every one of us was a philosopher. We took turns coming up with theories about why the world so royally screwed us. We were victims, but if you pressed us, we couldn't tell you who or what specifically was doing the victimizing. All we knew was that we were stuck, and it wasn't our fault. We also *knew* we couldn't get unstuck because there wasn't anything we could do about it. As artists, musicians, and writers, we thought everything we created was perfect. We didn't need to practice because we didn't need to change. We were already geniuses. The world needed to change. We were all sleeping beauties, waiting for the world to come to its senses and fall in love with us.

In Part 1, there is a chapter about mindset (page 44). If you've already read that chapter, you are one step ahead of me. For those who need a refresher, let me get you up to speed. The people I hung around with in my late teens (including myself) had a fixed mindset. A fixed mindset is someone who believes that people are born with natural talent (athleticism, creativity, intelligence, etc.) Their genetics define them. Much like the other unrecognized 19-year-old geniuses I hung around with, I believed I was a natural student, writer, and musician. When life got tough and I couldn't compete, it was never my fault. These were the cards I was dealt, baby, and I'm playing them the best I can. I thought, "If you don't see that I'm brilliant, just you wait. One day, the world will see me for who I am and you'll be sorry." And then I sat around and waited and waited. And waited.

The other mindset I talk about in Part 1 is the growth mindset. People with this mindset believe that skills are grown, and our genetics play a very small role in our physical and mental abilities. The growth mindset says that any skill can be learned, and it doesn't matter who your parents were or where you came from. When the going gets tough, people with a growth mindset see it as an opportunity to grow their skills. When they get cut from the team, they practice harder. When a publisher rejects their manuscript, they revise it and send it to the next publisher on the list and keep on writing. When the music label decides to pass on a record deal, they keep writing new material and practice their instrument. When a school sends them a rejection letter, they find another school to apply to and start studying to retake the standardized test. When life gets hard and they feel like they're two inches tall, they go back to the basics and strengthen their skills.

This chapter is about the science of successes: how practice leads to mastery. The catch is, you can't practice effectively unless you have a growth mindset. Before I get into strategies about how to practice, I want to address two myths getting in the way of good practice. The first is the talent myth and our culture's obsession with child prodigies. Wasn't Mozart composing music before he started kindergarten? We'll look at two examples of child prodigies and how some kids became very good at something in a short amount of time. The second myth is the myth of practice itself. Malcolm Gladwell popularized the 10,000-hour practice rule claiming that 10,000 hours leads to world-class expertise in any skill. If the average driver on the road has thousands of hours of practice behind the wheel, why do more than half of the drivers I share the road with suck? I'll unpack the 10,000-hour rule and clarify where people have taken Gladwell out of context. Finally, we'll move into how to practice and I'll pick up where I left off with mindset and the importance of attitude in deliberate practice.

The Talent Myth

People who have tied up IQ as their identity, as most scientists do, love the idea of emphasizing all the genetic components, because it makes them feel superior.
— SCOTT BARRY KAUFMAN

No one is born a genius, but everyone is born with the potential to become a genius. When we watch someone do a triple backflip on a motorcycle at the X Games or read about the recent Noble Peace Prize Winners, natural talent has nothing to do with it. What we are witnessing is hours upon hours of good practice. The dedication *to* practice is rare and that is what should be celebrated. The playing field is level and anyone with enough time and drive can become a master at anything.

I know what you're probably thinking: That's great and all, but what about child prodigies like Mozart? Can't someone be gifted AND have a growth mindset?

Okay. Let's talk about the big stinking elephant in the room: child prodigies.

First, let me ask you a question. Besides Mozart, how many child prodigies can you name? Or, is Mozart the most famous child in the last 250 years? Maybe there was someone you saw on TV? Or maybe you read about online? What happened to them?

Ellen Winner, director of the Arts and Mind Lab at Boston College, studies children who are gifted. In an article for the New York Times, she writes about how most child prodigies do not grow into adult geniuses. Many of them lose interest in their talent area and discover something new, where they start anew as beginners, just like everyone else. Some child prodigies rebel. Since many of them were forced (through extrinsic motivation, see Motivation in Part 1, page 95) to constantly study and practice their skill, they saw their genius as a curse and stopped practicing once they were old enough to take a stand. A majority of those who were motivated and chose to stick with their talent fell short of genius as adults, and became experts (not too shabby), because they only followed in the footsteps of the people they studied and never added anything novel to their subject area. Finally, there have been those who discovered something new or changed their domain, and these are the creative geniuses. Unfortunately, this is rarely achieved by any group (prodigy or not, there are few Steve Jobs and Bill Gates in the world) and prodigies do not historically have a leg up on us norm-ies when it comes to the creative genius.

I'll help you out with another child prodigy who, like Mozart, changed the game. Her name is Judit Polgár. If you're not familiar with Chess, Polgár has been called the strongest female chess player of all time. At the age of 15, she was the youngest person to earn the Grandmaster title, beating the previous record held by Bobby Fischer (considered by many to be the best chess player of all time). Let's look at these two childhood prodigies who changed the world and see what was really going on behind the scenes.

The Mozart Myth

Wolfgang Amadeus Mozart started learning the piano at the age of three, began composing at five, and was publicly performing at eight. He went on to create hundreds of works, many of them considered to be treasures of Western culture, and he did this before his early death at 35. You might be thinking, "If this isn't natural talent, I don't know what is."

You'd be right about one thing: There is no such thing as natural talent, even (or especially) when it comes to Mozart. According to music scholars, Mozart wasn't off-the-charts talented, but he was still able to become a world-class musician. Using a calculation called the "precocity index" to gauge how quickly musicians progress, researchers can place the skill level of any musician throughout history. The calculation is simple: the researcher adds up the number of years it took a musician to train before performing a piece publicly, and then they compare that number to the average length of time it takes a musician to learn and perform a similar piece. For example, if a musician spends three years learning to perform a piece and the average student takes six years, the musician has an index of 200%. Researchers have concluded that Wolfgang Mozart had an index of around 130%. Compared to twentieth-century prodigies, many of whom land between 300% and 500%, Wolfgang was better than average, but nothing to brag about. What's changed in the last 250 years is the advancement in training methods. Present day practice is more efficient than it was when Wolfgang was growing up. At the time, Wolfgang's training was far superior to his peers, and this is what separated him from other young musicians. His instruction began earlier than most children his age, and he had a world-class live-in teacher.

Wolfgang's father, Leopold Mozart, was an established composer and performer in his own right, and gained international success for his book on violin instruction, *Versuch einer gründlichen Violinschule* (A Treatise on the Fundamental Principles of Violin Playing). As an instructor, Leopold was interested in how children learned to play music. When he became a father, he could finally test some of his theories. Described as ruthless, Leopold was a strict disciplinarian and his all-day practice sessions were exhausting and described by some historians as abusive. Michael Howe, author of *Genius Explained*, estimates that before his sixth birthday, Wolfgang had already racked up 3,500 hours of practice.

When we hear that a child is composing music, it sounds remarkable. Digging a little deeper, it's not as amazing as it sounds. When Wolfgang began composing, Leopold always corrected the manuscripts before anyone saw them. This sounds a little like cheating, but from a practice perspective, Leopold's feedback was an opportunity to teach Wolfgang at the point of failure, so Wolfgang could see the error and fix it. The next critique is originality. Wolfgang's first four piano concertos, composed when he was eleven, didn't contain any original music. Instead, it was works from other composers chopped together. His next piano concertos, composed at age sixteen, were arrangements of work by Johann Christian Bach, one of Wolfgang's former teachers. His symphonies, too, which were written when he was eight, are Bach imitations with little original thought. Keep in mind that this is a child we are ripping apart, so let's put down the pitchforks. We shouldn't be too hard on Wolfgang, because this is how we all learn: by copying, re-arranging, and imitating the work of others. The only difference is Wolfgang has been put on a pedestal, and it's a letdown when reality doesn't meet our expectations. It wasn't until he reached the age of 21, 18 years after he began his study of music, that Wolfgang wrote his first masterpiece: Piano Concerto No. 9.

Let that sink in. Under the direction of an unruly and abusive teacher (his father Leopold) and a world-class mentor, Johann Christian Bach, Mozart's divine spark of genius took 18 years of extremely hard, expert training to ignite. And when it did, it was short-lived. Wolfgang never acquired the fame or riches we associate with genius. At the age of 35, he suddenly became sick and died. His funeral was small with only a few friends in attendance. In his time, Wolfgang wasn't rich or famous. The exact amount of wealth Wolfgang acquired during his lifetime is up for debate, but many scholars agree that he was paid about 10,000 florins/year, which is about $51,500/year in 2017. Critics at the time would have laughed if they were told that Mozart would be a household name in the 21st century, and that his music was still being performed by top musicians around the globe.

When you unpack the Mozart story, it's not as glamorous as those with a fixed mindset would like you to believe. I'm not trying to downplay Wolfgang's success or suggest that his works are anything less than remarkable (his music is remarkable). What I am suggesting is that Wolfgang Amadeus Mozart was no different than you or me.

The Polgár Experiment

Hungarian educational psychologist László Polgár spent years trying to convince teachers and local government officials, that anyone can train to the level of Mozart, because genius is grown, not born. He argued that every child has the potential to become a master at their craft and it's up to society to unlock it. When Polgár started sharing his research and theories on practice and child development, it was met with intense criticism. This was in the 1960's at the height of the Cold War, when radical ideas were met with caution so they didn't appear rebellious against the government. His papers were so controversial, a local official told him he needed to see a psychologist to treat his delusions. Polgár responded by upping the ante. To test his theories, he publicly asked if there was a woman who was willing to marry him, have children, and conduct one of the boldest human experiments of the 20th century.

László began corresponding with a number of women. In his letters, he wrote about his educational plan for when he had children of his own. A young Ukrainian woman named Klara matched his enthusiasm. They were married in 1967 and together, began designing a plan to test Polgár's practice theory of expertise.

In 1969, Klara gave birth to their first daughter, Susan. Klara and László spent a lot of time talking about what their daughter should study. The subject had to be something critics couldn't credit natural talent for. There also had to be hard proof of her skill that couldn't be debated. The Arts were thrown out because her progress needed to be objective, and people are constantly at odds over whether a work of art is world class or rubbish. That's when it hit László: chess. Chess is purely objective. You either win or lose, and there is a rating system based on performance. Critics couldn't credit his or Klara's genetics, because he was a mediocre chess player and Klara didn't play at all. In addition, if Susan became a successful chess player, she would not only prove the practice theory, but she would challenge the stigma and discrimination women face in the male-dominated sport.

László bought as many books as he could find about chess so he could learn how to teach it and began Susan's training program. By her fifth birthday, Susan had racked up hundreds of hours of chess practice. That year, the Polgár family put their theory to the test. Susan entered her first competition against girls twice her age. She was so small she could barely see over the table. Parents and other children watched with amusement as her tiny hands grabbed pieces and moved them on the board. Amusement turned into shocked silence. What was more impressive than Susan winning the tournament was that she didn't lose a single game.

That same year, Klara gave birth to a second daughter, Sofia, and two years later, Judit. The Polgár sisters were homeschooled and practiced chess for eight hours a day. Their family library had 10,000 books about chess, and a handmade catalogue of more than 100,000 games. At the time, the only place in the world with more chess material was the Soviet Union's restricted chess archive. In addition to chess instruction, all three sisters spoke several languages and the Hungarian authorities insisted that they all pass regular exams in school subjects.

The sisters excelled in chess, becoming three of the best chess players in recorded history. When Susan was 19, Sophia 14, and Judit 12, they competed as a team in the Women's Olympiad and won Hungary's first gold medal, defeating the Soviet Union (the first time the Soviet Union had ever been defeated). Judit (remember, she was 12) finished the tournament with the highest individual score earning her a gold medal. She also won the Brilliancy Prize, awarded to the best strategic plan made by a player in the competition.

Here are some of the sister's individual highlights: At the age of 17, Susan became the first woman to qualify for the Men's World Championship (unfortunately, the World Chess Federation wouldn't let her compete). Four years later, she was the first woman to ever be named a Grandmaster, which is the highest rank in chess. In 2003, the United States Chess Federation named Susan the Grandmaster of the Year. A year later, Susan worked with the U.S. Olympiad team, winning a silver team medal and an individual gold medal, bringing her total medal count to ten: five gold, four silver, and one bronze.

At the age of 14, Sofia blew away the chess world by her performance in Rome, later called the "Sack of Rome." She won the tournament defeating several Grandmasters. The magazine, *New In Chess*, pinned her performance rating for the competition at 2879, one of the strongest ever recorded.

Judit became a Grandmaster at 15, the youngest person ever to achieve the title. Before she retired, she was ranked as the best woman in chess. She is currently the coach and captain of the Hungarian National Men's chess team.

Watching children perform tasks better than most adults is entertaining. We like feel-good stories about people who can achieve unimaginable feats, but this can rob them of all the work they put into their achievement. Often, a young person's practice is downplayed, and their youth is what we focus on. The truth is, child prodigies do not have spectacular genes, they have spectacular training, including supportive parents and encouraging coaches. The child, too, is willing (or forced) to spend hours practicing. They sacrifice a large portion of their childhood in order to devote their time and efforts to a single activity. When a young person does something miraculous, our first thought should be: that took some serious practice. Instead of praising natural ability, we should be celebrating their effort and dedication *to* practice.

It's not just any kind of practice that leads to mastery. You can't just go through the motions and expect to become the best in your field. It takes a specific kind of practice to grow, something called deliberate practice.

The Practice Myth

Never mistake mere activity for accomplishment.
— JOHN WOODEN

I'm going to be blunt, if practice leads to mastery, why do so many people suck at driving? According to a survey from the AAA Foundation for Traffic Safety, the average U.S. driver spends about 300 hours per year behind the wheel. That's a lot of practice time. Malcolm Gladwell famously wrote in his book, *Outliers*, that it takes about 10,000 hours of practice to achieve world-class expertise in any skill. Logically, the average 50-year-old U.S. driver should be a world-class driving expert. To be clear, this is Michael Schumacher or Dale Earnhardt-level "expert" Gladwell is talking about. I don't know about you, but I think that more than half of the drivers I share the road with need to go back to Driver's Education. Most of the drivers I slam on my breaks for and flip off during my morning commute look old enough to have at least a couple thousand hours of practice. According to the practice rule, this doesn't make any sense when statistically 35% of drivers on the road should not only be good, but be top professional athlete good (35% of drivers are 50+, having 300 hours/year for >34 years).

Geoffrey Colvin, senior editor at Fortune, writes about the practice myth in his book, *Talent is Overrated*. He begins the book by asking the reader to think about their friends, relatives, co-workers, and the people they meet at parties. Many of the people in our lives spend at least 40 hours per week working. This means that after five years (40 hours a week, 50 weeks a year), they should be experts at what they do. Ask yourself honestly, how good are they? Sure, some of them may have received several promotions and are now in a high position in their company, but how good are they, really? Colvin writes that odds are, few of them are truly great at what they do:

> Extensive research in a wide range of fields shows that many people not only fail to become outstandingly good at what they do, no matter how many years they spend doing it, they frequently don't even get any better than they were when they started. Auditors with years of experience were no better at detecting corporate fraud—a fairly important skill for an auditor—than were freshly trained rookies. When it comes to judging personality disorders, which is one of the things we count on clinical psychologists to do, length of clinical experience told nothing about skill—"the correlations," concluded some of the leading researchers, "are roughly zero." Surgeons were no better at predicting hospital stays after surgery than residents were. In field after field, when it came to centrally important skills—stockbrokers recommending stocks, parole officers predicting recidivism, college admissions officials judging applicants—people with lots of experience were no better at their jobs than those with very little experience.

This probably isn't a fun fact you should share at dinner parties or family gatherings. But the reason you need to know it is that it says something important about practice: not all practice is equal.

A lot of people have misinterpreted Malcolm Gladwell's 10,000-hour rule. The rule *doesn't* mean that something magical happens after 10,000 hours. You don't "level up" like you do in a video game after you get enough experience points. However, something *does* happen along the way if your practice is effortful, concrete, precise, designed, and focused. Ten thousand hours is a large abstract number representing roughly the number of hours someone needs of *deliberate* practice (sometimes called "deep practice") before they hit mastery. Deliberate practice focuses on the quality of the practice you are doing. The practice must be focused, conscious, and goal-oriented. Often, deliberate practice is when you are in a flow state or "in the zone", laser-locked on the task you are doing. It's when the curtain of reality drops and you are in harmony with the task you are performing. Mozart had a leg up on his peers because his father understood deliberate practice (even though the name hadn't been coined yet) and implemented a training program based on effortful and goal-oriented practice. But modern training, as the "precocity index" suggests, may be as high as four times more effective than Mozart's training (remember, it took Mozart 18 years to write his first masterpiece). That's why all the numbers I'm writing about are subjective. Mastery does take years, and sometimes decades to achieve, but ultimately, your mastery depends on the quality of your practice: your intrinsic motivation, your coaches, and how effective your practice is. There are no exact numbers, only trends in the data. The hope in sharing the trends is that it will lend some insight into your life and, in this case, how you structure your practice. It's not gospel, it's data. And it's hard to measure how effective your practice is because so much of it has to do with your mindset and intrinsic motivation. Keep this in mind as you continue reading.

Some researchers estimate that an individual can only spend about three hours a day in the deliberate practice zone. It's too intense and the brain and body can only operate at this level of intensity so long before reaching fatigue. If this is true, and someone achieves three hours a day, every day for a year, it will take them roughly 10 years to become a master of their skill (this is in-line with Gladwell's rule). The 10-year rule can be traced back to John R. Hayes of Carnegie Mellon University. He was the first to identify the gap, which he named the "ten years of silence." He studied the lives of 76 composers throughout history and found that only three composed major works before their tenth year of composing (and these were composed in year eight and nine). Other researchers have confirmed Hayes' findings. In a study of 66 poets, 55 took ten years or longer to produce a notable work. In a similar study of 131 painters, there was only six years of silence, but still notable for Hayes' argument. In his book *Creative Minds*, Howard Gardner recognized the ten years of silence while examining the lives of Albert Einstein, T. S. Eliot, Sigmund Freud, Mahatma Gandhi, Martha Graham, Pablo Picasso, and Igor Stravinsk. Keep in mind, all these individuals grew their talent through deliberate practice, meaning they weren't jogging through life like most of us do, but consciously pushing themselves to be better every day.

When someone starts jogging through their skill, it means that they have hit a plateau. The only way they can get better is to push beyond their current skill area. In his book *Bounce*, Matthew Syed describes how people at the top of their field practice:

World-class performance comes by striving for a target just out of reach but with a vivid awareness of how the gap might be breached. Over time, through constant repetition and deep concentration, the gap will disappear only for a new target to be created just out of reach again.

If this sounds familiar, it should. In Part 1 (page 57), I wrote about something called the Learning Zone, which is the space between security (too comfortable) and panic (too much stimulation). What I didn't talk about in Part 1 is that the more time you spend in the Learning Zone, the more you change the structure of your brain. What deliberate practice does is strengthen the neural connections in your brain. When you repeatedly perform an action, a substance called myelin builds up around your nerve fibers and neurons, insulating the connection. The signal sends more efficiently, with the more myelin there is. For example, if someone has a wicked backhand in tennis, they had to perform the same backhand action possibly hundreds of thousands of times, in order to myelinate specific nerve fibers. And that's the downside about myelin, your brain needs to send the same signal over and over and over to grow myelin over a single nerve fiber. That's why practicing good technique is so important and why bad habits are so hard to break.

Chances are, I'm just as bad of a driver as the people I critique on my way to work. To be honest, I don't care about being a world class driver, I just want to travel to and from my destination in one piece. I've plateaued in my driving skills. I'm too busy listening to audiobooks or zoning out to push myself to be a better driver. Besides, I'd rather spend my deliberate practice time writing or improving my communication skills. The good news about practice is that anyone can become a genius at whatever they deliberately practice. It takes time and a lot of work, but it is within your reach. Vince Lombardi, arguably one of the best NFL coaches of all time, said: "Practice does not make perfect. Only perfect practice makes perfect." To get you on the right path, I put together a list of tools, tips, and suggestions to guide your perfect practice. Hopefully this speeds things up, and both you and I can become masters of our craft.

How to Practice Deliberately
Practice starts with attitude.
The greatest discovery of any generation is that a human can alter his life by altering his attitude.
— WILLIAM JAMES

When I was hanging around my I'm-so-counter-culture-I-hate-counter-culture friends, my attitude was holding me back. I wanted to make it as a musician and a writer, but I didn't think practice was going to make me any better. I thought, one day I was just going to wake up and write the great American novel. It would be that easy. I would put everyone in their place, and all the corporations and goody-goodies with their conformist clothing and posh lifestyles would realize they were all frauds, and rebels would take over the world.

At some point in my early 20's, the group I hung around with started to split paths. On the first path were those who continued to see themselves as victims. Every rejection was a personal attack and a confirmation of their fixed beliefs. On the second were those of us who got tired of waiting to be discovered. We started taking risks. We met people who were doing the things we wanted to do, and they gave us advice. And for once, we listened. We realized that we were the ones causing so much pain in our lives—our biggest fears were self-imposed, and the world was only as terrible as our imaginations dream it to be. Something happened. A switch was flipped, and we started doing things we had previously only talked about. We had discovered a growth mindset, and we began to practice what we loved.

A fixed mindset is not limited to the young or those in the Arts. I just happened to find them there because that's where I spent most of my time growing up. Since, I have found people young and old with a fixed mindset, ranging from business to sports, politics, and even education. I'm happy to report that many of my fixed-mindset misfit friends became growth-mindset misfit adults and have shaken the world in business, music, writing, and philosophy. It doesn't matter who your parents are, your income, or status in society. What matters most is your mindset. Once you have a growth mindset, you can start to practice.

Understand your coach or mentor's role in practice.

There was a day when I realized that no one was going to knock on my door and give me a book deal. I critically looked at my life and my goals and I accepted that I needed help. I also knew that there were people in my life who I could learn something from, but that meant going outside of my comfort zone and asking for help. I gathered myself together and I asked. It was hard. It was humbling. But when they agreed to have coffee with me, I listened. I really listened. I practiced what they told me and asked for feedback. And then I listened some more. I am still asking for help, still practicing, and still asking for feedback, because it works.

When picking a mentor or coach, Daniel Coyle, author of *The Talent Code* and *The Little Book of Talent*, says that a good mentor shouldn't be like a restaurant waiter, catering to your every need. If anything, they need to be a little intimidating. If your coach/mentor smiles a lot and says things like "Don't worry, no problem, we can take care of that later," they aren't going to give you the immediate feedback you need to grow. A good mentor will push the bar higher and higher and you are expected to meet them, not have them come down to you. A good coach will know where your comfort zone is and push you out of it into the learning zone as often as they can. They will ask you to take risks they know you are capable of, even if you don't know it yet.

Your coach or mentor should know the skill you are working on in-and-out. They may not be the highest paid person in the company, but they are the subject matter expert. If you've ever watched the Olympic Games, you've probably noticed that each athlete had a coach. That's because even world class performers need feedback and advice from experts. Tom Brady, who has won five Super Bowls quarterbacking for the New England Patriots, still relies on coaches to keep his technique in check. Tom Martinez has been Brady's coach since he was 14, and up until 2012 when he passed away, Brady regularly checked in with Martinez for a tune-up. In scientific terms, he visited with his old coach to repave his myelinated neural highways.

(We'll unpack mentoring a little more in Part 3.)

Practice the fundamentals.
Many of us view practice as necessary drudgery, the equivalent of being forced to eat your vegetables, far less important or interesting than the big game or the big performance. But in the talent hotbeds I visited, practice was the big game, the center of their world, the main focus of their daily lives. This approach succeeds because over time, practice is transformative, if it's the right kind of practice. Deep practice.
—DANIEL COYLE

Every great athletic coach (John Wooden, Vince Lombardi, and Phil Jackson, to name a few) will tell you that the fundamentals are at the core of your skill. The truth is, it's not only sports, it's everything you do. From music to sales to web design, if you get too caught up in the details, you'll forget what you're doing. That's why Tom Brady has the handwritten piece of paper in his wallet, to remember that no matter how complex a play gets, it all falls back on the basics.

Practice where you are.

I've had people come up to me and tell me about the New York Times Bestselling novel they have brewing inside of them. The only problem is, they can't start working on it until they have a vintage mahogany table to write on. Or a new laptop. Or when they can move out to the country because the city is too loud for beautiful writing.

I've met people who pay a monthly storage fee for a busted up classic car they plan on restoring. Problem is, they can't do the work unless they have a temperature controlled garage or top of the line tools or the perfect piece they still need to order. So, it sits and sits, and they keep paying their storage bill.

You can exchange writing or classic cars with pretty much anything, I have heard excuses for not going back to school, for not joining an apprenticeship program, for not applying to new jobs— the list goes on. If you wait until you have the perfect gear, the cleanest most impressive office, or "the right time", you are focusing on the wrong thing.

In the early 1970s, George Lucas wrote drafts for all six *Star Wars* movies on a desk he made from three doors. Stephen King wrote his first novel, *Carrie*, in the back room of his trailer on a makeshift desk between the washing machine and dryer. The North Baltimore Aquatic Club, which could pass for an underfunded YMCA, has produced 10 Olympians, including Michael Phelps. Google, Apple, Microsoft, Amazon, Disney, and Hewlett-Packard (HP) were all started in garages, and Wordpress, Yahoo!, Dell, Facebook, and Napster were started in dorm rooms.

You shouldn't wait until you can practice in luxury, because practicing in luxury is not going to make you successful. If anything, being a little uncomfortable will inspire you to work harder because you will want to get out of your trailer, basement, garage, dorm room, etc. There's never going to be a single "right time" to start something new, because it's always the right time to start doing the thing you care about most.

Steal, err… borrow practice techniques.

Good artists copy, great artists steal.

— PABLO PICASSO

You don't need to reinvent the wheel. Practice what works and the technique will transfer over to your original work. This is why chess players replay classic games and its why musicians cover their favorite songs. Hunter S. Thompson rewrote entire books to get the rhythm and style of an author he admired. While writing his magnum opus, *Fear and Loathing in Las Vegas*, Thompson frequently typed out pages from *The Great Gatsby* to get the feeling of the style and flow.

When you borrow, you model precise behaviors—the angle of Serena William's elbow when she does a backhand or the word order in a Hemingway sentence. You shortcut your practice by practicing what works. Daniel Coyle makes the following suggestion in his book, *The Little Book of Talent*:

Ask yourself:

- What, exactly, are the critical moves here?
- How do they perform those moves differently than I do?

I will touch on modeling again in the last chapter of Part 2 when we get into routines and rituals. In the meantime, if you want to learn more, check out the book, *Steal Like an Artist*, by Austin Kleon.

Repetition is key.

I fear not the man who has practiced 10,000 kicks once, but I fear the man who has practiced one kick 10,000 times.

— BRUCE LEE

Weight lifters don't say, "I've lifted enough pounds in my life, I think I'm at where I want to be." They know that if they don't maintain a certain level of activity, they will lose their strength. In other words, you have to work each day to maintain where you already are. Regularly engage with your skill: read blogs, read books, watch videos, attend conferences, and expand your network.

What's most important is sticking with it: getting up each morning and dragging yourself to the office or gym to work on your skill, whether you feel like it or not. One of my friends who was on the swim team in college told me that he hated waking up at 5 a.m. for morning practice. He would suit up and jump into the water, cursing the whole way. Once he started swimming, things changed. He would get out of the pool and walk to his first class feeling like he could take on the world because he already accomplished something while the rest of campus was asleep.

Each repetition makes a pathway in your brain stronger. It's just like adding a piece of electrical tape around a wire—each repetition wraps another piece of myelin around a neural connection in your brain. Each repetition insulates the connection, so it can send faster and with better accuracy. Remember, it takes a lot of repetitions, but every rep counts.

Focus on small daily achievements.
Don't look for the big, quick improvement. Seek the small improvement one day at a time. That's the only way it happens—and when it happens, it lasts.
— JOHN WOODEN

When it comes to practice, it's better to snack than binge. You build skills quicker practicing five minutes every day than 35 minutes in one weekly chunk. Your brain needs repetitive motion and repeat exposure to build neural connections.

To do this, try setting one small goal. It could be to get one perfect chunk done: one chorus of a song played through once without a mistake, one perfect line of code, one perfect email to a client, or three perfect swings of a golf club in a row. For the author Terry Pratchett, it was 400 words.

Before receiving a knighthood and winning the British Book Awards (among many other awards), Terry Pratchett began his writing career with 400 words every day. That's it. Eventually, he finished his first book: *The Carpet People*. Legend has it, the only reason he wrote a second novel is because he finished the book and still needed to write a couple hundred more words that day. Before his death in 2015, Pratchett published more than 70 books in total. Here's Terry in his own words:

> For more than three years I wrote more than 400 words every day. I mean, every calendar day. If, in those pre-portable days, I couldn't get to a keyboard, I wrote hard the previous night and caught up the following day, and if it ever seemed that it was easy to do the average I upped the average.

For Terry, 400 words was his small daily achievement—less than one single-spaced page (roughly 500 words).

The more you struggle, the more you learn.
It seems the harder I work, the more luck I have.
— THOMAS JEFFERSON

Never take a first mistake personally. Mistakes are part of learning, and it's healthy to distance your personality from the normal mistakes that come along with learning something new. Avoid negative self-talk like: "I'm not a good writer, that's why no one responds to my marketing emails". Instead, reframe the feedback so it encourages practice: "writing good marketing emails takes a lot of practice and every piece of feedback I get is making me a better writer." All feedback, positive and constructive, should be analyzed so you can learn from it.

First mistakes happen in the learning zone (see the Learning Zone in Part 1, page 57) when you step away from the outer ring of your comfort zone. Whenever you enter your learning zone, you are going to start feeling your muscles work a little harder. It will get tough and sometimes you'll want to give up, but if you push through the growing pains and see your practice, task, or project to completion, you'll gain a lot of experience points.

Hang around people who are better than you.
Judit Polgár is a more successful chess player than her sisters, and it's not surprising that she is also the youngest. Historically, younger siblings who study the same skill perform better than their older siblings as adults because they grew up competing against opponents who were stronger than they were. In addition, younger siblings grow up watching their older brothers and sisters make mistakes, and try to avoid making the same mistakes. Serena Williams grew up serving and volleying against her older sister, Venus. Both are two of the best tennis players in the history of the game, but Serena has the better record. Nick Jonas, the youngest Jonas brother, has had a more successful career than his brothers. And both Janet and Michael Jackson, both two of the youngest siblings in the famous Jackson family (Janet youngest, Michael third youngest), have outshined their siblings.

Since we're a little past the age of asking our siblings to play a pick-up game of basketball, we should hang around people in our own field who are better than us so we can act like a sponge and learn whatever we can from them. I've felt like the dumbest person in the room many times, and every time I've left with a wealth of information and new strategies for my own practice. It's a cliché, but it's true. You don't get better beating people who are not as good as you. You only get better when matched against someone who is slightly better than you.

Keep your goals to yourself.

After a concert at Skeletones in 2009 (I'll talk more about Skeletones in Part 3), I was hanging out with the band Showbread in the parking lot before they left town. Josh, the lead singer of the band, had recently run a second printing of his first novel, *The Spinal Cord Perception*. I loved the book. I was 19, in a local band (trying to make it big) and I liked writing fiction as much as I liked playing music. Josh was exactly where I wanted to be in a few years, so I asked for some advice. He started with a caution: how you talk about your goals can make or break you. He said something like this (not a direct quote, but as close as I can reconstruct from the notes I made that day in my notebook):

> Right now, I'm working on a book and it's named after a state. But that's all I can tell you. If I tell you anything else, I won't be able to write it. Whatever project you're working on, whether it's writing fiction or music, don't tell anyone about it until you're finished. Think about your idea or concept as a bubble. Each time you write or work on a song, you poke a hole in the bubble and a little bit of the creative energy comes out that you can turn into words, notes, art, etc. When you talk about your concept, you let energy out of that bubble, but it doesn't turn into anything. The goal is to turn as much of that initial idea bubble as you can into art. A lot of people, all they do is talk, so their bubble is gone before they can even start. If you have a novel you're writing, don't tell me about it. Don't tell anyone else about it until you're finished. Don't even release the title until you're finished.

His advice came true. At the time, I was working on a bizarro punk-style novel about a famous porn star turned serial-killer. She falls in love with a man after his sex doll is stolen. It was violent and disturbing, but at the same time, funny and symbolic. More importantly, it was fun to talk about at parties. I liked watching the shock on people's faces when I told them the plot. Talking about writing the book became more fun than sitting down and doing the work. Ten years later, it's unfinished.

It feels good sharing a goal we're working on. So good, it tricks our brain into thinking we've already accomplished it. That's why every year the same person at the holiday meal says this is the year they're going back to school. It's why year after year the same friend tells you they plan on quitting their job so they can start their own company. And it's why your childhood friend shares monthly Facebook statuses about the new diet they're on and how this time it's going to work. Sometimes you need to go silent and do the work. It's more fun to share accomplishments than working plans. Talking is pre-game stuff, doing the work is where the action is. There is one exception: Sharing with a mentor or partner is completely fine—it's heathy to have someone to confide in and a mentor will help keep you on task.

The best way to practice is to teach.
When I was a student at Valley View Elementary School in Rockford, MI, every year we were assigned new "reading buddies." Apart from the kindergarteners and 5th graders, everyone had a reading buddy who was older and younger (5th graders only had younger reading buddies and the kindergarteners only had older reading buddies). Once or twice a month, an older grade would visit a younger grade. The students would pair off with their buddy and take turns reading to one another. The older student would help the younger student read a book at their grade level, and the older students would take a turn reading a more advanced book, so they could teach the younger student what the grade above was learning.

As adults, we should continue the practice because when you teach, you learn the material better yourself. As soon as you grasp your skill, you should start teaching it to others. If you are becoming established in your field, reach out to younger professionals in your company so you can start sharing your knowledge with them. If you have only worked a few years in your field, reach out to a new hire who is making the same transition from school to work that you made not long ago. If you are a rookie, go back to your school or reach out to people interested in your line of work and share the skills you developed to get to where you are now. If you are still in school working on a degree, go to high schools and share your experiences and the tools you used to find your passion and start heading in the right direction. You can do the same in the Arts. If you play guitar and your goal is to be a self-sufficient musician, you can become an instructor for children and adults. If you are an aspiring novelist, you can work in a university writing center or volunteer your time at high schools. Like the reading buddies at

Valley View, the goal is to always have a mentor and to always be mentoring.

Let your lower consciousness chew on it a while.
When I was in school and still worried about exams and regurgitating information on multiple-choice tests, I would read all my notes aloud before bed. Every time I did this, I woke up the next morning with better recall than reading my notes during the day.

I learned the practice from my dad. When my dad was in school, he studied physics and mathematics and would often work late into the night trying to solve a problem he was stuck on. He would fall asleep with the problem unfinished (sometimes accidentally) and would wake up in a panic, scrambling to find a pencil so he could write down the solution that popped from the lower conscious to the upper conscious.

A 2015 study at Brigham and Women's Hospital in Boston confirmed an increase in memory and recall after sleep, though it's not a new concept. The study references other studies, one dating back to 1973, that show a link between sleep and working memory.

I've found that my brain gets stuck on whatever activity I do before bed, as if the last few minutes are on repeat. When I'm working on a communication or organizational issue at work or when I'm writing fiction and I'm trying to figure out what a character in a story does next, I sit back on my bed and run through it once in my head. When I reach the point where there is an issue, I turn off the light and let my lower consciousness take over. It doesn't always work, but more often than not, I'm pleasantly surprised with my thoughts on my way to work the next morning.

Turn practice into a game.
Your drive to practice should be intrinsic (see Motivation in Part 1 on page 95), but that doesn't mean you are going to wake up every morning excited to work. When practice gets boring or feels meaningless, you can give it meaning by turning it into a game. If you cold-call every morning, track your progress. How many calls can you do before lunch? What's your success rate? If you're not having much luck, count the number of people you talk to for a few minutes before saying "no" vs. people who hang up immediately. If you're trying to learn how to play a few bars of music, see how many times you can play them in a row without messing up.

It's all about flipping your perception: drills kill your willpower, but if it can be recorded, it can be turned into a game. And when it's recorded, you can track your progress and try to do a little better each week.

Keep practicing, even when you win.

After writing his fourth novel, *American Gods*, and 75 issues in the comic book series *The Sandman*, Neil Gaiman told friend, author Gene Wolfe, that he had finally learned how to write a novel. Gaiman recalls Wolfe's reaction: "He smiled at me and said 'You never learn how to write a novel. You just learn how to write the novel that you're on.'"

Every event is an opportunity to grow new skills and sharpen the ones you already have—no matter your age or existing skill level. When you get a promotion, keep on practicing. When you win a big award, stick to your practice routine. When your skill provides you comfortable living, wake up early and practice.

Practice in the Dock Model

The Practice Pillar in the Dock Model represents the repetition you should be doing every day. It's important to have frequent interactions with the skill you are building because every time you practice, you also reinforce your pillar. Like Health, Practice is an important foundational pillar because it anchors your dock to the shore. Practice is where you build stability: when times get tough and you get pushed closer to shore, your practice will keep your dock strong, so you can weather the storm.

GOAL FOR TODAY: Daily practice starts today. Can you think of one daily repetition you can start doing as part of your daily routine? I recommend starting with one small daily achievement. If you're having a hard time thinking of one, break the skill you are working on down into small, achievable goals and pick one to focus on each day of the week. When you get into the swing of daily practice, push yourself a little further each day, to keep your momentum moving forward. Finally, don't forget to track your progress! Not only will you see the results, but you can make a game out of your practice when the drills start to kill your motivation.

If you are interested in learning more about how practice leads to mastery, check out my sources and the Suggested Reading & Listening page in the back of this book. Most of the source material in this chapter comes from the works of Geoffrey Colvin, Daniel Coyle, Malcolm Gladwell, and Matthew Syed. They are the true pioneers of practice.

PLAY: THE THIRD PILLAR

Newton was at play in his mind when he saw the apple tree and suddenly conceived of the force of gravity. Watson and Crick were playing with possible shapes of the DNA molecule when they stumbled upon the double helix. Shakespeare played with iambic pentameter his whole life. Mozart barely lived a waking moment when he was not at play. Einstein's thought experiments are brilliant examples of the mind invited to play.
— DR. EDWARD M. HALLOWELL

What was your favorite subject in elementary school? Most kids I ask tell me recess, which was mine also, with lunch coming in a close second. So, what happened to recess? Somewhere between kindergarten and high school, recess is phased out of our day. By the time we get our first full time job, breaks are used to catch up on side projects, to schedule appointments, and frantically check bank accounts so our bills get paid on time. There is little room for us to work on creative projects, play games with friends, or socialize—the very same things we loved to do when we were kids during recess and at lunch. We've been told that life isn't all fun and games, but it isn't all work either. And not having free time to play is hurting us in ways we didn't previously account for.

Sleep researcher Kristen Knutson at Northwestern University

analyzed sleep diaries from several studies involving thousands of participants from the year 1975 to 2006. She found that people have been consistently getting the same number of hours of sleep. Meaning, modern society isn't sleeping less. Why, then, do we all feel so tired? Knutson found that although we are not sleeping less, full-time workers are working longer hours. According to a 2014 Gallup poll, the average full-time worker is putting in 47 hours per week, nearly a full work-day more than the traditional 40-hour week. If we are working more, this leaves less time for recess and lunch, in other words: play. Having free time for play invigorates us with a new perspective on life and it bonds us with others. It gives us a break from the stress at work and invites us to use our imagination. Play was something we never had to account for, and now with the average worker spending more time in the office, play may be the key to treating workplace fatigue and disengagement.

So, what is play? In its most basic form, play is anything we do for the pure enjoyment of it, not because it is a means to an end. As simple as it sounds, behavioral researchers were all wrong about why we play until Harry Harlow observed some peculiar behavior at his University of Wisconsin-Madison lab in 1949.

Harlow was a psychologist, famous for his research in cognitive development. If you ever took a class in psychology, he's the one who discovered that caregiving and companionship in infants is more important than food (wire monkey mother with bottle vs. cloth monkey mother). One morning, Harlow walked into his lab and found the rhesus monkeys solving wood puzzles that were accidently left in their cage by researchers. This was odd, because the monkeys were doing the puzzles without any rewards. The monkeys were working purely out of curiosity. After some time fiddling around with the puzzles, they figured out how to solve them. There wasn't a reward for solving the puzzles, no food, affection, or applause. Up until Harlow's observations, the scientific community only knew about two drivers to action—pain and pleasure—and both were externally driven. For example, if a stick hits a tree, fruit will fall, and the monkey can now eat a sugary treat. The monkey will hit the tree again when they are hungry because they know hitting a tree with a stick brings pleasure. Here's another example. If a male monkey makes advances towards a female that are not reciprocated, negative actions follow, usually involving a stronger dominant male. When the monkey is physically injured and feels pain, he learns to never go near that monkey again. If action x is performed, y is the reward (positive or negative). Harlow offered a new perspective: the performance of the task itself could be a motivator. In other words: curiosity and play were as strong (or stronger) motivators than pleasure and pain. Thanks to some 13-pound primates and a wooden puzzle, we now know that play in itself can be a reward, and this is where intrinsic motivation begins.

Like the rhesus monkeys, we do not need to be taught how to play because it's something we're hardwired to do. Play *should* come naturally to us. As adults, we've been shuffled through our factory-style compulsory schooling and come out the other side forgetting what play was like as a child and some of us need help getting back there. Before we get into all the benefits play has to offer our health and our work, let's get back to where it all began: the playful mind of a child.

Rediscovering Play

Play provides the emotional spark which activates our attention, problem solving and behavior response systems so we gain the skills necessary for cooperation, co-creativity, altruism and understanding.
    —CARLA HANNAFORD

As a child, I could lose myself for hours roleplaying and taking on new identities. I built huge structures out of cardboard in the basement of my childhood home. When I was older, I went into the woods and hammered bent nails into trees, and called the uneven 2x4's a clubhouse. In my free time, I was quite the inventor, and drew designs no matter how crooked the lines were. I also played sports and invented games with my pack of neighborhood friends when the traditional ones had too many rules—or needed a few more. At sleepovers, we made up stories about spirits and ghosts, and ancient creatures who lived in the forest on the edge of the neighborhood. Since they only came out after dark, we dared one another to walk through the woods after the clock struck midnight.

What made play so easy was the lack of judgment—especially from ourselves. Not many of us had been told that some things are impossible. If anyone told us that there were things that were impossible, we would have said that an adult hadn't asked a smart kid to discover a solution yet. Over time, the small voice in the back of our heads that dared us to run through the woods at night without a flashlight changed its tone. It started saying things like: "You can't do that. You're not good enough. It's not scientifically possible. That's stupid. That will never work. If it's such a good idea, someone else would have already done it." Instead of fearing our imagination, we started fearing reality. Instead of focusing on what was possible, we started thinking about all the reasons why something was impossible. The voice of adventure became the voice of caution.

If you are having a hard time rediscovering your old childhood joy for play, try giving yourself "play breaks" during the day. You can start small with doodling in a notebook or by placing an assorted box of LEGO® bricks in a disorganized pile on your desk. For social play, join a community ultimate frisbee team or ask friends to play a pickup game of basketball. During your lunch break, eat outside and toss rocks in a pond. These small steps will help you remember what it was like to be in that child-like mindset again. Little by little, it will come back.

If you put up a mental barrier against play in hopes of being more productive, it might be working against you. What researchers are finding is play, especially when learning a new hobby or when coupled with movement, has been shown to decrease depression, induce positive mood states, and improve overall quality of life. Play is also associated with alleviating the negative impact of age on the body and the mind. Finally, those who play are more productive, have a better eye for detail, and are less stressed.

Preparing Your Mind for Play

A lack of play should be treated like malnutrition: it's a health risk to your body and mind.
—DR. STUART BROWN

Sometimes, I have a hard time relaxing and getting into a playful mindset because I am always overthinking everything. I'm so good at thinking too much about something, I don't even know I'm doing it. I'll get distracted with a fleeting thought for minutes before I realize that I'm off task. Sometimes, one of those thoughts leaves a mark that lasts longer than a minute or two and it makes me angry, worried, or sad. When this happens, I use the Shelf Metaphor to get back to work, let myself play for a while, or engage in playful work.

Here's how it works. In your imagination, create your very own shelf. Feel free to make it as simple or elaborate as you'd like. My shelf looks like the one in *Indian in the Cupboard*, but that's just me.

When designing your imaginary shelf, build it so it can be moved out of your direct line of sight. Mine is just above my head and out of my way when I need to work (this is important).

Next, imagine what your distraction looks like. In the past, I have put the following distractions on my shelf: unrelated side projects (an image of me sitting at my laptop typing), a relationship (the person in miniature form), family health issues (usually a body part—a lung, kidney, heart, or hips), and waiting for news about something or someone (fireflies in a mason jar). What I do next is take the image of the distraction, reach above my head, and put the distraction on the shelf where it is out of the way but close enough, so I know I didn't abandon the thought (it feels good knowing it's close, but it's out of sight so I can still do my work). Whenever I feel the urge to think about my distraction, I tell myself that it is right there on the shelf and I can take it down and think about it later. I tell myself that right now, for the next hour, it's going to stay on the shelf. If I can't last an hour without thinking about it, I'll try for 20 minutes. And if 20 minutes is too challenging, I try five. When the time is up, I let myself think about my distraction, but only for a few minutes. When time is up, back on the shelf it goes.

When I put my distraction on the shelf, I know I am not abandoning it—I am setting it down, so I can pick up the rest of my life and move it forward, even if it only happens five minutes at a time.

Work as Play

Don't make a distinction between work and play. Regard everything that you're doing as play, and don't imagine for one minute that you've got to be serious.
—ALAN WATTS

I'm a freshwater Midwesterner. No matter where I go, my friendly roots have followed me as I set up camp in new cities across the country. I grew up talking to service workers at the gas station, making small talk with the grocery clerks, asking baristas at the local coffee shop what books they were reading. I usually start with an open-ended, "Hiya, how's it go-in?"

In the last few years, I've picked up on a more somber and disengaged attitude. People may have always been this way, and I am now just picking up on it? Regardless, what I do know is that it's not only in the one state, it's all over. When I ask people how their day is going, most of them respond with: "Well, I'm at work…" or "It will be a lot better in x hours" (when their shift is over).

Dr. Stuart Brown, a pioneer in research on play said: "The opposite of play is not work—it is depression." What we call "work" encompasses whatever we do between the time we get up in the morning and before we fall asleep, and how we do that work defines who we are. If your job is the worst eight hours of your day, you are going to feel more drained of energy after your shift than someone who has worked the same amount of time at a job where they are able to play. If you don't enjoy your work, start thinking about a job where you can apply skills and knowledge that will allow you to be more playful. If you can't find new work or need to stick this job out a little longer, try making your work more playful. The only way I was able to survive a few jobs in the past was to think of it all as a game. I thought only about what was right in front of me, one customer at a time, one project at a time. This idea comes from Alan Watts. In a lecture, he describes the chore of washing dishes. Instead of thinking of a towering stack of dirty plates and bowls waiting to be washed, one should only think of the dish they are currently washing. And then, the whole act of taking a dish from the stack, wiping it down, rinsing, and moving onto the next becomes a kind of dance. Instead of it being a chore, it turns into something playful.

As we get older, play becomes something taboo: a time-wasting activity that takes us away from *real* work. This kind of thinking couldn't be more wrong. Steven Johnson, author of *Wonderland: How Play Made the Modern World*, writes that innovation hasn't only followed money, war, or sex. According to Johnson, innovation is based in playfulness. Johnson writes: "You will find the future wherever people are having the most fun." Some companies have caught onto this idea because there is a direct correlation to increased productivity. Studies have found that employees who work for companies that support healthy habits like play are eight times more dedicated and more than three times more creative. This means that if you want to be more productive, you also have to be more playful.

Game of Life

Play is the highest form of research.
— ALBERT EINSTEIN

In the summer of 2009, game designer and researcher, Jane McGonigal, suffered a concussion that didn't heal properly. A month into her recovery, she still couldn't read or write for more than a few minutes at a time. She had constant headaches, nausea, and vertigo, and had a hard time remembering things. Most days she was too sick to get out of bed. Jane felt anxious and depressed, and experienced suicidal thoughts, a side effect of traumatic brain injuries. To reduce the symptoms, her doctor told her all the things she should avoid doing: reading, writing, running, playing video games, working, using email, and consuming alcohol and caffeine. Jane jokingly responded: "In other words, [I have] no reason to live."

McGonigal was the first person in the world to earn a Ph.D. studying the psychological strengths of gamers and how those strengths translate to real-world problem solving. When she was injured in 2009, she had nearly a decade of game research under her belt, and out of this grew an idea.

There isn't any real treatment for post-concussion syndrome. You can only rest and wait, with recovery taking sometimes over a year. One day she hit a breaking point and told herself, "I am either going to kill myself, or I'm going to turn this into a game." Building on gaming principles she learned from her research, McGonigal created a real-life recovery game called "Jane the Concussion Slayer" where she took on a hero's identity and battled anything that triggered her symptoms. She named these "the bad guys" and together with her allies (friends and family members) they battled the bad guys and collected powerups: anything that would make her day more enjoyable or speed up her recovery. Within a couple of days of playing her real-life game, Jane noticed her depression loosening its grip. It was a lot of work, and by no means a miracle cure, but Jane felt stronger and in more control of her life.

McGonigal made a full recovery and has shared her game with millions of people under a new name: SuperBetter. In her own words, she writes:

> I knew from my years of research at the University of California at Berkeley that when we play a game, we tackle tough challenges with more creativity, more determination, and more optimism. We're also more likely to reach out to others for help.

In 2015, McGonigal published a book about her experience under the same title as her game: *SuperBetter*. Both the book and app were released in the same year and are based on five years of research. This research included a randomized, controlled study with the University of Pennsylvania and a clinical trial at the College of Medicine at Ohio

State University and Cincinnati Children's Hospital, which was funded by the National Institutes of Health.

Play and gamification reframe our chaotic world into one we are more familiar with: a video game world with patterns, rules, hacks, and secret identities. When we see the world as a game, our challenges become quests that build experience points and lead to overcoming a larger goal—what Jane and SuperBetter call an Epic Win. Our friends become our allies, and together we are stronger. Our lives are more manageable and more fun as we become the hero of our lives and live more playfully.

> To play SuperBetter, visit superbetter.com/want_to_play or visit your mobile app store for a free download.

Play as a Creative Escape

Fairy tales are more than true – not because they tell us dragons exist, but because they tell us dragons can be beaten.
— G.K. CHESTERTON

What you do outside of the office influences your creativity and productivity in the office. When you play, it's an escape into a less serious world where you are free to explore without having the stress of a deadline. Here are some things you can do to remain playful at home:

Read more science fiction & fantasy books. Reading fiction of any kind can be a healthy escape. You are transported to another world where your imagination leads the way. Have you ever watched a movie of a book you read? It was terrible, right? Because nothing can compare with the movie you made in your mind as you read.

Specifically, I'm suggesting sci-fi and fantasy because those genres push your imagination to create images of things that don't exist (yet) in our world. In these books, characters are not bound to the same rules and laws we are. They can move through different worldly dimensions and use magic. It pushes us, the reader, to question our own world, and to believe that anything is possible.

In 2007, the author Neil Gaiman visited China for the country's first-ever state-sponsored science fiction convention. At the event, he began talking to a party official about why they decided to put on the event. Up until this year, the government had disapproved of science fiction, and Gaiman asked why there was such a big change—not only to allow the convention but to sponsor it? The official responded by saying that China manufactures many wonderful things, but they don't come up with any of the ideas. On a government tour of America, officials spoke to employees at Microsoft, Google, and Apple, and asked a lot of questions. What they found was, all the people they interviewed read science fiction when they were teenagers. That's when China decided that maybe science fiction and fantasy are good things after all.

Thrift store game night. One of my friend groups meets one night a week to play board games. This isn't poker or Magic the Gathering, though I do have friends who meet regularly for those games. My thrift store game night friends meet-up and play the games they grew up with like Pictionary, Cranium, Scattergories, Charades, and Bananagrams (usually purchased at a thrift store). These are short games that involve bursts of creativity and sometimes moving out of your comfort zone to act a little goofy. Having a weekly game night is a good outlet to blow off some steam and be a kid again, especially in the middle of the week when it's easy to feel like a cog in the machine.

Trade night. One of my other friend groups meets once a month to learn something new. They spend Saturday afternoon learning how to do something they have never done before, like learning how to knit, throw clay, or perform a new dance step.

It all started when I was living in Seattle and realized that there were things I've always wanted to do, but I had no reason to go out of my way and learn them on my own. I could very easily live the rest of my life not knowing if I liked ballroom dancing or making tiramisu. Besides, who knows, maybe I have a secret knack for something I never knew about?

How it works is someone in the group will say something like "I've always wanted to ice skate," so the next month we will all meet at an ice rink. Usually, there is one person in the group who has done the activity before, and they have the opportunity to teach the rest of the group. What I've learned is, sometimes you love it, sometimes you hate it, but it's better to try it and hate it than not know what you're missing.

Here are some ideas to get you and your friends started:

Karaoke	Dancing
Squash (game)	Making a short movie
Woodworking	Archery
Sewing	Crocheting
Beekeeping	Cooking

How Play Fits in the Dock Model

Do not take life too seriously. You will never get out of it alive.
— ELBERT HUBBARD

Within the serious rules of life, play encourages you to test the limits and reframe what is possible. Play lets you experiment with your skills and challenges you to grow them by going on quests and collecting power-ups. You can gain experience points, conquer new territories, and fight the bad guys. When you play, you get to come up with your own life strategy and become the superhero you have always wanted to be.

Unlike the Health and Practice Pillars, Play is the first pillar that is not connected to the shore. Play is facing open water, symbolizing a full range of opportunities. Once you are healthy enough to use all of your faculties to their fullest (Health, Pillar I) and have a solid foundation to connect to (Practice, Pillar II), you are ready to explore new territory. In Play, you experiment with your skills, break rules (and know why you are breaking the rules), and extend your dock, opening it up to an ocean of possibilities.

GOAL FOR TODAY: Find one thing you can start doing today that will make your life more playful. If your job is a drain, what can you do to turn it into a game? This weekend, is there something new you can explore with your friends? Or, do you have time during the week to host a thrift store game night?

REFLECTION:
THE FOURTH PILLAR

We come from a generation of people who need their TV or stereo playing all the time. These people are so scared of silence. These soundaholics, these quietophobics.
— CHUCK PALAHNIUK, *Lullaby*

We do not learn from experience ... we learn from reflecting on experience.
— JOHN DEWEY

During his time as Microsoft, CEO, Bill Gates, would periodically leave for a week to be alone in the woods. Apart from one caretaker who provided two meals every day and a steady stream of Diet Orange Crush, Gates was alone in a mystery location in the Pacific Northwest. This was something he called Think Week. Twice a year during each Think Week he would dive into papers written by the Microsoft community. He scribbled notes, mapped out ideas, and wrote summaries for executives. For Gates, this was a time of deep thought, reflection, and goal creation, and he credits his Think Week process for many of Microsoft's most successful innovations.

It wasn't until 2005, when Gates was in his 11th year of doing

Think Weeks, that he shared his long-time secret with the *Wall Street Journal*. Since, his Think Week practice has taken off like wildfire. Many top professionals including Michael Karnjanaprakorn, CEO and Co-Founder of Skillshare, have adopted Think Week strategies into their own reflection practices. In an article published in Fast Company, Karnjanaprakorn writes about how he has tweaked Gate's practice and made it his own:

> If you haven't taken a week off to reflect on your past and your future, it's something I highly recommend. If you can't take a week, I'd encourage you to take a day, or even a few hours. ... For each 'Think Week,' I create a life to-do list, do a lot of research, and think through big ideas and challenges deeply.

Unfortunately, many people and companies believe they are too busy to reflect. An hour spent thinking about what they have done, analyzing the present, and planning for the future, is considered a waste of an hour. Francesca Gino, professor at the Harvard Business School, says thinking you're too busy to reflect is a huge problem in business:

> I don't see a lot of organizations that actually encourage employees to reflect—or give them time to do it ... When we fall behind even though we're working hard, our response is often just to work harder. But in terms of working smarter, our research suggests that we should take time for reflection.

Reflection is an important part of the learning process, and even doing a little goes a long way. According to the dual-process theory of thought, there are two types of learning processes. In the first, called Type 1, people learn by doing. The more someone does a task, the better they know how to do it. In Type 2, someone builds on Type 1 by doing and then pausing to consciously reflect. Instead of only doing, the individual thinks about the past, takes in present data, and makes a choice based on how their choice will affect the future.

To test the effectiveness of these two types of thought processes, Gino studied new employees at a business-process outsourcing company based in Bangalore, India. In the experiment, new employees training at a tech support call center were put into three different groups: a control group, a reflection group, and a sharing group. In the control group, employees were given no additional instructions besides the standard training. In the reflection group, employees were given training and told to spend an additional 15 minutes at the end of each day writing and reflecting on the lessons they learned. In the third group, sharing, the new employees were given training, told to write a reflection for 15 minutes (same as the reflection group), and were then told to spend an additional five minutes explaining their notes to a fellow trainee. A month later, the three groups were tested on their performance. All three groups made improvements, but the biggest improvements were made by the reflection and sharing groups. The reflection group had an average performance 22.8% higher than the control group, and the sharing group performed an average of 25% higher than the control group. Gino says that this should be a wakeup call for both employees and managers. Using reflection is not about working harder, it's about working smarter. The two groups who had an increase in performance spent an additional 15 to 20 minutes reflecting or sharing, respectively, each day, for 11 days, which should be an indication of little investment for a high return.

Reflection is important for learning new skills and for creating and revising your goals. During reflection, you are actively disconnecting so you can purposefully and critically look at your work and life from a distance. Reflection is not a vacation, even though afterwards you may feel inspired and refreshed. Reflection is not meditation, although meditation could be part of your reflection practice. Reflection *is* about taking inventory of where you are and where you want to be, and designing a path that leads there. It's like you're floating 100 feet above your life with the ability to press rewind, pause, and fast-forward.

I call my regular think time Deliberate Reflection, because my reflection (like my practice) is specific and structured. Here's my process.

Do.
During your normal day-to-day interactions, put your best foot forward, always do your best, and live in the present moment. This is something you are probably already doing. The only difference is you need to be a little more observant: Take notes and record impressions about how things went throughout the day, and save them to look at later.

Think deeply.
During this part of Deliberate Reflection, you take all the notes and impressions from weeks or months prior and see if there are any

trends. You celebrate bright spots and use failure as feedback. With this information, you ask: do my actions align with my goals? Are my feelings and impressions consistent with the path I want to follow? If there are any differences, what needs to change?

Plan.

Using the trends in the previous step, Think Deeply, create a new path to the end goal you have been working towards. The new path you create will allow for plenty of wiggle room to account for the natural changes you and the world go through.

Do better.

Using the insights gained from reflection, you will be more confident and knowledgeable, and have a renewed sense of direction. As a result, you will avoid making choices that might have previously gotten in the way of you reaching your goals.

Repeat.

You repeat the process over again, because you are never finished growing. You know that there is always something to learn and you can always improve. True masters always have a goal they are working towards and never reach what they call perfection.

Next, I am going to unpack my process, step by step, so you can see how each part is critical to the Reflection pillar. When you see all the moving parts and the reasons behind each step, you can decide how often you want to use reflection in your own life. I suggest taking time to reflect at least two times a year and no more than once a week. If you chose to reflect twice a year (like Bill Gates does with his Think Week), set aside a few days or a week to do so. If you do a reflection at the end of every week, I suggest spending no longer than an hour doing so to avoid overthinking. Overthinking can lead to spending too much time in the past or future, which will take you away from the important work you are doing in the present.

Using Think Time for Deliberate Reflection

Do.
While you are doing what you do best, carry a small notebook with you (like I suggest in the introduction to this book) and write down anything that sparks your interest. Random thoughts, to-do lists, observations, etc. After a big event, key interaction, or something that happens that makes you feel more emotional than usual (good, bad, or mixed) write down your thoughts and feelings. For longer reflection pieces, feel free to type it out. What you are doing is gathering notes on how you felt in that moment, so you can reflect on them later during your weekly, monthly, or yearly reflections.

Think deeply.
You can do this two different ways, alone or with others. I suggest trying both.

Thinking deeply alone:
Shut your door and find a space to concentrate free from distraction. Bring your notebook and any other information you have gathered in your **Do** step. When you look at all your feedback, take note of any trends you see.

When you are thinking deeply, this is your time to get away from distractions like people and deadlines. You don't need to be extreme and hide under your desk, but find a comfortable location that works for you. There's a philosophy myth that René Descartes spent an entire day in the damp, cramped space of a stove, meditating, before coming up with his most famous philosophical idea: cogito ergo sum— in English: I think, therefore, I am.

I do my best reflecting in the unfinished upstairs of my 1927 house. It's one medium-sized room with a piece of plywood resting on some two-by-fours in a corner. I use it as a desk and it's big enough to hold a few stacks of books, several piles of paper, a laptop, and my pile of small notebooks. It's not anything special to look at, but that's the point: there are zero distractions.

Thinking deeply with others:
Reach out to mentors, colleagues, and friends and broadly share your goals and observations with them. In **Practice**, I wrote about how

sharing your goals might get in the way of working on them, that's why your approach to this is important. If you are working with a mentor, they can help keep you on track with regular check-ins to make sure you are following through and doing the work. If you are sharing your ideas with friends, only tell one or two people. If they are willing, have them check-in with you so you are held accountable. The more you share, the harder it is to get motivated and do the work.

Your friends and mentors will help you put your life and goals in context. It's the old saying: if you were to see your clone on the street, would you recognize yourself? Friends and mentors are able to mirror things back to you that you cannot see. With their input, you will be able to craft a more complete plan for the journey ahead. Remember two things: 1) Don't take anything they say personally. 2) You asked for an honest opinion, so don't get mad if you get an honest opinion that's hard to hear.

Plan.
This is your game plan, the stage where you take what you have learned and make a new plan to account for the trends noticed in your past behaviors. For example, let's say I have a goal of getting into an apprenticeship program at my work. Through the step of **Think deeply**, I see that I tend to get very frustrated with my coworkers and react in ways I regret later. Management may see this and worry about my success in the program. To account for this in my plan going forward, I would take note of my short temper and make it a goal of mine to reduce my frustrations with coworkers or devise a better way to cope with them, so I don't outwardly display them.

When you take notes of the impressions you have while you **Do** your work, you will have a lot of information to **Think deeply** about. Comparing your actions and feelings against your goals, you will be able to craft a **Plan**. When you are finished reflecting, you will **Do better** than you would have just going through the motions. And when you do better, you will see the value in **Repeating** the process.

What to Watch Out For
Deliberate reflection ≠ vacation.
During your reflection, you may be using vacation time and you may be in a remote location away from people and deadlines, but you are

not relaxing. A vacation is when you emotionally and physically remove yourself from work or regular responsibilities. Deliberate Reflection is the opposite of a vacation. Deliberate Reflection is about diving into the work you are doing, have done, and want to do. You are critically looking at the past, honestly evaluating the present, and creating a roadmap for the future.

During Gate's Think Week, he spends up to 18 hours a day working. That's how serious it is. You are creating your future, so be prepared to work.

Reflection ≠ living in the past.

It's okay to visit the past, but make sure you don't get too comfortable there. You are a visitor, not a resident. I've caught myself thinking about the past and longing for those days to return. I'll walk through the day reminiscing and miss out on all the cool things I'm doing in the present moment. What I realized when I was reflecting on my time was, the reason I get caught up in the past is because I didn't appreciate past moments when they happened—and I wish I would have. Me spending time in the past with those moments is me trying to make those moments more meaningful. The problem is, I can only be in one place at a time. When I'm reminiscing, I'm not appreciating the present moment, so a month from now, I'll look back and realize I didn't appreciate the moment and agonize over it. This causes a delay in my life where I am always one step behind the present, always in the past and never enjoying what is in front of me.

I sound like a broken record, but it is worth repeating. You are only a visitor in the past, your home is in the present. The present is where the work is done, and living in the present is the only way to change the future.

Reflection ≠ living in the future.

I read somewhere that the average adult has three million-dollar ideas per year. ... So everybody's got ideas. Ideas are cheap. What's unique is the conviction to follow through: to work at it until it pays off.

— MAX BARRY from his novel, *Syrup*

I've met some very charismatic people—I'm sure you know who I'm talking about. The friends who get so excited it's contagious. Whatever they're talking about rubs off and you immediately want to jump in, get your hands dirty, and help out. And then, later that night, something peculiar happens. You think to yourself: well, that was odd, why would I ever want to help start an organic sherbet company? (No offense to those whose dream is to own and operate an organic sherbet company.)

I know those people, because I am one of them. I have a Roughneck® Rubbermaid® container full of unfinished books and failed companies (let's say I'm easily excited and I'm easy to persuade). These friends of mine, as well as myself, have the best of intentions, but spend too much time living in the future. We only think about the benefits of the great products we are going to make, not the work to get there. It's great to think about traveling the world, buying cars and houses, being recognized by the media, and changing culture, but it's quite another thing to sit down and do the work.

Reality may ≠ your plan.

During your reflection, you may realize that you are not following your original plan. Or you may discover that if you follow your plan, it will no longer lead you where you want to go. Don't worry, this is completely normal.

Never be married to your plan. Things change, and when they do, your plan needs to change too. When your goal or environment moves, your path (your plan) needs to change as well. This means a couple of things. First, you need to reevaluate where you are spending your time (look back at the Time Management section in Part 1, page 100). Second, you need to be honest with yourself so when you course-correct, you are still doing something you value and have a passion for (see Section 1.3, page 65).

Let's work through a few examples. Let's say you know that you want to work in the medical field and eventually have an advanced degree working as a nurse practitioner. After working with teens in an adolescent rehabilitation unit as a nurse, you may learn that you like working with teenagers, but don't like working in an in-patient rehabilitation setting. Since you like the nursing model and want to advance in your field, when you go back to school for a Master's in Nursing, you will want to spend your clinical hours working with adolescents outside of an inpatient rehabilitation setting. This means having the courage to change where you work and the drive to learn a new routine and skillset.

What if you put in all the work, graduate with a degree in something you loved learning about, and realize in the first year at a job in your field that what you loved learning about isn't fun in practice? Each morning, you wake up before work and feel disembodied and desperate. Your job is the identity you've been repeating to yourself every day for the last four years. You have family, friends, and teachers excited for you and wishing you on your way. Not to mention all the loans you took out, and you've got six months before you get the first repayment bill in the mail. This is going to be a big course correction, but it's not unmanageable! No matter your age, you are never too old to change your career to something you have a passion for. In this example, since you already have a degree, there is a wider door of opportunities available to you. The good news is you know that you can make things happen. You earned a degree, which is like the marathon of education, so you know what it's like to work hard and follow through with something you care about. What you need to do now is discover where that new goal is hiding. Go back through the exercises on page 75, and reflect on careers where your interests intersect with your skills.

Finally, let's look at a change you can't control. What if the goal you're working towards becomes obsolete? If you are a farmer by trade, your parents were farmers, your grandparents started the farm and built the barn, and so on, you are probably concerned about being absorbed by a large farming corporation (if not willingly, then forcefully). The problem is, you can't produce enough to keep up with the low prices of the big corps. If you're on a dairy farm, this might mean that you can't sell milk in the quantities you used to before the corporations took over. If your farm is something you love, you need to find your niche. Seth Godin, founder of the altMBA workshop and daily blogger (and a totally freak'n awesome business writer), has some advice. He writes: "There's no such thing as a niche that's too small if the people care enough. ... You might only need to produce more value for those you already serve."

If you can't compete with quantity, what about quality? Can you be the best tasting grass-fed dairy in the state? If you grow corn or soybeans, what would you do if corn drops to under $2/bushel? Is it worth starting up the equipment if you're going to lose money at harvest? You could change your business model to accommodate for a corn maze or other fall festivities. Is your barn picturesque? You could host weddings or work with a photographer to host photo shoots. Finally, could you grow other crops that are more profitable? The organic market is steadily growing—could you transport vegetables to farmers markets around the state?

The only thing we can count on is change. Knowing this, we should always be open to revising our plans. I've always liked the U.S. Marines mantra: Improvise, Adapt, and Overcome. This is exactly the kind of thinking one needs to stay afloat in the Age of Agility.

Reflection in the Dock Model

Do you remember the story *A Christmas Carol*? It's the Charles Dickens classic about the old miser, Ebenezer Scrooge, who doesn't donate to charity or let Bob Cratchit, his underpaid clerk, have Christmas Day off (Dickens breaks your heart when you learn about Cratchit's ill son, Tiny Tim). In the story, Scrooge is visited by four ghosts: the first is his old business partner, Jacob Marley, who is tangled in chains. Marley tells Scrooge that if he doesn't change his ways, he too will have the same fate in the afterlife. Scrooge is then visited by the Ghost of Christmas Past, the Ghost of Christmas Present, and the Ghost of Christmas Yet to Come.

Ebenezer Scrooge's ghosts live on the Reflection pillar (past, present, and future). In the Reflection pillar, you are standing at your Dock with the open water behind you as you look at the other pillars: Health, Practice, and Play. After looking at the other pillars, you turn around and gaze into the open sea. Take this time to think about your goals: where are you now and where do you want to be? What are your priorities? When you spot one of your goals on the horizon, strengthen your Dock. Keep building. As your Dock becomes stronger, it will be like a lighthouse, attracting big ideas to your shore. Take advantage of the opportunities that come your way. Each one is a chance to extend your Dock for bigger adventures in the future. There are endless opportunities sailing around, looking for a Dock like yours to drop anchor. And sometimes they appear when you least expect it, completely out of the blue.

Better now than never. Ask yourself, where have you been, where are you going, and what tools do you need to get there?

GOAL FOR TODAY: Find a space where you will be free from distraction and interruption (go for a walk, put in some ear plugs, or go to a coffee shop and sit down with your notebook). Close your eyes and take two deep breaths. Use this time to think about how you can use reflection in your life. Is there one thing you can start doing today that will help you focus on the big picture? Can you set a date for a big reflection? What resources should you start gathering to aid in your reflection?

BUILDING YOUR DOCK

We are what we repeatedly do. Excellence then, is not an act,
but a habit.
— ARISTOTLE

The last four chapters provide a lot of information about how to
keep your life—your Dock—balanced. But that's only the first step;
knowledge is only useful when it's acted upon. That's why I've added
an additional chapter on building your Dock so you can put your
knowledge into action.

Our lives are filled with habits, though we may be unaware of
what those habits are. We wake up at some point during the day, eat
a few times, and spend most of the day working or going to school.
What happens between waking up and walking through the front
door at work may be a blur or a chaotic scramble (especially if you
have kids or roommates). Like most of the population, you may be
stuck in passive routines. Using the Dock Model, you can create
active routines that consciously move you closer to your goals.

If you don't have a daily routine already, it's not too late to start.
In this chapter, we'll look at how single meaningful actions can be
strung together into a supportive routine. Routines come in a variety
of forms. Some routines actively support your goals through time
management or practice. Others are considered mindful routines

(also called rituals) and these routines focus on the breathing and reflection portions of your Dock. All routines can be modeled after patterns of success. Instead of reinventing the wheel, you can borrow routines from people who have achieved the same goals you are working towards. Once you have a daily routine, you won't need to think about living healthily and achieving daily goals, it will become a thoughtless part of your life.

How Habits Work

Trigger, behavior, reward. (Repeat). Remember this progression.

A few years ago, I moved to a different part of Seattle and found myself in an unfamiliar part of town, meaning I needed to find a new place to get my morning caffeine kick. Every day, I would try a new café in the neighborhood. On the third day, I walked into a small coffee shop a few blocks away from my new apartment and my senses were immediately overcome with memories of snow covered mornings in West Michigan. There were days when so much lake effect snow fell, we couldn't leave the house, so my mom, sister, and I would stay inside and bake. That day in Seattle, I looked to see where the smell was coming from and I saw a worker standing behind the counter, lifting chocolate chip cookies off a baking sheet and placing them in a glass paneled display case. In that moment, time slowed down and I was the only one left in the café. The rest of the room darkened except for the light on top of the display case. A silent sigh escaped my lips.

I made my way up to the barista and ordered my drink. And then, I hesitated. "Anything else?" the barista said. I felt myself begin to stutter so I pointed to the display of baked good. It took half a second to find the words: "Those cookies, they smell really good. Do you bake them here?"

People in Seattle aren't as patient as they are in the Midwest. The barista gave me an eye roll. (Communication! Usually I only get a blank stare when I ask questions in public!) I lean to my left and peer behind the cash register. There are two people mixing batter and dough.

"They're organic, if that's what you're asking," the barista said, "We also have vegan options."

I heard the person behind me breathing heavily. In Seattle, this means I needed to speed up the pace. "I'll take two." I hesitated again, "Two, *with* the animal products in them."

The next morning, I saw the cookies from a distance before I could even smell them. I remembered the previous morning sitting down and slowly savoring each melt-in-your-mouth bite. It was a Friday so I decided to buy two more. (What? Don't judge me, it was a Friday.)

Monday morning, I bought cookies. I bought cookies every single day that week.

The following week, I felt myself standing up straighter in line. I was feeling a little more confident. I turned around to the person behind me: "They smell great, don't they? I can't believe it. Every single day, it smells like cookies in here. I love it." There was no response. My new-Seattleite-(not)-friend turned 90 degrees and started playing on their phone. *They don't know what they're missing.*

I was all giddy when I made my way up to the counter to order my drink. "Two cookies?" the barista asked. And then it hit me. My stomach dropped and it felt like it landed somewhere around my knees. I felt a knot the size of a walnut forming in my throat.

"...N-no cookies today. Just the drink."

In the movie version of my story, the room turns black again and it's just me and the display case. We stare longingly at each other as the distance grows between us. A chocolate chip cookie stands up and rolls to my feet. It winks its chocolate chip eye at me and rolls away into the horizon. I whisper a small farewell to the cookies that brought me so much joy these last two weeks. Goodbye, friends.

Trigger, behavior, reward. (Repeat). That's all a habit is, and I caught myself as I was starting to form a very unhealthy one. Let's break the habit down a little further so we can see how we pick up habits without even thinking about it.

The first part of developing a new habit is the trigger. Side note: Triggers have recently popped into news because of "trigger warnings," which alert readers or viewers to potentially distressing material—for our purposes, we are only going to talk about triggers as they relate to building habits. In its simplest form, a trigger is an event that stimulates us to perform an action. Sometimes the trigger is so strong we don't realize we're performing the action. A smoker, for example, has a lot of triggers (that's why it's so hard for smokers to break the habit). For many smokers, the first cup of coffee in the morning is a trigger for a cigarette, and those who have quit smoking will tell you how hard it is to drink alcohol without fighting back the urge for cigarette. (If you've ever been to a bar with a tipsy ex-smoker, you've probably watched them as they circled the bar asking to buy a single cigarette for what an entire pack costs.) Likewise, when I smelled the baking chocolate chip cookies, I was triggered because of my positive associations from my childhood.

Eating food is often the behavior associated with a trigger: stress, anxiety, depression, celebration, the list goes on. The action, step two, is what happens because of the trigger. It's Friday, so I'm happy **(trigger)** and excited for the weekend **(trigger)**. On Fridays, I let myself splurge a little **(trigger)**, so I buy two cookies **(action)**. What happens next? It. Tastes. Wonderful. My brain is firing pleasure chemicals like crazy and I'm off in la-la land enjoying my snack. This is the reward. The reason habits are hardwired into our brains is that building good habits was once imperative for our species thousands of years ago. When our relatives were walking through the woods and came across a fruit tree, they built a habit. They knew to come back to that place for food. Nowadays, we don't need to build the same habits for finding food, but the wiring remains the same. The good news is, since we know how habits work (trigger, action, reward), we can manipulate them to create positive habits.

Habits can be good or bad. On the other hand, routines and rituals—what we're developing in this chapter—are purposeful. They are made up of good habits you intentionally create to support a lifestyle that meets the needs of your goals. Let's take a closer look at why we need routines and how using routines can direct your energy to the things you care about most.

Why We Need Routines

...you have a routine that allows you to preserve your decision-making and your creativity hit points...for the things that actually matter so that you're not waking up and every morning deciding what to have for breakfast. You're not waking up every morning and maybe deciding what to wear. So, in what ways can you preserve your decision-making budget, your creativity budget, for the things that you are uniquely good at and that really matter? And the answer seems to be, you have a lot of routines.

— TIM FERRISS, *How to Cage the Monkey Mind* from Talks at Google

A routine starts with one habit. The completion of the first habit is the trigger for the second, and from there, you create a habit chain a.k.a. your routine. You can improve your daily routine by adding a habit to an existing habit chain or by starting a new chain of habits. If it sounds overwhelming now, know that it gets easier. Every habit becomes easier the more times you do it. Take your commute to work or school as an example—the first week on the job, you might have needed to use a navigation system in your vehicle or look at a public transportation map. After a week or two, you became more familiar with the route and ditched the map or navigation system. Now, the map is burned into your head, you could probably drive there in your sleep. And that's because it literally is. Your brain changes the more you do something. Like we discussed in Practice, your brain changes with repetition. That's why it takes a few weeks for a habit to become second nature, because you are building new pathways in the brain. And that's why it's so hard to break new habits, because you don't ever break the connections you have already made. Those triggers will never go away. However, your new connections will get stronger and more favorable than the old ones.

Once you become comfortable in your new daily routine, you will gradually be able to take on more each day. That's why some people like Bill Gates or Steve Jobs appear to be like super-humans. In reality, they have spent decades adding powerful habits to their daily routines. Here are two more reasons why routines are so important.

Everything you do affects the goal(s) you are working towards.
In the summer of 2010, I signed up for a writing workshop lead by a local writer and educator in Grand Haven, Michigan, located about a half-hour drive away from my off-campus college apartment. When I walked in the door of the home where the writing instructor lived, she gave me a folder. Inside was the day's schedule, a packet of notes summarizing the main points we would cover in the workshop and various pamphlets about upcoming events. I quickly flipped through the folder and closed it. I couldn't help but notice a bulge the size of a pen at the bottom of the folder. I took a seat and opened the folder again, reaching under the bottom flap. To my shock, it was a toothbrush.

When everyone arrived, the instructor explained why she had given each of us a toothbrush: "This is one of the most important writing tools I can give you. Use it twice a day: once in the morning and once at night." She explained that the toothbrush did two things:

1. It provides a routine to follow every day. Just like brushing

your teeth, you should be writing every day, even on days you don't feel like it. Brush your teeth twice a day at the same time each day. Write twice a day at the same time each day. Brushing your teeth is a **trigger** for the **action** of writing.

2. Routines keep us sane and grounded. If you get caught up in your writing and forget to go outside, sleep, eat, or talk to other humans, this routine of brushing will give you some stable ground to stand on. We get so caught up in the work we're doing, we lose perspective. Brushing your teeth is a small routine to keep you grounded in your other daily routines.

The toothbrush was the biggest take-away from the workshop. It was a reminder that the skills we learned in the workshop only help us become better writers when they become part of our daily routine. Additionally, if we want to produce good work, we need to break habits that keep us from performing at our peak. All of our habits affect our work, and replacing bad habits with good routines will keep us grounded and moving forward.

Here is reason number two.

We have a limited amount of decisions we can make per day.
If you wear clean socks every day, do you get your work done on time? In the 1970s, Stanford social psychologist, Daryl J. Bem, assumed that he would find a positive correlation between students who changed their socks and those who turned in their homework. His reasoning was that both actions stem from the same underlying trait: conscientiousness. What he found was the exact opposite: either students changed their socks, or they turned their homework in on time. It was as if students chose to do one or the other. Bem didn't think much of the small study until a couple of decades later when researchers started testing students' willpower.

Multiple studies have found that during exam time, students reduce the amount of time they spend exercising, they smoke more cigarettes, and their caffeine intake doubles. This makes sense, anyone who has been under the exam crunch knows that students are spending more time studying (so they can't go to the gym), and using stimulants like caffeine and nicotine to stay focused. If their behavior change was purely for the sake of productivity, we wouldn't see an increase in alcohol and junk food consumption, which detract from learning and leave the student feeling more tired—but we do. The study also found that students are less likely to respond to phone calls, wash their dishes, floss their teeth, shave, and yes, change their socks. The big question is, what's happening inside the brains of students during exam week?

After an intense day at the office, do you ever come home feeling drained, even if you didn't do anything physically exhausting? I'm sure every one of us can empathize with students during exam week. We've all given into cravings and skipped chores so we could relax (or at least really wanted to). The bigger question is, why do we have a shorter fuse at the end of the day? Why do chores like laundry and washing dishes feel so much harder to do at night? And why does junk food sound so much better after a long day? John Tierney and Roy Baumeister, authors of the book *Willpower: Rediscovering the Greatest Human Strength*, suggest that it's because of these two reasons:

1. You have a finite amount of willpower that becomes depleted as you use it.

2. You use the same stock of willpower for all the tasks you do.

What's happening is we are spending all our willpower on work or studying, so when we go back home, we make poor choices about food and can't find the motivation to return texts and phone calls.

Researchers call this Decision Fatigue. It refers to the finite amount of willpower each of us has each day. Every time we make a decision, we use some of our willpower. Not every decision uses the same amount of willpower—some drain us more than others, but it's enough for some people to alter their behavior. Former U.S. President Barack Obama, Steve Jobs, and Mark Zuckerberg only wear one or two outfits. When they open their closet, there's no deciding what to wear for the day, it's already planned so they don't waste any of their willpower on deciding what to wear. The idea is, if you reduce the amount of decisions you make on things that don't matter to you, you will be able to spend your willpower on what does matter. The best way to reduce your willpower is to turn things like what you wear, what you eat, and what time you go to sleep, into a routine.

The Difference Between Routines and Rituals
(and why we need both)

Daily rituals, especially walks, even forced marches around the neighborhood, and schedules, whether work or meals with non-awful people, can be the knots you hold on to when you've run out of rope.
— ANNE LAMOTT

Routines and rituals (R&R for short) are similar in structure, but they center on a different part of the action. Rituals focus on performing a task and routines place an emphasis on completing the task. In other words, rituals are about the experience and routines are about the end result. This might be confusing, because what one person calls a ritual (for example, washing dishes) someone else may call a routine. It's all about where your head is when you are performing the action. Let's unpack this a little further.

Rituals engage the body. They are meaningful to you and you do them because you are intrinsically motivated to do them. A ritual brings awareness to your day and gives you a sense of belonging. Routines, on the other hand, can be done on autopilot. Your body follows the motions and your brain is turned off. Routines are not especially meaningful because you are extrinsically motivated to complete them. The kicker is, we need both.

Routines keep us on track, so we can make daily progress on our goals. And because routines can be done without thinking, it helps us save our willpower energy for when we need it most. Unlike routines that don't require a lot of thought, rituals energize us by grounding us in the moment. Our brain is awake, but the eyes are flipped, looking inwards. We can focus on our breathing and take in the world as it is.

To get you thinking about some of the routines and rituals you can implement in your life, I created a list of routines and rituals I've used in my own.

Routines (automatic/second nature)
- Going to bed and waking up at the same time every day
- Eating your meals around the same time every day
- Exercising at roughly the same time every day
- Taking prescribed medications at the same time every day
- Brushing your teeth, shaving, cleaning, and cooking at the same time every day

- Preparing lunch for the next day while cleaning up dinner
- Setting your clothes out for the next day so you don't have to decide what to wear in the morning

Rituals (mindful)

- Having a special drink each morning or afternoon (lemon water, tea, or coffee)
- Stretching your muscles when you wake up or after a meal
- Going for a walk alone or with a friend
- Setting time aside for meditation
- Listening to music or an audiobook on your way to and from work (a pre-work playlist and an after-work playlist)
- Writing down one goal you want to focus on throughout the day, such as being more present, actively listening, or being more patient (I try to focus on one of Benjamin Franklin's 13 virtues, like humility, temperance, or sincerity)
- Making a list in the evening of your next day's objectives so they are in your notebook, not in your head; this will clear your mind before bed

Now that you know the importance of routines and rituals, the next step is coming up with specific behaviors that support your goals. With all the self-help business books out there, it's hard to know which routines and rituals work. It gets frustrating, especially when two books contradict each another. Since you need to do what works best for you, it may take trying a few routines on for size and seeing if they improve your day; and if they do, how? Instead of reinventing the wheel, you should start with borrowing routines and rituals that have worked for the people in positions where you want to be. You don't have to limit it to one person or one industry. For example, I borrow Steve Job's clothing routine, Joe Sweeney's ritual of doing one unexpected favor for someone (like buying a coffee for the person behind you in line), and Terry Pratchett's writing 400 words per day routine. When you model routines, you can become a "best of" version of the people you respect most.

Modeling Routines & Rituals

Be wise, because the world needs more wisdom, and if you cannot be wise, pretend to be someone who is wise, and then just behave like they would.

— NEIL GAIMAN

In Play, I wrote about gamification and how you can live your life more playfully if you view it as a game. I wrote about Jane McGonigal and how she created a real-life game, called Superbetter, to help her recover from a concussion. Let me let you in on a little unknown secret: McGonigal wasn't the first person to use the video game model of gamification to achieve a real-life goal. A year before Jane McGonigal's head trauma that lead her to the creation of her game, there was Steve Kamb's Nerd Fitness and his game: The Epic Quest of Awesome.

Like most kids in the 80's and 90's, Steve Kamb grew up glued to a TV. In college, he became an avid gamer, spending 10-12 hours each day playing online with friends until one day, the motherboard on his computer fried and he didn't have enough money to fix it. That's when he realized that his character in the game, *Everquest,* was leveling up and developing new skills, while he was sliding backwards. The more time he spent developing his video game character, the less time he was spending on developing himself.

Steve knew he should be exercising more and building his confidence, but didn't know how he would find the motivation to start living a healthy lifestyle and exploring the world beyond the screen; so, he began thinking about his life as a video game. He named the game: The Epic Quest of Awesome. Steve started blogging about his experiences playing his real-life video game where he leveled up each time he stepped into his learning zone and tried something new. His blog EXPLODED because it resonated with some many online gamers. Soon, other bloggers were sharing their experiences playing The Epic Quest of Awesome. They were getting up and off the couch, trying new things, and leveling up their life.

In 2008, it became official when Kamb launched his website Nerd Fitness, where he encouraged other gamers (who are called Rebels—inspired by Star Wars) to go on quests, face their fears, and start gaining real-life experience points. Or, as Steve Kamb and the rebellion put it, you can become a superhero in your own personal Hero's Journey. When you become part of the Nerd Fitness rebellion, you get to become a superhero. This is based on the idea of modeling: you can model your behavior after certain traits you value or after someone you admire to create a path to a new skill, habit, or lifestyle. In techie-speak, when you model someone, you rewrite your source code to match the person you are modeling. The idea is, there are patterns to success, and if you adopt those same patterns, you too will be successful.

How Modeling Works

We are what we pretend to be, so we must be careful about what we pretend to be.
— KURT VONNEGUT JR., *Mother Night*

If you have an older sibling (like I do), you may remember following them around and trying to do everything they did. Or, if you have a younger sibling, you probably remember the shadow that was on your tail wherever you went, doing everything you were doing, and it probably got super annoying—sorry Katie (that's my older sister). Modeling works the same way. As adults, we shouldn't follow our company's VP around mimicking every single move they make (that might get a little weird), but we can replicate the routines and rituals that lead them to a VP position. Instead of years of trial and error, modeling cuts directly to the successful behavior patterns so you can reach the same level, faster.

Children are excellent at modeling (walking, talking, using a fork or chopsticks) because they are learning how to do something for the first time. Modeling in adults is harder because we have to break away from the old behaviors we have grown accustomed to. Remember the flying horses in Part 1 (page 40)? Change is tough because you have to get both horses on board with the new behaviors. If we think of our modeling-self as a persona, as Steve Kamb suggests in his game, we are free to take on a new identity, one that is powerful, confident, and successful.

To start, imagine you are in the shoes of the person or superhero you are modeling (you can create a new superhero if you'd like). Think about what it would feel like to use your new skill or routine (presenting in front of people, writing an informative blog post, or leading a team are a few examples). In your persona, what kinds of new things do you hear when you listen in a conversation? What new things do you pick up on when you look at a document or walk into a room? What kind of new movements are you making? What tone of voice are you using? What kind of language (vocabulary) are you using? It's helpful to ask, "What would this person do if they were in my situation," because it helps us see the problem from another angle. For example, when I know I need to be more confident and detailed-oriented, I ask myself what Steve Jobs would do if he was in my situation. I take a step back and look at my situation through a new lens. My impression of Steve Jobs is that he was no-nonsense, highly passionate, confident, and a perfectionist. When I look at the dilemma I'm in through his eyes, I immediately become more confident and assume the positive traits I associate with Jobs.

You can channel any person or character, real or imaginary, alive or dead, for the specific superpower you need to handle your tough situation. Meaning, you can model several people each day to help you face your unique daily challenges.

Good Modeling/Bad Modeling

By three methods we may learn wisdom: First, by reflection, which is noblest; Second, by imitation, which is easiest; and third, by experience, which is the bitterest.
— CONFUCIUS

One of my favorite authors, Charles Bukowski, started his daily writing routine in his teens. It wasn't until the age of 51 when he published his first major work, a novel titled *Post Office*. That's over 30 years of daily practice. The reason it took so long is that his practice wasn't efficient. His lifestyle got in the way of racking up hours of deliberate practice (page 207). He was a proud alcoholic who frequently got into bar fights and couldn't keep a job. Practice was interrupted by hangovers, bad relationships, and trying to find his next meal. The problem with modeling is, too often people model the wrong routines. Drinking like a fish isn't going to make you a writer, if anything, it's going to cause the same issues that delayed Bukowski from achieving his goals.

Good modeling copies strategies a person used to move from one life event to the next, not the surface behaviors. Too often, people look at a successful person's achievements and make inaccurate conclusions based on the limited details in their biographies. If there's a news story about a successful entrepreneur who had a paper route as a child, it doesn't mean that every child who had a paper route grew up to be successful. The strategy behind the behavior leads someone to success. A child paper carrier who grew up to be a CEO of a Fortune 500 company might have learned the following strategies: 1) the benefits of a routine, 2) to deliver all the newspapers on time, and 3) developed the people skills to interact with their customers, so they were paid every month.

This kind of thinking is easy to get caught up on. For example, going to a "good school" doesn't make you employable—there are plenty of graduates from top schools who cannot find a job because they expected one to fall into place with little effort. The same is true for bands who like to party—doing a bunch of drugs isn't going to turn you into a Rock and Roll Hall of Fame musician.

The biggest modeling blunder I come across is the drop-out myth. Just because many successful entrepreneurs have a history of dropping out of school, doesn't mean everyone who drops out of school will go on to become successful entrepreneurs. To achieve success in modeling, you need to look at the strategies: the what, why, and how. For example, why did the person drop out of school? How were they able to network and make connections? And finally, what did they see that others overlooked? Let's take a look at Steve Jobs. Here is a very short four-point list of events in Job's life:

1. Drops out of college.
2. Sells his smart friend's product and creates a billion-dollar start-up.
3. Gets fired from the company he created.
4. Starts a company that was just as successful as his last and then gets rehired by his previous startup.

These specific behaviors are not the whole picture of what accounts for his success. For a more efficient approach to modeling, we need to focus on the patterns leading up to the event (the whats, whys, and hows).

1. *Why did he drop out of college?*
   Because he discovered his passion at a young age and the field of computer science was too new of a subject. Because he knew dropping out wouldn't be easy, he made a lot of sacrifices to achieve his goal.

2. *Why did he sell his friend's product for billions?*
   Because he was passionate about the product and believed in what he was selling. He also saw an opportunity that had yet to be tapped by others in the market, what Renée Mauborgne and W. Chan Kim call a Blue Ocean Strategy.

3. *How did he rebound after getting fired from the company he created?*

He admitted to himself that he needed to tweak his business model when his current model stopped working. He needed to spend time reflecting on his values, life goals, and the path that connected the two.

4. *What brought him to success as he started his new company?*
    Setting unheard-of goals and surpassing them. He relied on the connections he made with others and inspired them to always do their best.

Once we know the full picture, we can better understand what behaviors to model.

If you read the news headlines, you know that successful people have good and bad habits. Your heroes, no matter how much you love their work, are human. They are human just like you. That means you too, have the potential to be remarkable. Let your heroes be your teacher first, and as you get better, your competition. In modeling, we stand on the knowledge of those who successfully came before us. As the saying goes, we stand on the shoulders of giants. My goal is to one day surpass my heroes. Since they did the hard work for me, their landing pad is my launching pad.

(Public domain image, Library of Congress, Rosenwald)
The metaphor of dwarfs standing on the shoulders of giants (Latin: nanos gigantum humeris insidentes) expresses the meaning of "discovering truth by building on previous discoveries".

Making Your Rituals and Routines Stick

Motivation is what gets you started. Habit is what keeps you going.
— JIM ROHN

What happens when you come up with a really good plan, but you can't seem to put it into action? The biggest complaint I hear about starting a routine is sticking with it. There have been a lot of business books that give numbers for how long it takes to develop a habit. I've read anywhere from 21 to 30 days before a habit is automatic. I think placing a hard number on habit adoption can be dangerous, because there are so many factors involved. What I can offer you is the latest from scientific literature: In a study published in the *European Journal of Social Psychology*, health psychology researcher Phillippa Lally observed a wide range of habit adoption. In the study, it took anywhere from 18 days to 254 days for people to form a new habit. What made it so hard was overriding the old neural pathways. Creating new neural pathways in your brain takes time, especially when the old ones have been in use for years or decades. It's the same concept you learned in Practice: with the right mindset and if your new habit is deliberate, it will become automatic. To help speed this process up, I put together a list of tools to help you incorporate your routine and rituals into your everyday lifestyle.

Find your "I want" power. Sure, we may want to exercise more or practice a skill, but if we don't spend time investigating *why* we want to adopt a new routine, we will break it as soon as we are hit with resistance. Kelly McGonigal, health psychologist at Stanford University (and sister to Jane McGonigal, who created the game Superbetter) suggests finding your "I want" power. You should ask yourself: why do I want to exercise? What is my desired outcome? It might be because you want to be able to play with your kids without getting tired and losing your breath. Or it could be, so you can one day take your dream trip to Rome and walk the streets without needing to take a break to sit down. If your new routine supports advancement in your career, ask yourself, what specifically is motivating you? Who are you trying to help? Whatever your reason is, identify it and write it down because when you have a "why" to do something, you are more likely to follow through and achieve your desired outcome. Ask yourself: "why do I want this?"

Roll with resistance. When legendary Russian novelist Leo Tolstoy was growing up, his brother told him to stand in a corner, and he could only leave the corner if he didn't think about a white bear. His brother came back much later to find Leo in the same place, paralyzed because he couldn't stop thinking about a white bear.

This is called Ironic Process Theory. The theory suggests that the more someone tries to suppress a thought, the more likely it is to surface. An example might be not wanting to think about sweets because you have cut them out of your new diet. In thinking, "don't think about the pastries in the bakery at the grocery store," all you can think about is freshly baked sweet rolls. The more you try to suppress thinking about sweet rolls, the more you will drain your willpower and the more likely you will give in.

When you are faced with resistance, don't try to suppress it. One of the reasons why diets statistically cause people to *gain* weight is because dieters are spending all their willpower on suppressing thoughts instead of acknowledging them (acknowledging them does not mean giving in). One way to deal with resistance is to stop what you are doing when the feeling hits you, acknowledge the feeling as an observer while it passes through you, and once it has passed, move forward. Once you have acknowledged the feeling, instead of thinking, no, I can't do that, think about what you can do. Instead of saying, "I can't think about X", say, "I can think about Y."

Before I talk in front of an audience, I am stuck thinking about how much I hate being onstage. I know I shouldn't be thinking about how much I hate talking in front of people, because thinking about it only makes it worse. Instead, I acknowledge the feeling and think about the people I intend on helping with my words (my "I want" power). When I think about what I *can* do, I stop thinking about my white bear and focus on what is important.

Develop good triggers. Triggers make us spring into action, and creating strong triggers will propel you into your routine without having to think about it.

One of my friends travels a lot for work. Until a few years ago, the airplane was a great place to get work done because it forced her to sit with her laptop—no distractions, not even the internet. When airplanes upgraded their entertainment systems, adding small TVs behind every headrest with many channels to choose from, and Wi-Fi on every flight, she noticed a drop in her productivity. She was getting caught up watching movies and browsing the web instead of getting her work done like she used to. That's when she decided to create a new habit. Now, when the airplane reaches cruising altitude and the fasten seatbelt sign goes off, *ding*, instead of flipping through the channels on the small TV in front of her, the *ding* becomes a trigger to pull the laptop out of her carry-on bag and start working (work, and only work, so the action does not include grabbing her credit card and buying in-flight Wi-Fi).

When you find your trigger, perform the action immediately after. For example, if you are building the habit of brushing your teeth every morning, and putting your shoes on is the trigger, you may want to lace up your shoes in the bathroom, so you don't forget to stop at the sink and brush before you leave.

Use a checklist (triggers #2). Having a checklist for your routine is also a good idea. In his book, *The Checklist Manifesto*, Atul Gawande writes about how important checklists are even in routine tasks. From landing an airplane to performing a surgery to constructing a skyscraper, pilots, surgeons, and engineers follow a checklist—even if they have performed the same task ten-thousand times before. The reason being, even though the task may be simple, there are a lot of pieces to it, and if one thing goes wrong, we may forget a step. Likewise, when you start your routine, you may forget to pack your salad for lunch or grab your daily reflection notebook off your nightstand.

When I started my new morning routine, I created a checklist using note cards. I punched a hole in the corner of each notecard and put them in order on a keyring. Every morning when I woke up, I went through the cards and followed them in order all the way from getting dressed to leaving with everything I needed for the day. I also put a time limit at the bottom of the card to keep me from leaving too late. For example, at the bottom of Card #6, which is my Five-Minute Daily Journal Reflection card, I have the time 6:05 written on the last line. While I am doing my morning reflection, I am also steeping tea that I will bring with me when I leave the house (Card #7 pour morning tea in to-go bottle), and if I go longer than 6:05, the tea might steep too long and be bitter. Seeing the time at the bottom of the card is a reminder to keep me on task so I can move on to the next card on time. Eventually, pouring hot water into my French press to make tea (Card #5) became a trigger to write my journal reflection (Card #6), and ending my journal reflection became a trigger to pour my tea into my to-go bottle (Card #7). The notecard checklist were the training wheels that helped me develop the triggers I use every day.

Plan around your window of peak productivity. Each of us has a peak time of productivity. Some people work better in the morning, some are productive after lunch, and others work the best in the evening or at night. Most people find that they have about a four-hour window of productivity, when they can complete more during that time than any other time during the day. We are still productive outside of the window, but inside the window of productivity things run a little more smoothly. During this time, tackle the hardest part of your day. Outside of the window, this is where you can afford to take your time. When planning your routine, schedule the heavy lifting in your window of peak productivity and your second-tier priorities outside of the window. Likewise, if you find that there is a time of the day when your productivity dips below normal (if it takes you a while to get going in the morning, you like to take a nap after lunch, or get tired as soon as you come home from work), schedule the part of your routine that doesn't require a lot of brain power. Knowing when you are and are not most productive will allow you to conserve your energy so you can power through the hard stuff and take your time when you need to.

Your environment should support your new behavior. Your environment is one of the most important factors in having success in your new behavior change. You can put reminders all over your home, office, and technology to reinforce good routine building behaviors. For example, you can put a picture of your goal as the background on your phone or laptop, so every time you unlock the screen, your goal is staring back at you. If you are making a dietary change, you can put pictures or motivational quotes on your refrigerator or cupboards to reinforce smart snacking. If you are concerned about eating too much junk food, don't buy any at the grocery store and toss out any remaining you have in your kitchen. You can't give into your sweet tooth at 10:30PM if you don't have any sweets. If your goal is about reinforcing a career move, buy books about your goal and leave them around your home. If you are struggling to remember something and checklists aren't your thing, leave post-it notes in key areas (like the front door handle and the bathroom mirror) so you don't leave your home without something important. Your goal is to create an environment that supports your routines and rituals surrounding your career and personal goals.

Ease in, start with one routine. Don't try to do too much at once, because this will lead to burnout (remember, we only have so much willpower throughout the day). Focus on incorporating one or a few routines or rituals into your life at a time. Once those have become automatic, it is okay to move on to others.

Navy Admiral William Harry McRaven, ninth commander of U.S. Special Operations Command, spoke about the importance of routines in his 2014 commencement speech at The University of Texas at Austin. His advice to college graduates was to incorporate one morning routine: Make your bed every morning.

If you make your bed every morning you will have accomplished the first task of the day. It will give you a small sense of pride, and it will encourage you to do another task and another and another. By the end of the day, that one task completed will have turned into many tasks completed. Making your bed will also reinforce the fact that little things in life matter. If you can't do the little things right, you will never do the big things right.

Waking up is the trigger to make the bed. The action of making your bed becomes the trigger for the rest of the days tasks. Let this small habit be the start of your daily routine.

Be patient. One of my mentors told me a story about the gym he worked out at in New York City. Since the facility was on the top floor in an older building, it took a few minutes for the water in the showers to heat up. Even though it didn't look like anything was happening, the warm water was slowly making its way up from the basement to his floor. This is how routines and rituals work. You may not see immediate results, but a lot of things are working hard and defying gravity.

What to Do When the Unexpected Happens

What happens when something unexpected comes up and you can't stick to your daily routine? We are living in an Age of Agility, after all, where change is an expected part of our daily life.

When the unexpected does eventually happen, you should first determine the impact it is going to have on your routine. Is it going to be short-term, moderate-term, or permanent? Short-term changes are the daily hiccups that occur on a regular basis. For example, an unexpected project might pop up and need to be dealt with by the end of the day. Sometimes, a daily change can grow into something much larger. Let's say your daily change is staying home from the office due to illness. This is a short-term change, but what if your one-day flu bug turns into a week of bedrest? Now you need to respond to a moderate change. Finally, how would you respond if it turned into something more serious and you needed to change your whole way of life? This is a permanent change, and your approach is going to be very different than the first two.

The next step in determining your approach is to check your frame of reference. At first, change of any kind is a shock to our way of life—remember, our dark horse is resistant to change (Part 1, Change, page 39). Since change is hard, most of the time we avoid it, stress out about it, or write it off as bad. Instead, I recommend viewing change as an opportunity to grow. I've noticed in my own life (and in the lives of many others) that after time has passed, the event that prompted the change motivated me to respond in a way that improved my life, even if at the time it was incredibly difficult. Even "good" change like winning the lottery or getting a job that we've been working towards come with its own unique blessings and challenges. That's why having a positive frame of reference (one that says: I will get out of this, there is a solution, this is the world providing me with an opportunity) is so important.

Let's look at how you might respond to each length of disruption.

Short-term (< 1 week)
If the disruption is only a road bump, you'll deal with it because you probably deal with minor interruptions every day. Anything larger, like your vehicle breaking down on the way to work, getting busy with an unexpected request, or going on vacation, you will need to consider the impact it will have on your routine. It might be as simple as pushing something around in your schedule (can you go into work earlier and go to the gym after work?) or removing something from your schedule (working later instead of watching Netflix for two hours in the evening). A good rule is, for anything shorter than a week, pause your routine and focus on removing the roadblock as quickly and efficiently as possible. Once you have dealt with the issue, return to your routine. If the issue becomes a regular disruption, it's no longer a short-term problem, it's been upgraded to moderate-term.

Moderate-term (>1 week, < 6 months)

If a week-long road bump turns into a month-long pothole, it's going to get harder to power through the bumpy road and you'll need to navigate around the pothole. First, you need to determine what the impact will be on your routine and how much effort it is going to take to deal with the new temporary lifestyle. At this point, take a moment to think about how much you are willing to let this externally-controlled disruption influence your internally-controlled plan. Remember, there are things you can control and things you can't. For everything you can control, determine the level of mental impact you are willing to give the disruption. That will determine your path and approach to incorporating the change into your routine. Ask yourself, is there another action I can perform to get the same benefits? Or, can part of my routine temporarily be changed? For example, if you break your arm and can't lift weights for three months, you need to adjust your workout routine. You can still go to the gym, but you may need to seek other workout options. If you move to India for six months, it might be hard to stick to a low carb diet. What are you willing to give up and how much effort are you willing to spend on finding low-carb foods?

Permanent (> 6 months)

When potholes become road closures, you need to rethink your routine. For example, if you get put on your dream project, you may want to start working 60 or 80 hours per week on it, so it gets done right, instead of your usual 40 hours. The hours are longer, leaving you less time in the morning and you will come home at the end of the day with less willpower. This is when you need to go back to the drawing board and decide what routines and rituals you need in your life to support your goals, and then strategically place each routine or ritual in your day based on how much willpower you have left in reserve.

During a permanent life shift, there is going to be a lot of energy and new feelings. Sharing your next steps with mentors, friends, and your loved ones is important. Their support will help you through this, whether you were just given a MacArthur fellowship or recently diagnosed with cancer. Once you have your support people, make your first move. As harsh as it sounds, there is going to be a point when people stop listening if all you do is talk. Instead of relying on others to do some of the work for you, begin searching for it inside yourself. It's there. You may be going through the most difficult and/or exciting time in your life, and this is exactly when you need to be strong. If you perceive the change-event as bad, it's easy to become a victim, and once you see yourself as a victim, it's much harder to rise to the challenge. Always remember: you are in full control of how you respond to the world around you and will remain in control regardless of what you may encounter.

In the past, I faced some road closures that represented a permanent change in my life (and I'm sure there are more ahead of me). When I went to my mentors, they told me to be strong. It wasn't exactly what I wanted to hear them say, but it was what I needed. One of them told me:

> There are few people who want to hear how you were impacted and your plans derailed, so save it for a memoir and just get it done. I know this sounds cruel, but there are no guarantees and you are not a victim.

During a different permanent change, another mentor told me:

> The world is not going to sugarcoat anything. It is going to give it to you exactly as it is. Andy, the world gave you a very kind and loving mother. Be thankful you have her. When you need to hear something nice about how well you are doing, talk to her. The world is not your mother, so don't expect a 'good job' every time you do something right.

My mentors were tough on me because they were building my emotional resilience. I may have struggled at the time, but I grew into a stronger person because I was encouraged to deal with the change instead of running back to bed and hiding under the covers. With an attitude that embraces resilience, you too will be able to face the challenging permanent changes that come your way.

Whenever you encounter something that breaks you away from your normal routine, determine whether it is going to have a small, medium, or permanent impact. Then, adjust accordingly and move on without whining. If a small change lasts longer than a week, bump it up to a medium-impact disruption and start looking for ways to creatively alter your routine. Anything longer than a week is going to have a longer-term impact on what you do, so accept it, own it, and limit how big a deal it is.

Final Thoughts

In the Dock Model, every pillar (and the activities they are made of) can fit into a routine or ritual. The pillars are the raw material you hammer and chisel into a foundation that keep you strong when you are met with the challenges the world throws at you. The routines you create around these four pillars will maintain their structural integrity by creating planks that bridge the gap between the pillars. The stronger your routines, the more stable your Dock will become. With time and repetition, you will build an unbreakable structure that will be able to withstand any storm that might come your way. Your platform will be a safe and secure place for boats filled with great opportunities to tie onto, and you will be able to move about the waters, sharing ideas with other secure Docks, creating a harbor of innovation.

GOAL FOR TODAY: Think about one new habit you can incorporate into your daily routine. What trigger can you use? How does your new habit support your career path?

Part 3:
Reinforcement

By now, you have a growing foundation, big enough to support a goal or career path. You know how to manage your time. You have a schedule. You know about emotional intelligence, neuro-linguistic programming, and how to use motivation. Every day, you are building your skills and you have a framework to add structure to them. Whether your next step is going to college, dropping out of college, getting an advanced degree, entering an apprenticeship program, starting your own company, or making a career change, the following chapters will help you prepare for a career in the working world. These tools will build the additional reinforcement you need to thrive in the Age of Agility.

3.1 NAVIGATING THE WORKPLACE

At work, you may find yourself spending a lot of time doing something besides what's listed in your job description. This might be figuring out your company's internal politics: such as, who to talk to, about what, and when, in the unofficial chain of command. You may also reach out to others to help make sense of your role in the company or to understand how your position lends itself to your greater goal. Other times, you may have to pick up the broken pieces of a project you didn't start and try to put it back together with no instructions. This next section is all about the work you do that's not part of your job description. In the next four chapters, you will learn about mentoring and how mentors provide critical experience-based insight that will guide you on your career path. Next, you will learn about working with tough colleagues, and what to do when they get on your nerves. You will also learn how to motivate others, so they can make the changes they know they need to make. Finally, you will learn how to remain in control while working for a company with strong (cult)ure.

MENTORING: NO ONE IS 100% SELF-MADE

Colleagues are a wonderful thing – but mentors, that's where the real work gets done.
— JUNOT DIAZ

Mentoring is one of the oldest forms of teaching, dating all the way back to Greek mythology with Odysseus (remember Homer's Iliad and the Odyssey?) and his friend Mentor who helped raise his son, Telemachus. In the last few years, mentoring has been getting a lot of attention because of the phenomenon sometimes referred to as the "silver tsunami". It refers to a large percentage of the population who are getting older, retiring, and exiting the workforce. While this is great news for healthcare workers and Florida retirement community owners, it's frightening to many business owners. Most of the management positions today are held by baby boomers who are going to retire in the next few years. In the decades of watching their industry change, these baby boomer managers have gained unique insight and wisdom that have made them the respected workhorses they are today. After all, that's why they're still around. They learned how to be agile and respond with change instead of pushing against it.

Since many of these managers want to leave their respective

industries in good hands, they are reaching out to the next generation and teaching them the agile skills of success, so we too can thrive in the industry we love most. They need us, and we need them.

Experts—the ones doing all the cool things you want to be doing a few years from now—want to teach you. It is their way of handing off the baton. Working one-on-one with a master of their craft who has knowledge and experience in a skill you are building will give you quick and direct feedback, so you can learn the skill deeply. Working with a mentor is deliberate practice in action, and if you're willing to listen, you will streamline your success. What might have taken you years of trial and error can be achieved in a matter of months with a good mentor.

Before we put the cart in front of the horse, let's get clear on one thing. Your mentor is not going to fight your battles for you. They will make suggestions about the best paths to take and the appropriate armor to wear, but that's where it ends. If you go off course and make a mistake, they will be there with advice for getting back up and on the path. The character Yoda in the Star Wars series did not fight any battles for Luke, he helped Luke become the best he could be by providing skilled training and direction. That's exactly what your mentor will do for you.

Benefits of Mentorship

You can think of a mentor as being a database of specialized knowledge. They are people who are encouraging and offer guidance. Not only are they people you can count on to be on your side, cheering you on, they can help you develop your skills in a specific area and give you a glimpse of the world you are working to become a part of.

When you work with a mentor, you get a chance to talk about yourself, your goals, and your future. Once you have your plan on the table, a mentor will offer advice about potential pitfalls to look out for, so you don't make the same mistakes they made. More importantly, a good mentor will be there when you do make a mistake. They will have the experience and knowledge to help guide you out of a crisis. In addition to knowledge, mentors are also a database of connections. When you are ready, they will open doors for you in their network.

How to Find a Mentor

You can't choose your parents, but you can choose your mentor—or so the saying goes. When you start looking for a mentor, make a list of the qualities you are looking for. Are you looking for someone to push you harder than you would normally push yourself? Or are you looking for someone who can take a step back with you and look at the whole picture? Also, keep in mind that a mentor/mentee relationship is not a one-way street; it is an explicit relationship that must be voiced and agreed on up front. It should be right for both people. When a mentor decides to take you under their wing, establish the boundaries of the relationship. Talk about where you see the mentoring going and what specific areas you want to work on. This can change as you become more comfortable in your mentor/mentee relationship, but having some solid ground rules to grow around will avoid awkward conversations in the future and provide the best experience for both of you.

When you're ready, here are some places to start looking for a mentor:

Your extended network. This may be someone you respect or look up to in your friend-and-family network. Talk to this network about your goals. If someone in this network cannot provide you with the mentor relationship you need, a friend or family member may know someone in their own network they can introduce you to.

Current or former school. Ask a professor, former high school teacher, or coach you have a strong connection with. If you are not currently one of their students or players, send them an email. I have had great conversations with these educators well after being in one of their classes or teams.

Where you work. This may be someone in your office who is in a position you would like to have one day. Your company may have a mentorship program already in place. If so, I encourage you to look into the program and meet a few of the mentors one-on-one for lunch to see if one clicks.

Conferences, meet-ups, and relevant events. Take a risk. Start a conversation with someone who makes an impression on you. If you feel a connection with someone, ask them about mentoring and invite them out for coffee.

A word of advice: When you ask for someone's time, be respectful. Mentorship is not a business transaction; it's an open space to share knowledge and offer guidance. They are not a paid career coach; most of the time a mentor is giving back to the younger crowd, pro bono, because they want to invest in the next generation. They love what they do, and they are excited to share what they know with people who are just as eager.

You Can Have More Than One

Luke not only had Yoda, but also had Obi-Wan "Ben" Kenobi. In the movie, *The Empire Strikes Back*, Luke crash-lands on the swamp planet Dagobah and seeks out the wise mentor Yoda to build a specific skillset. Yoda was a great mentor, but Luke's relationship with him was brief. On the other hand, Ben was a long-term mentor and continued giving Luke guidance after his death.

When you are searching for a mentor, you should have an idea of what kind you are looking for and know that one mentor doesn't have to do it all for you. There are people you may want to talk to a few times in preparation for a test, a new position, or before starting school. There are others who you meet up with on an informal basis. This is typically done with a former manager, co-worker, or teacher. Every few months, you catch each other up on what you've been up to, and you're able to ask their opinion about something you've run up against. These people also are always accepting of an out-of-the-blue email about advice, networking, or for emails/letters of recommendation. There are also people you want to grow with. Usually, you have something specific you are trying to work on. This is someone who holds a position you hope to grow into one day or is an expert you look up to.

Hints and Pitfalls

- **Your mentor is a sounding board.** Your mentor should give you advice and help you talk about your goals, setbacks, and work ethic, but they should never tell you what to do. The end decision should always be left up to you. If you make a mistake, it is a good opportunity for your mentor to step in and help you reflect on a recent decision.

- **Age difference benefits both the mentor and mentee.** Gina Amaro Rudan calls millennial mentees "fat brains" in her book, *Practical Genius*. She writes,

    ... every practical genius needs some percentage of their tribe to be at least half their age. ... A Millennial's digital fluency, gamer's problem-solving skills, and scrappy creative resourcefulness can change your DNA, making you nimble, adaptive, and more comprehensively exposed to the broadest spectrum of cultural influences.

    On the flipside, as a mentee, working with someone who is a master of their craft with decades of experienced-based knowledge will accelerate your learning. Let's face it, there's only so much books, blogs, and videos can teach you.

- **Clearly communicate your goals to your mentor.** Make sure your mentor knows what skills you want to grow. If you get derailed, remind your mentor of your goals and have a conversation about how you feel they can help you best.

- **Be mindful that your mentor isn't reliving their glory days.** This rarely happens, but it's worth noting just-in-case. If your mentor is spending more time reminiscing and using you to accomplish failed goals of their youth, you may need to start looking for someone else.

- **Be prepared to work.** A mentor will not want to invest time in you if you don't invest the time in yourself. This may mean reading books suggested to you, reading a few new blogs per week, or doing some deep introspection and writing about what motivates you.

- **Be open to a new approach.** Just because something is new doesn't mean it won't work. Some of your mentor's ideas may sound foreign to you at first. Just like in the movie, *The Karate Kid*, a mentor's value is only recognized months (or years) later. Wax on, wax off!

Take note of what works for you and share these ideas with your mentor. Eventually, you too will become a mentor. Both roles are crucial and having a chance to wear both hats will give you valuable insight into how you and others learn. As a rule, I try to always have one mentor and one mentee. This way, I can play both sides of the relationships, having a chance to grow in my career and help someone grow in theirs.

Key Takeaways

o Find one or more mentors, and once you have some experience, become a mentor.

o Agree and commit to an explicit mentoring relationship.

o Expect feedback and suggestions, not someone that will tell you what to do.

o Be open to doing things differently and committing to work.

GOAL FOR TODAY: Make a list of potential mentors to reach out to. Prepare a list of questions you would like to ask them during your first meeting. This will guide the conversation. See if they are a good fit, and show them you are serious about your career goals.

WORKING WITH TOUGH COLLEAGUES

I will not let anyone walk through my mind with their dirty feet.
— MAHATMA GANDHI

When I was seventeen, I started working at a large grocery store chain in West Michigan. Previously, I had mowed lawns for neighbors, shoveled snow, and worked for a family-friend's company doing manual labor on construction sites. This was my first time working a job with co-workers who were not friends or temp workers. Shortly after being hired, I realized that it takes all kinds of people to get a job done, and some of them are harder to work with than others.

Every other day, I would walk into the break room and find one of my managers sitting at a table with a nail clipper. This was the same room where everyone had a locker, where we ate, and sat around texting on our T9 keyboard phones. Instead of jamming buttons on a phone, he would read the newspaper and clip his nails one by one and leave the stray clippings on the table. After a couple months of dodging stray nails, I spoke up.

"You going to clean that up?" I asked one afternoon, taking a sip of my drink through a straw (as a precaution, I had started using plastic lids on my fountain drinks during break).

"Why should I?" he said, sweeping the clippings with a slack hand into a pile, half of them overshooting his mark and landing on his lap. "That's why we have a janitor. I don't have time to clean up. If they expect me to clean up, then I expect a longer break."

Since nail-clipper-guy, I have encountered my fair share of coffee slurpers, open-mouthed chewers, arm-on-your-shoulder "buddies", natural deodorant users, never serious jokesters, strung out Adderall junkies, as well as the nitpicky, mean, arrogant, negative, rude, gossipy, conniving, and otherwise toxic people that are a naturally occurring part of associating with humanity. From all these experiences over the last decade, I have learned to accept two things. The *first* is that you are not going to love everyone you work with—and that's okay. The *second* is that you don't need to be friends with every one of your co-workers—or even like the person—in order to work well together and get a job done.

What you do need to do is treat people like human beings. Shaming or making the person feel bad often creates more problems than it solves. When someone doesn't feel validated, or if they feel like the butt of a joke, they are going to feel threatened. That's why you should never bully (even jokingly) to get your point across. When someone is operating from a point of defense, they are more likely to lash out and halt progress, making your life more frustrating. When in doubt, keep it professional. You are in control of how you respond to a situation. If your working environment becomes unsafe or if someone is keeping you from getting your work done, you should always address the issue with the person first, and then a manager. Depending on severity, you may want to go directly HR.

Since you have to work with this person, and you will probably never escape at least one person who gets on your nerves, here are some guidelines for working with tough colleagues.

- **Never bond over negativity.** Don't use gossip as a way to bond with your co-workers. This will only encourage negativity. The break room at any retail store, the kitchen at any restaurant, and the kitchenette in any corporate building have the potential to be a hive of positivity or negativity.

- **Nip it in the bud.** Although direct confrontation can be intimidating, it is your quickest and most efficient solution for solving a conflict. Go directly to the person you are having the conflict with, and calmly but firmly tell them what the problem is and pitch potential solutions. If you don't want to call them out directly, you can talk about how your team's cohesion is important and solving this conflict would contribute to a better working environment and/or higher productivity.

- **Watch your words.** Never say anything behind someone's back that you would not say to the person directly. How someone talks about another when they are not there is how they talk about you when you are away. Picking up on patterns like this will go a long way in reading people and judging what you should and should not say in their company.

- **Do not respond to negativity with negativity.** When someone gives you hostile feedback, it says more about the person giving the feedback than it does about your performance. Criticism is one thing—storming around and making ad hominem attacks is another. If you can, ignore how they are giving you feedback and look at the actual claims. If their inappropriate behavior continues, you need to confront them and go to HR. Part of changing culture in the workplace is standing up for what you know is right.

- **You win more battles if you choose your battles.** Your co-worker who slurps their coffee probably has no idea they are annoying you. They have probably been a slurper their entire liquid-drinking career, and chances are you are going to offend them if you bring it up. Me calling the nail clipping manager out in the beginning of this chapter probably wasn't worth it in the end. Decide if something is reasonable or unreasonable to call to someone's attention by thinking about how your relationship may change after the thing is said. When giving someone feedback, it's always best to critique the behavior (like a technique or strategy), never their character.

- **Don't burn any bridges.** Whenever I get frustrated, I think about this Thomas Jefferson quote (I also referenced this in the chapter on Emotional Intelligence, page 126): "When angry, count to ten before you speak. If very angry, count to one hundred." If you catch me on an off day and I'm slow in responding, look closely and you'll see me counting, calming myself down so I don't say something I will regret later.

Key Takeaways

o   People have habits that will annoy you, and you have habits that will annoy others.

o   Choose your battles based on their impact to your work environment and job performance.

o   If you give feedback, focus on behaviors, never the person's character. Critique the technique, not their personality.

o   Never respond when angry. First calm down, then respond.

o   Try to resolve an issue with the individual first before going to a manager. If it is a serious issue, like bullying, discrimination, harassment or sexual harassment, contact HR immediately and go to a place where you feel safe.

GOAL FOR TODAY: Working with tough colleagues requires a high level of emotional resilience (if you need a refresher, flip back to page 52). Knowing that the two are related, think about a time you used emotional resilience with a tough colleague. What went well? What didn't?

MOTIVATIONAL INTERVIEWING

When we are no longer able to change a situation—we are challenged to change ourselves.
— VIKTOR E. FRANKL

Have you ever worked with someone who is so stuck in their ways, they have become a boat anchor, slowing down everything they touch? Or, have you ever watched someone going down the wrong path, ignoring advice and support from others? How about, the I AM NEVER WRONG co-worker, who will tell you that everything is fine as you watch them sink further and further into quicksand with every step they take?

In the past, when I noticed a friend or co-worker was doing something that was holding them back, the first thing I tried to do was give them advice, and this only made it worse. I would take out my toolbox and show them how I would deal with the issue they were struggling with. I gave logical arguments and talked until I was blue in the face. Most of the time, I walked away exhausted, all my good intentions falling on deaf ears. Occasionally, it completely backfired. What I did next was ignore my impulse to reach out to others. I stood by and watched as people sunk or swam. That's when I realized that change wasn't something I could force on people, they had to do it for themselves and only when they were ready. I realized that when I tried to give advice, it wasn't that my peers didn't understand my message, it's that they didn't have any motivation *to* change. The change I was suggesting felt like more work than the baggage they were already dealing with. My new approach isn't to force change and it isn't to stand by and watch, it is to ask questions.

While I was a student at Grand Valley State University, I had the opportunity to start and manage an alternative zine that was fully funded by the university. We were an outlet for some really creative ideas and a home for artists and writers that lead the way for counter-culture thinking on a relatively conservative campus. As we came together to work on a project, it was a great experience watching my peers practice what they were going to school for: photography, graphic design, journalism, creative writing, and marketing.

One of the biggest challenges I ran into was having to talk with writers about the difference between being angry about a current event and being clever. It's easy to write an article condemning others, but it takes real craft and skill to write a piece that doesn't offend your readers and instead invites them to think differently about a popular topic or current event. Back then, I needed a way to help my friends see the value in writing good-humored articles instead of reactive twenty-year-old punk-infused ramblings. I was at a loss. As much as I tried to point out that a well-written article would be more effective and reach a wider audience, I was often met with firm resistance. *If people don't understand or get offended, it's their fault. They're not smart enough.* Or: *If I change something, I won't be doing the topic justice.*

I first heard about Motivational Interviewing from a friend who uses the practice in the medical field, where it was first coined and is still used today. In a clinical care setting, medical personnel will talk with a patient about a life change they need to make, for example, reducing or ceasing substance use, healthy eating, taking medication regularly, or starting a new routine after a medical procedure. Instead of telling the patient they need to stop smoking and become more active, they will ask targeted questions that will help the patient discover the need to change within themselves and the motivation to follow through. Motivational Interviewing spans a larger audience than just the healthcare field and can be applied to the workplace and in our own interpersonal relationships.

Most people don't want to be told what to do, they want to make their own choices and feel like they are in control. All you can do is influence someone's willingness to make a change on their own. Most people know they need to make a change, but are not willing to take ownership of it, because it may be a very big change and possibly part of their identity. You can inspire action by asking questions so they can reframe the issue—this gives the person agency to achieve the change on their own. Best of all, they will know that you support the change, and even though they'll be doing all the work, you will be there supporting them as an ally by withholding judgment.

How It Works

Motivational Interviewing helps refine an idea or problem by strategically asking the person to clarify it. When they do this, they also define the steps, bring light to possible obstacles, and as a result the change feels more obtainable. Here is the approach I followed with a few of the writers who wrote at the zine with me at GVSU. The same steps can be applied to your own situation:

1. **Make it casual:** Ask your friend or coworker to meet one-on-one in an open and familiar environment. When I thought it was necessary to speak with one of the zine writers, I would meet them on campus in the dining hall, a coffee shop, or at a happy hour nearby.

2. **Don't follow a set agenda:** When you start your conversation, don't begin with the issue right away. You should have an end-point you want to reach but it shouldn't be forced. With the zine writers, I thought: Ok, eventually I need to steer the conversation to the piece they just submitted to me, but I'll let them take me there and when they do, I'll start asking my questions.

3. **Ask questions:** Start the conversation by asking open-ended questions or by asking your co-worker to reflect on the area you want to see changed. How do you feel your piece was received in the last issue? How do you think things are going? I know both of us want this to be the best program it can be. Do you think there are any areas we need to focus on? Most of the time, there is a lot blowing off steam and both us agree to problem areas. While you are listening, it is important to express empathy and build rapport with the person you are speaking to. The speaker needs to know that you are not attacking them, only trying to

come together to work on a problem. In my example, after the writer responded to my questions, I followed with this: *Based on what people have been saying, I don't know if we are reaching as many people as we can. Did your last piece achieve what you set out to do?*

And if I was talking to a stubborn writer: *It sounds like some people didn't understand your piece, which is a bummer because it has some really powerful ideas in it. Why do you think people are not understanding it?*

Or: *Since not all people are as well-read as you are, they need help understanding the idea. I don't think you should dumb down your piece, I only want to talk about why you think others are not understanding it.*

4. **Look for inconsistencies:** Identify discrepancies between what you hear the person say their goals are and their behaviors. If your co-worker/friend/mentee's goals do not match their behavior, repeat the discrepancy back to them <u>in their own words as they told you</u>. When I spoke with the zine writers, I did so in a way as to not start an argument. Any resistance came from their own personal discrepancy between goals and actions.

   You said that you want to change how people think about [issue] on campus. You also said that people don't understand your article? Is there a way you can write an article a lot of people can understand that also changes how people think about [issue]?

5. **Roll with resistance:** You shouldn't argue or be pushy; instead, be curious and accepting. Resistance is part of the change process and it's better to downplay the issue than push it. With the writers, I made sure to validate their skills and build their confidence based on past projects. I also matched their present excitement and did so with a positive attitude. The bottom line is: Change is hard, however small it may be. It is important to be supportive of any willingness to try a new approach.

Motivational Interviewing is the process of affecting change that allows the individual you're attempting to influence feel agency and ownership over their evolving ideas. Rather than telling, you are leading people to change instead of forcing it on them.

Tips

- Motivational Interviewing is best done one-on-one.

- Don't be judgmental.

- Don't argue.

- Ask open-ended questions rather than "yes" or "no" questions.

- Use reflective listening by repeating in your own words what the person said to make sure you understand what they mean.

- Be honest and genuine rather than trying to push forward your own personal agenda.

As much as you want someone to change, you can't do it for them. Change only happens when someone discovers the drive to do it on their own. Motivational Interviewing enables someone to discover the drive they need to make a change. In doing so, it validates their decision to change by letting them know there is someone who supports them.

Key Takeaways

o   To make Motivational Interviewing work, stay calm and casual, ask, and don't tell.

o   See and point to the positive, and use introspection to focus on how to best land the message.

o   Do not ask closed-ended questions or use a question to trap someone in a corner.

GOAL FOR TODAY: Think about a situation where you could have used Motivational Interviewing. What was the change you were trying to encourage? What open-ended questions would you have asked? How do you think asking these questions would have changed the outcome?

ECHO CHAMBERS &
COMPANY CULT-URE

If you live your whole entire life according to the Walmart culture and three basic beliefs, life becomes a lot easier.
— LOIS GIVENS, Walmart Personnel Manager at Store Number 992

Rule 1: The Best Startups Work a Lot Like Cults.
— PETER THIEL

If you are educated or have above average intelligence, you are statistically more likely to join a cult. Wait! Before you stand open-mouthed in front of your microwave cranked on high in an attempt to dim down your too-smart brain from tricking you into joining a cult, let me explain.

The word cult (from the Latin *cultus*, meaning 'care') is the root word in culture and describes the communities we live in, both small and large. Although the first is associated with small new-thought movements and the other describes larger communities, both cult and culture influence how people talk about their view of reality. The question is, when does a company's culture turn into a company cult, and how does this change their version of reality?

A key indicator of a company culture becoming cult-like is the promotion of a false reality: what they think is true about the world becomes narrow-sighted. The company cult-ure may have started out as good ideas and with the best of intentions, but somehow it ran wild and into a downward spiral of falsehood. Employees (especially long-term employees) become complacent and lose sight of the full picture. Instead of bouncing ideas off the market, they keep it internal, creating an infinite feedback loop. A company cult will believe that only their ideas influence the marketplace. They put blinders on and believe that nothing the company does is wrong, because only they know the truth.

As a larger business community (full of many companies with unique cultures), we are aware that cult-companies exist. It's prevalent enough to joke about, and we are now entering a time when we are ready to confront it. Language from cults has now entered our business community lexicon. If you listen to people you work with, or, if you are a consultant, listen to how each organization you work with talks about their organization:

(overheard at a large tech organization in Seattle)
You're a new hire? You drink the Kool-Aid yet? You will. You'll come over to the dark side.

(overheard at a bar in Seattle)
What a waste! You bought the watch?! Or did you get it when you paid your [company name] membership dues?

It's not only big corporate culture that is at risk for creating a cult-ure. The business ecosystem is changing. Startups are becoming wildly successful in what seems like overnight while established corporations head towards bankruptcy. Instead of moving from a small or medium sized company to a big corporation, the current trend in some industries is moving away from big business to small startups. In 2014, 47% of Millennial workers were employed by companies with less than 100 employees. In Peter Thiel's book, *Zero to One*, he argues that the best startups work a lot like cults—and this kind of thinking is a slippery slope. As a free-agent, self-branded, worker in the Age of Agility, you need to be able to identify cult-thinking, so you know when a company is benefiting from it and when they are at risk.

"Cult-Thinking" Causes an Echo-Chamber Effect

How do good ideas get out of control? The Echo-Chamber Effect is a fairly new term that is slowly gaining traction in fields like mass media, journalism, and sociology. In an article published in *Wired*, Alan Martin explains the phenomenon:

> If you surround yourself with voices that echo similar opinions to those you're feeling out, they will be reinforced in your mind as mainstream, to the point that it can distort your perception of what is the general consensus.

Before applying the concept to business and company culture, I want to give a few real-life examples to clarify what an echo-chamber is.

Social media: Your social media is tailored to your interests. If you have a belief about the world, say, all cats should be able to wear pajamas if they so choose, the algorithm used by social media sites will pick up on this and tailor your newsfeed accordingly. Every time there is a story about cats wearing or not wearing pajamas, it will come up on your newsfeed. Not many people care if cats should wear pajamas or not, so if you are seeing news stories about it daily, it distorts what you think is mainstream.

News organizations: Some news organizations frame stories to gain a specific audience. Let's say you really like Cats United Together Enterprises (CUTE). CUTE is known for covering what you believe is the truth, which is, that all cats should be able to wear pajamas. If you only get your news from CUTE, you will only hear one side of the story. You don't hear about the cat-snob problem associated with cats wearing pajamas or how cats who wear pajamas become finicky eaters and demand tuna for dinner every night. Since you are only going to CUTE for your news, everything you believe is being echoed back as reality.

Comments/discussion boards: After reading some news or viewing a video on CUTE, you scroll down to the bottom of the page where you can leave comments and have a discussion. Let's say that you just read an article about a cat who wasn't allowed to wear pajamas. In the comments below, other CUTE readers will echo back all your same beliefs. (No one mentioned that when the cat in question had previously worn pajamas, it locked itself in a cupboard for three days demanding king crab for supper).

Let's apply this to business: As you walk around the office this week, you bump into a few different people who all give you a slightly different version of the same story: customers are buying anything that is in the color red. In your next meeting, someone asks about color options and you immediately say: red. Another person in the meeting says that a recent market survey shows that blue is favored over red (2:1). You respond by saying that everyone you know has been saying that red is the best color for new products. Everyone else agrees because they, too, have heard the office rumors.

Alex "Sandy" Pentland writes about this in an article published in the Harvard Business Review:

> ...[W]hen engagement is high and intensely concentrated within a group, the same ideas often circle around to you again and again. But because ideas usually change slightly as they go from person to person, you may not recognize them as mere repetitions of ideas. You may think that everyone has independently arrived at a similar strategy, which might make you more sure of those ideas than you should be.

If there are too many people in the room echoing back what the company wants to hear, the products and services will be limited to a narrow, like-minded audience.

Do Cult-Companies Have Their Benefits?

You can have a productive career working at cult-company so long as you have the right checks and balances. Make sure you are bouncing your ideas off of colleagues, mentors, friends, and family members. Very bright people often spend a lot of time in their head, spinning ideas around and around. This is the type of person who, by accident, convinces themselves of something against their best judgment by merely thinking about it for too long. The people in your social circle can see things you can't, just as you see things about them they can't see. Listen to their feedback. Together, you will keep your sanity, dignity, and freedom from cult doom.

Short-term effects of cult-thinking can be good because it allows a company, team, or individual to focus on a project and stay on task. Long-term effects can be catastrophic. Employees detach themselves from the marketplace, they lose their sense of reality, and begin to follow one they have invented.

How to Avoid Cult-Thinking

- **Beware of echo chambers.** Have a diverse group of people who are giving you feedback. Sometimes, the best way to get feedback is to bounce an idea off of someone who is part of a different team, company, or industry. Getting the perspective of someone who is not in your field may be the sobering eyes you need to bring your idea from abstract to concrete.

- **Be open to criticism.** If you hear yourself saying, "Nobody understands my idea; it's brilliant; they just can't see it because they're not as smart as me!" then take a step back from yourself. Ask friends, coworkers, or your mentor exactly where they are getting tripped up by your idea. Open yourself (and the idea) up to others instead of closing yourself off.

- **Beware of single leadership.** Never rely on a single leader or idea to guide the way. A successful organization and a good team doesn't let one idea dominate their time or define them. Likewise, a good employee should wear many hats and have more than one project they are working on, so they don't get caught up in a single idea.

- **Beware of confirmation bias.** A confirmation bias is when someone interprets new evidence in a way that confirms their existing beliefs or theories. This means that you can prove just about anything with a confirmation bias. Just because something happened once does not mean it is industry standard. Feel out the industry, keep tabs on your competition, and share your observations.

- **Beware of easy cheese.** If something sounds too good to be true, investigate. There are simple answers to hard problems, but they may not be easy to implement. You should always question everything, especially when the solution promises everything from world peace to clearing up the weird fungus you don't tell anyone is growing between your toes. Watch out, there's always free cheese in a mousetrap.

- **Beware of perfection.** Don't trust anyone who says their company is the best. Trust the company who is always working to become the best. As soon as a company declares they are the best, they have lost sight of their competition.

If the road to hell is paved with best intentions, the road to cults is paved with creative ideas thought up by brilliant people. There are benefits to cult-like thinking, but to reap those benefits, you need to have checks and balances. When you are standing at the bottom of a well, knee-deep in work, don't confuse the echo of your voice with the voice of reason.

Key Takeaways

o   No matter how smart you are, you can get caught up in the false reality of cult thinking.

o   Cult thinking can help bring a group of like-minded people together, however, there should be checks and balances in place to stay grounded.

o   Short bursts of cult thinking can be positive, but long-term cult thinking can be catastrophic.

o   To avoid cult thinking, surround yourself with a diverse group of people who offer you feedback, and always be open to criticism.

GOAL FOR TODAY: Any company has the potential of turning into a cult no matter how big or small. Ask yourself: who are some good people to have around you to check in with, so your work doesn't become an echo-chamber? Having a community of people outside of your company will diversify your influences, making you and your team more well-rounded.

3.2 SCHOOL NEVER TAUGHT YOU THIS

While writing this book, I frequently visited my mother-in-law at my wife's childhood home in what I call—but the rest of the family isn't too fond of—out-in-the-sticks Minnesota. In the kitchen, sitting at the island counter in a bar style chair with my head in my hands, I would tell her about the struggles and pleasures of writing this book. She would listen and nod in all the right places, something she does well, having raised four children, all the while preparing the evening meal or an afterschool snack for her grandchildren. Our conversations often drifted to the heart of my career goal, the subtle messages this book only hints at: education and the complete reworking of our schools from kindergarten to college.

One memorable story my mother-in-law told me was this past October, as the last of her garden was being picked before the first autumn freeze. At the cutting board, fresh carrots were piled high off to the side. She started telling me about the influential teachers she had and why some information stuck and why most of it didn't. Pausing to think, the knife reflecting in the overhead light, winking at me (was that a power move or just my imagination), she told me that the most useful thing she learned in high school was when a teacher went off script for a couple days and taught all his classes how to do their taxes. That was something, she said, that immediately became useful after graduation.

Schools, the places that are supposed to train us for life as an adult, do a good job at teaching us how to sit and take tests, but rarely do they teach us any practical life skills. My mother-in-law and I could talk your ear off with our ideas for education reform. Since this isn't one of those kinds of books, I'll spare you (for now) from our long monologues and the totally awesome research we've come across. What I do want to include are a few more skills I think are incredibly important for being successful and productive that are not traditionally taught in schools, even in college, unless you have an outstanding professor (I was lucky to have a few at the University of Washington).

There are many important skills our schools need to be teaching including some I have already covered in this book. This section will cover the skills I think are necessary for reinforcing the foundation and structure. Here is what will be covered in the next few chapters:

- o Interviewing

- o Writing a weekly blog

- o Creating a productive workspace

- o Combatting overthinking

- o Learning a lot quickly

- o Managing your money

To learn more skills schools didn't teach you, like personal finance, communication in business and personal relationships, finding a romantic partner, reasoning, self-awareness, finding a job you love, and being calm under pressure, just to name a few, I recommend starting with Alain de Botton's School of Life. Here are some links:

theschooloflife.com/london/

thebookoflife.org

Alain de Botton has written several books, and I have listed my recommendations on the Suggested Reading & Listening page. His books include topics such as: relationships, art, travel, social status, happiness, work, religion, and the news.

INTERVIEWING AS A SKILL

There was a point when the idea of the job for life disintegrated. Now no one has any expectation of lifetime employment.

— DOUGLAS COUPLAND

This is probably a refresher, but I want to include interviewing in this section of the book because rarely do we think of interviewing as a skill. Since it is likely that you will change companies every few years, finding a position that aligns with your skillset and meets your goals is incredibly important. Not only do you have to know what you want in a company, but you have to sell it. In Seattle's fast-moving tech industry, people are always interviewing. Most people I hung around with were interviewing at least once every three months, even if they were not actively looking for a new job. There are two reasons for this. First, interviewing is a skill that needs to be kept finely polished. If you want to move with the industry, you will likely have to change positions at the company you are already working at, change companies to follow the technology, or change industries because the technology has changed. All require interviews. Second, interviewing is a great way to grow your network. As business continues to grow and change with technology, every industry will have to respond with changes of their own. Having a large and diverse network will keep you plugged into how each industry is adapting to change.

As you read, think about how you are going to grow your personal brand though the interview process. You may switch uniforms over the years, but your brand is who the company is buying. Employees in the Age of Agility think of themselves as professional athletes do, signing contracts with teams (companies) and based on their performance, staying with the team, getting let go, or choosing to sign with a different team. The difference is, we are all free agents and most of us can choose to work at another company when the opportunity arises. Freelancers who run from gig to gig are not the only free agents any more. We all are.

This chapter provides the fundamental skills you need in order to prepare for an interview, be confident in a phone interview, and know what to expect from an in-person interview.

Before your Interview
1. Research the Company
Skim the company's SEC 10-K Statement. This is a report required by the Securities and Exchange Commission for publicly traded companies in the U.S. The SEC 10-K Statement is the company's annual report to their stockholders. If they are a publicly traded company, they are required to provide this information. You can find this information on the investor page of their website. While skimming, pay attention to their Business Overview and Industry section. If anything catches your eye, bring it up during the interview, when they ask if you have any questions. If the company you are interviewing for is private or a startup, read their mission statement, skim through their blog posts, and look at their social media pages.

When you join a company, you enter a culture of people who share a goal. Research how the company culture fits into the industry at large. Ask yourself, does this company have a culture you want to be part of or will you be bringing in a new type of culture? If you come from a different culture are you willing to adjust, or do you expect their culture to change? Also: does this company's mission align with your career path? Finally, ask yourself: is change and innovation at the heart of the company or do they only talk about it because it's trendy? Look up recent articles about the company, research the CEO, visit employee forums like Glassdoor, and ask questions about the company on Quora.

2. Research Who You Will Be Interviewing With

Usually, this is a hiring manager and someone on the team you are interviewing for. Find their LinkedIn profile and read up on them. If they blog, read the last two or three blogs they posted so you can discover what's on their mind. Additionally, try to find any publications or videos of them speaking at a conference. Familiarizing yourself with the person you are talking to is the best way to calm your nerves. Instead of going in blind, you will have a good picture of the person you are speaking with.

3. Craft a Narrative

Use your skills and experiences to craft a narrative that lines up with the position you're applying for. Your narrative should include how you intend to add value to your employer, your personal goals, and how you are responding to industry change.

4. Simple is Better

When it comes to a resume, personal statement, emails, or anything else in written form, you should focus on giving the right answer without giving a long answer. If Twitter has taught us one good thing, it is how to be precise. Think: How can I say the most with the fewest words?

During the Interview

The reason why you do so much work before the interview is so you can be prepared for any question the interviewer asks. It's almost certain that you will be asked an open-ended question like, *tell me about a time when…* or the dreaded *so (pause) tell me about yourself.* When this happens, you will have something prepared to say ahead of time, and this will give you some control to direct the interview. For example, you could talk about a recent project you worked on, and in talking about the project you can highlight the strengths you think would be good for the position you are interviewing for.

Avoid peacocking and groundhogging. Peacocking describes someone who is intentionally trying to stand out by making themselves look more impressive than they really are. These are people who sell themselves with achievements and disguise a strength as a weakness. When you're peacocking, your light horse (page 40) is usually leading the way with arrogance and overconfidence. Someone who is peacocking will say (with words or an action): I am overqualified to work here. You should be thanking me for walking through your door.

Groundhogging, on the other hand, describes someone who is shy, insecure, and self-conscious. They are waiting for opportunity to knock on the door, and they will only open the door when an opportunity that meets all their special criteria knocks, which will probably never happen. When you're groundhogging, your dark horse is leading the way with negative thoughts about how hard it is to look for a job and be an adult. Someone who is groundhogging might say (with words or actions): I just want this to be easy. If you want to know about me, read my resume or call my references. I will only take the position if it's an easy transition from what I'm already doing.

To avoid peacocking or groundhogging, keep these four traits in mind:

1. Always be honest. Being honest is a sure way for your confidence to shine through without looking like you are trying too hard.

2. While answering an interview question, don't rely on looking for ways to tie-in your resume or awards—the people interviewing you have your resume, cover letter, and a list of references. Since your time together is limited, you should talk about what isn't on there. Talk about a challenge someone in the position you are applying for might face on a regular basis and how you would go about confronting that issue. Show who you are; don't tell them.

3. Be the employee you would want to work with. This is a good way to feel out the company culture and see if your values and the company's values align.

4. Don't try to stand out—stand up for who you are. Make sure you are who you are selling.

Phone Interviews

Phone interviews, also known as phone screens, are usually the first round of interviews. They are going to be your toughest interviews because they are intended to weed out the people who look good on paper but who cannot carry a conversation. One of the hard parts is overcoming the phone/person barrier: you are talking to someone you don't know and can't see while you sit or pace in a room answering questions about your skillset and work history. I do three things before every phone interview:

1. I get in control of my breathing.

A few minutes before the phone call, I become aware of my breath and practice mindfulness. Taking control of your breathing will regulate your heart rate and reduce anxiety (Breathe in Pillar 1, page 192). I don't always close my eyes, but you can if it helps you focus. Take full, deep breaths and count one on the inhale, two on the exhale, three on the inhale, four on the exhale, and start again at one. Mindfulness is becoming aware of yourself and your environment. This allows me to become comfortable in my own skin and aware of what is around me. Even two minutes of breathing clears my mind and centers me in my body. I am at my best and ready to talk about myself, my career path, and the position I am applying for.

2. I make notes to reference during the interview.

Before the interview, I write out notes I want to use during the interview. Usually, I never look at the document I have prepared, but the act of writing down notes helps me commit my main talking points to memory. I also make a list of questions I want to ask the interviewer about the position and company.

3. I find an image of who I'm talking to.

Talking to someone you don't know is difficult. On the phone, not being able to read their body language, or even seeing who you are talking to can make for awkward pauses and can be all around disorienting. What works for me is finding a picture of the person I am interviewing with. I can usually find a picture on LinkedIn, and having this open in a tab on my computer gives me a visual of the person I am talking to.

The purpose of this interview is for the company to get to know you better and see if you have the basic characteristics of a candidate they are looking to hire. The interviewer will ask you why you're interested in the position and why you're leaving your current job. They want to know where you're looking to grow in your career and to address any red flags in your work history. The second half of the interview is about the company and the interviewer will be looking to see if you have done your research. Knowing who the key players are in the company, recent news, and accomplishments will tell the interviewer that you are truly interested in the position. The final part of the interview is, "Do you have any questions?" The answer: Always have questions. Having questions and being enthusiastic about the company is a way to show that you are strong candidate.

In-Person Interviews

The first in-person interview is usually done with the hiring manager who you had your phone interview with and a manager on the team you are applying to. During the first part of the interview, you will be asked to validate parts of your resume by giving examples from your work history. One of the things the interviewer is looking for is how you respond to unexpected problems. They want to know if you have encountered any setbacks and how you overcame those setbacks. As you learned in the chapter on Failure (page 50), setbacks are good if you can learn something from them. Talking about the lessons you learned and the struggles you have encountered in the past will show the interviewer how you handle stress and give insight to your personal work ethic.

In the next part of the interview or second interview if the first interview is short, you will learn more about the position you applied for. The manager will tell you what they are looking for, and you should honestly respond with your career goals. Interviews are not only the company interviewing you, but you are also interviewing the company. The opportunity has to be a good fit for both you and the company, so make sure you understand the role and responsibilities of the position and if it aligns with your career path.

In the final stage of the interview process, you will meet the team's immediate manager, their director, and will likely interview or job shadow someone on the team. The interviewers are looking to see if you are a good fit for the company and if your skills, character, and work habits will add value to the team.

After the Interview

You're not done yet. At the end of each round of interviews, it is good practice to send thank you emails to the people who interviewed you. They took time out of their day to meet with you, and a quick thank you is always appreciated.

After each interview, make notes about your impressions of the company. What do you like and what are your concerns? Are any of the concerns deal breakers? Reflect on the whole interview process from preparing for the interview to leaving the building after your last in-person interview. What went well? What could you do better in the future?

If you get the job and realize that it's not a good fit, you should take time to write an email to the hiring manager or the manager who emailed you. In your email, tell them you appreciate the opportunity to apply for the position and thank them for the time they took with you during the interviewing process. Let them know why you are deciding not to take the job and wish them the best. As a rule, you should never burn any bridges because you might meet these people again in a different position or at a different company. People talk, and it's best to treat everyone with respect. If you don't get the job, more than likely it's not because they didn't like you (you should never take it personally), it's because they found someone who fit the position better—and this might be a good thing. If your career goals did not match the position, you're better off finding one that does.

Key Takeaways

o   Treat interviewing as a skill you must have, maintain, and grow.

o   Don't be a peacock or a groundhog.

o   Prepare for the type of interview you will participate in. Not all approaches work for all styles of interview.

o   Treat every interview as though you are interviewing the company. You want to know if you are a good fit as much as they do.

GOAL FOR TODAY: It's always easier to find a job when you already have one. It puts the ball in your court and allows room for negotiation. Make a list of companies you are interested in working for and pick one to start researching today. Do they have an SEC 10-K Statement? What can you do to add value to their company?

If you want to learn more about the art of the interview, I suggest reading Chapter 8 in the book *The New Rules of Work* by Alexandra Cavoulacos and Kathryn Minshew.

HOW TO WRITE A BLOG

Blogs matter. If you want to grow, you'll need to touch the information-hungry, idea-sharing people who read (and write) them.
— SETH GODIN

"It's been great talking with you. Do you have a card so we can keep in touch?"

"Uhh… I have a website…? If you have your phone on you, open a new tab and type it in for later. It's my full name .com. Feel free to connect with me on (social media site). All my social media profiles have links to my website and all my contact info will be there as well. Now, what kind of card were you talking about?"

Business cards are on the decline, although, I still wind up with a handful of them after attending an event. Most of the time, the cards end up in between the seats of my vehicle, or I find them later after they've gone through the wash. (Business cards are expensive clutter.) For this reason (and probably a few others), it's becoming more and more common to have a website or use a social media site as a landing page for your personal brand. In addition to a website, I challenge you to also start a weekly blog to strengthen the identity of your brand and share the ideas you are thinking about. This doesn't mean that you have to start frequenting coffee shops and smoking clove cigarettes. You don't need to think of yourself as a stereotypical "writer" to create great blogs and you most definitely don't need to spend hours every week working on a meaningful blog post. Some of the best blogs I've read were written in 15-minute intervals, on the way to and from work on public transportation, and are less than 200 words.

Blogging does three important things that will help you grow into your path and inspire discovery. First off, writing about a topic or idea forces you to think about your job or industry critically and in a new (or new-to-you) way. You can play with the idea, piece it together however you like, and take a stand. Second, sharing your thoughts with the world makes you more confident. Even if you need to go back later and change a mistake, blogging lets you have a voice—and often, discover what your voice sounds like. Finally, your blog is sent out around the globe, and it is free to anyone who wants to learn from it or give you feedback. Positive or negative, feedback strengthens your ideas.

Below is a guide to help you as you begin writing your very own blog. I hope this gives you the push you need to join the rest of us. We'll be waiting!

1. Defining Your Purpose: Why Are You Writing a Blog?

There are many reasons why you might want to start a blog. You might be an expert and want to share a new theory you are playing with. Or a blog might be a place where you can catalogue your observations in the industry you work in. You might be interested in starting a blog because you may want to fill a knowledge gap and inform others who are new to the topic. If writing about topics you already know about doesn't interest you, you may want to write about your experience learning a new skill. Before starting, you should begin shaping your blog by asking the following questions.

- **Who is your audience?** Do you have a size you're writing for? Many bloggers I know write for less than 100 people, but of those, there are a handful of people who share the post with their networks, and it gets passed along. Usually, these people are writing to a specific audience, and they would rather have the right people reading their blogs closely than having hundreds or thousands of views by people who don't care.

- **What topics are you going to cover?** Is this a topic you know well and will be an expert on or is it something new you are currently learning? I know someone who writes multiple blogs per week. She has one that relates to her job, another for crafting and food, and one about being a working mom and raising her kids.

- **Why are you engaging with your readership on this topic?** Do you want to join a community? Be an authority on a topic? Ask for help? Document your journey? Share your thoughts with friends?

- **Where are you going to publish?** Are you going to use a blogging site or blog attached to your website? Popular options include Wix, Wordpress, Blogger, Tumblr, Medium, and Squarespace.

- **When are you going to publish?** Weekly? Bi-weekly? Daily? If you are going to write multiple blogs, will this change how often you publish?

If you don't know specifics yet, that's fine—use large brush strokes in the beginning and a finer brush as you get into a rhythm and feel out your topic and audience.

The questions listed above will help you get started building your personal brand. If you are looking for more resources to build a brand, check out Quick Sprout's free branding e-text (probably the best resource around, free and otherwise). Visit: quicksprout.com/the-complete-guide-to-building-your-personal-brand/

2. Coming Up with a Topic

The next road block many people run into is coming up with ideas. Here are some prompts to get you started:

You have 200-500 words to tell this week's most important story about your industry. Go!

What changes need to be made in your industry? Your topic is the "who"; now think about what, where, why, and how.

What happened this week (or last week) that will change how you do business?

What articles or blogs have you read recently that you could write better? Rewrite a new version.

What predictions do you have for the future of business and

technology, and how will this affect your company or people with your job description?

3. Weekly Blog Writing Schedule

Blogging doesn't have to be a time-consuming process—you can use your small breaks throughout the day to work on your blog, such as the 10-15 minutes between meetings and during a scheduled break. You can also mentally prepare in the car (or public transit) or when you are getting ready in the morning. In the past, I have used brewing my morning tea to signal my blog writing time.

Here's one way you can break down your effort into small chunks, spread over a week.

Day 1: Start by brainstorming a list of ideas and topics you feel comfortable writing about. The format is up to you. You can make it formal, in a text document or excel spreadsheet, or informal, in a notebook or on the back of napkin. The point of this exercise is to give you some options to think about throughout the day.

Day 2: Pick the most appealing idea from the list you made in Day 1, and write why it is the most attractive.

Day 3: Write an outline: introduce the idea, provide some context, and tell us (the reader) why we should care about it.

Day 4: Finish the missing pieces in your outline. Connect the ideas in your outline with transition paragraphs or sentences so there is a consistent flow to your piece. As you do this, you will be turning your outline into your first draft.

Day 5: Reread your post, correcting and expanding on what you have already written. When you finish, send it to a friend, colleague, or editing service to look it over for mistakes.

Day 6: Read over your editor's comments and address any problem areas.

Day 7: Read your post one more time and make sure this draft is what you want to publish. Post your blog to your personal or company website/blog/LinkedIn/Medium/etc., and share a link on your social media sites like Facebook, Twitter, and LinkedIn. Additionally, if you work for a company that has rules you need to follow for writing personal blogs, make sure you are staying within those lines. More and more companies are adopting social media polices that include what you can and cannot write about online. Look in your employee handbook for rules and guidance.

4. Overcoming the Blank Page

My creative writing friends call writer's block "writer's constipation". If you sit down and the words are not coming, don't try to force it out. Knowing when to keep writing and when to take a break is important. If putting words on paper is a struggle, set what you're working on aside instead of trying to force it.

You should still shoot for trying to write for 10-15 minutes a day, but if you cannot think of anything in the first five minutes, chances are it won't come in the next 10. Try again later in the day. If nothing comes, try again tomorrow. If after a few days you are still having a hard time getting into the groove, refer to the chapter Getting Started (page 115) in Part 1 for ideas that will help spark your creativity.

Remember: you only need 10-15 minutes a day. Breaking a blog into small, workable segments makes it less intimidating and easier to work with. If you do a little each day, writing will become a routine and you will be joining your peers in contributing to the global conversation.

Once you have your topic and schedule, and are confident to move forward, you're ready to start your blog.

5. If You Don't Like Your Topic, Your Audience Will Know

You should be writing blog pieces you would want to read. If you are not excited about your topic, not only will it be a pain for you to write, it will be a pain for your readers.

A lack of interest can lead to something called "thin content." Thin content is when your webpage or blog offers little value to your visitors. Why is this bad? There are a number of reasons, but for the sake of space and the theme of this chapter, I will touch on two. First, it hurts your search engine optimization (SEO); meaning, your blog will get buried under thousands of other blogs and you'll have a hard time reaching your audience. Second, if you are not adding something new to the conversation or restating something more clearly, your blog content will not stand out, will likely be tagged as a content farm, and your credibility will be questioned.

6. Posts Should be Measured in "Skimmability"

Forget what you learned about essay writing in high school and/or college—a blog does not follow the same format. There are important formatting guidelines to follow, but for the most part, a blog is going against all the formal formatting rules you learned in compulsory education. A blog post should be written to skim first and read second. This allows your reader to skim the bullets until they get to ones that apply to them.

Your blog post should be visually appealing with a variety of fonts and media. The last thing you want is a block of text. Consider adding media such as pictures, videos, quotes, and free downloads.

7. Outlines are Important

Creating a map for your blog will help you visualize your story and aid in developing a consistent flow for the piece. When I am teaching the principles of writing, I usually take a short essay, cut out each paragraph in the paper, and have students arrange the paragraphs in an order that reflects the best flow for the paper. You can do this too, while writing and outlining your blog. Here is a picture of my handwritten outline in the cut-up exercise.

While writing my outline, I sometimes have holes I fill in later after I've thought about or researched my topic. When there's too many things I want to write about, I put a word limit on the blog so I don't overload my readers. This also helps me stay on topic, and sometimes the content taken out is a good starting point for next week's post. The point of a blog post is keeping it short and sweet with one nugget of information per post.

8. You Get Better with Practice

The more you write, the more confident you will be in your writing. After a few blog posts, you will become more familiar with the structure. You will develop your style and will understand the boundaries of the space you are writing in.

There is a lot of freedom in blog writing, and at times, it's hard to find your voice. What works for me is practicing often by writing a little every day, reading other blogs to see how my peers are writing, and listening to the feedback I get from friends, emails, and comments. If you need honest feedback, ask a friend or family member you trust for constructive criticism.

9. Engage Often

When I was writing a blog at Sustainable Evolution Inc., we tried to post twice a week. This is the sweet spot for most company blogs: you don't lose your readers and it's enough to remind them you're still around. If twice a week is too much of a time commitment, posting once a week is a good number for a personal blog.

You may find yourself writing in different styles to fit your schedule; this kind of diversity is welcomed. Examples of different styles are: long form posts, summary posts (where you point to other blogs), list posts, "how to" posts, reviews, insight and opinion posts, "update me" posts (summarizing any recent updates with you or your brand), and "roundup" posts (this is when you ask a few gurus in your field one question and post their replies).

10. Titles are 80% of Your Piece

When you are coming up with your title, use buzzwords and **nerve pinching** adjectives to make your titles **magnetic**. Unfortunately, good content gets ignored because of bad titles. Think about it. If a title doesn't draw you in, you don't click. David Ogilvy, often called the father of advertising, said: "On the average, five times as many people read the headline as read the body copy. When you have written your headline, you have spent 80 cents out of your dollar." Here are three resources you can use to bulk up your title:

- Find trends associated with your market to reach a larger audience with feedly.com
- Find title ideas using Portent's Content Idea Generator
- Find words and associated tags, using hashtagify.me

11. Pictures/Media/Copyrights

You are going to need some media to spice up your post. According to a HubSpot post on content marketing,

> ...[M]arketers who are leveraging visual content are seeing significant increases in their blog traffic, social media engagement, visitor-to-lead conversion rates and inbound customer acquisition results.

There are some great places to connect with photographers who allow us to use their images for free or a small fee.

- gettyimages.com *$$$ but worth it if you have extra money in your budget*
- canva.com *$1 photos*
- pablo.buffer.com *Free photos*
- flickr.com *Paid and Free (creative commons) photos*
- commons.wikimedia.org *(public domain) Free*

If you are using a creative commons image, make sure you are citing it correctly. Remember to cite the title, author, source, and license. There is a link to a guide in the Notes and References section at the end of the book.

12. You're Going to Need a Good Editor

After writing a blog for about six months, my posts started looking and reading a lot more professional. My secret? When I realized my writing was lagging, I reached out to three people. The first was an old college writing buddy, Jason, who read my blogs in draft form and gave me much-needed feedback. Second, my wife, Megan, began copyediting everything I wrote (and everything I wore before leaving the house). Finally, when I was stuck, I didn't hesitate to bounce ideas off of my mentor, Andy Ruth, and other employees at Sustainable Evolution Inc. Advice is always helpful, and verbalizing areas where I am stuck helps me reframe the problem.

In addition to the help I received, I also made a point to read and reread my blog to catch as many mistakes before sharing my draft with others. It's embarrassing to read through an old post and find grammar and spelling mistakes. Luckily, my worst mistakes were filtered out before I clicked publish. To help catch errors, I use an editing app called Grammarly to look for potential errors. You can download a free version at app.grammarly.com. Your blog posts may never be perfect, but you're in good company—everyone has a mistake slip through once in a while. Even big-name book publishers print books filled with errors. Luckily, if you spot an error in your blog post, you can edit your post in seconds. In print, it's not that easy.

13. First Year Marketing/Getting Hits

The goal for most bloggers is to get to a point where they have a dedicated audience that will advertise for them. This happens when the content you're posting is worth sharing and when you have spent the time building your readership.

When I say advertise, I'm talking about a more grass roots form, a technology-based word of mouth. The top seven places I see traffic coming from are not paid advertising sites (because I don't pay to advertise my blog). They are:

1) Reddit
2) Stumbleupon
3) Google
4) Bing
5) Twitter
6) Facebook
7) LinkedIn

There are a number of companies you can pay to direct people to your blog, but this goes back to point one: defining your purpose.

14. Stick with It

Writing a weekly blog post is hard. Some Monday mornings, I open my laptop and start writing, hoping that something salvageable comes from my day one free write. If you build it, they will come. My posts a few months into blogging were largely ignored, I was lucky to have ten views unaccounted for. About six months into blogging, my best daily view count was in the hundreds, and at around the year mark, I had one post break 3,000 views in one day. Keep in mind, this was after nearly a year of writing. If you write good, clean content, market it well, and use the resources I pointed to in the post, you will have no problem getting views and drawing attention to your blog.

Here's the key: You've got to stick with it. If you want to develop an audience, you need to be posting regularly, writing content people want to read, and telling people where to find your blog. Will it take time? Yes. But once you find your rhythm, it will feel like no time at all.

Key Takeaways

o   Your professional calling card is quickly becoming your social footprint.

o   A good blog post can be under 200 words.

o   You don't have to be a writer to write a good blog post.

o   Blogging is a muscle and requires regular exercise.

o   Frequently engage with your readers to retain your audience and to stay current with your position, industry, or interest.

GOAL FOR TODAY: If you don't have a blog, take some time today to define your blog's purpose. Why would writing a blog benefit you? Who would you write to, and what type of content will you write about? If you have a blog already, what can you start doing today that will attract more of the right readers to your posts?

WORKSPACE

There is one way to radically change your behavior: radically change your environment.
— B.J. FOGG

The moment you walk into a casino, your senses are being manipulated. The color, crowding, and symmetry in the layout. The low ceilings, elegant lobbies, themed slots, and don't forget, the beautiful staff who come bearing gaudy drinks with exotic names. Have you ever wondered why there aren't any windows or clocks? The environmental cues in a casino stimulate your senses so you can have what the owners might call a more enjoyable experience, but what the rest us, back in the hotel room later that night, call acting without good reason. This environment: bells ringing, elegant décor, and flashing lights, is how people get caught up in the moment and end up gambling more than they intend to.

Casinos manipulating people? "That's a given!" you might be thinking. I can feel your fists shaking at me, dear reader. It's the deal we make when we walk through their doors. But what about your local grocery store?

The bakery at your local grocery store doesn't make a profit. It loses money, quarter after quarter, but every day the ovens are on and they're baking. The reason why grocery stores are willing to take a hit at the bakery is because the smell of baking bread encourages

316

people to buy more groceries by stimulating their appetite. They end up making what they lost in additional sales. In fact, the entire store is hacked to make you spend more. The aisle junk, the corner displays, even the free samples! Ever wonder why the fruits and vegetables are located in the place with the highest traffic where they are likely to be bruised (the entrance of the store)? It's the first thing customers put in their cart. Research suggests that if a customer puts healthy foods in their cart first, they are more likely to splurge when they get to the boxed cakes and greasy snacks (where the profit margins are higher). Feel violated?

If companies ranging all the way from casinos to your local grocery store are doing this, what other companies are? Movie theaters? Waiting rooms? Churches? Absolutely. What about where you work?

Having a well-defined goal and healthy work ethic can only take your productivity so far. Depending on where you work, you might have some cues to stimulate productivity, but I'm guessing they could be better. If nearly every building you walk into is trying to impress your senses, why let it stop there? In this chapter, I'm going to share some tricks rooted in peer-reviewed research I use to boost my focus and creativity, increasing both the quality and quantity of my work.

Two Types of Thinking

Before I get into the science of engineering your workspace, you need to know a couple things about how your brain works. We use many different types of thinking every day, often employing multiple styles in tandem. I am going to boil them down to two: creative thinking and critical thinking.

Creative thinking is not just for the Arts. It also relates to idea generation, first drafts, and abstract problem solving. When a realtor is creating a strategy to show a house to a client, this is creative thinking. When a company is developing an online ad campaign, this is creative thinking. When an HR recruiter is reviewing potential candidates for a job opening, they visualize a future state to see if a candidate's skills and work history will meet the demands of the open position. This is creative thinking.

Critical thinking, on the other hand, is more analytical, focused, and organized. When a realtor is going over property values and tax information, this is critical thinking. The marketing team uses critical thinking when they are sifting through consumer analytics. Likewise, when an HR recruiter is reading resumes and work histories, they are using critical thinking.

Both types of thinking are important for working on complex tasks, and both require different environments.

Green, Blue, and Red

You can take control of your thinking by choosing the right color for your workspace. When determining what color to choose, you first must determine what type of work you will be doing: creative, critical, or both? Below are the three of the most studied colors in workplace efficiency and the benefits each brings to a space.

Green (*creative*): Green is an important color and resonates with our natural roots. Our ancestors relied on green plants for survival because the color signaled water, which meant food and safety. The human eye has evolved to distinguish between 2,000 shades of green, a much more impressive number than the 100 shades of red we can see. Research shows that when someone is in a green environment, they're more creative than those in other environments, because the color green triggers our hunter-gatherer roots.

Blue (*creative*): Similar results have been linked to the color blue. Researchers believe this is because the color signals openness. Looking at the sky and ocean gives us peace and perspective, evoking calm feelings of safety, fostering creative thought.

Red (*critical*): On the critical thinking side, the color red is linked to precision and analysis. In a study at the University of British Columbia, those who were exposed to the color red outperformed the blue group on tests of recall and attention to detail. The participants had an easier time remembering words, and had fewer errors in their spelling and punctuation. This might be because red triggers a heightened awareness to possible danger, and this awareness prompts us to pay more attention to detail.

Here are some ways that you can add color to your workspace:
- Choose a computer background with a greater amount of the desired color.
- Shine green, blue, or red lights on a white wall (depending on the type of thinking you are trying to do).
- Hang colored curtains (or bed sheets) in your workspace.

- Use picture frames, plants, or other desk objects to stimulate creative or critical thinking.

- If you're on a campus (college or corporation), work near a window that looks over nature when you are working on a new project or using creative thinking. When you are revising or working on a critical project, sit in a place that closes the world off from influencing your thinking.

Lighting

According to a joint study between the physics department at the University of Stuttgart and the school of Business and Organizational Psychology at the University of Hohenheim, dimming the lights promotes creative thinking. Even telling a story about the dark can spark creativity. This is because dim lights heighten the perceived freedom of constraints. When we are in the dark, we suspend judgment and feel more open to creative possibilities.

Working on the other end of the spectrum, bright lights foster better results in critical and analytical thinking. According to an article in the *Journal of Environmental Psychology*, those working in moderately and brightly lit rooms fared better on tasks that required analysis and implementation. Simply put, brighter light levels promote more focus on detail.

Here's a way to remember it: be creative in the dark and critical in the light.

Noise

Noise plays a huge role in focus and concentration. According to a study published by *Journal of Consumer Research* (part of the University of Chicago Press), participants who were exposed to moderate levels of noise around 70 decibels (similar to the noise level in a coffee shop or a television in the background) came up with the most original ideas in response to a problem-solving task, compared to those who were exposed to sound levels of 85 decibels or higher (the noise level of an idling bulldozer). Participants who were asked to come up with ideas in silence fared better than the group at 85 decibels, but the ideas were not as creative as the groups exposed to 70 decibels. When it comes to critical thinking, like proofreading or doing your taxes, the researchers in the same study found that a quiet environment fosters better results.

Creative thinking = ≈70 dB, Critical thinking = <70 dB

I listen to ambient music like Brian Eno's *Thursday Afternoon* for critical concentration. For idea generation, I like to listen to experimental artists like Tom Waits and Godspeed You! Black Emperor. What you choose to listen to doesn't have to be the music we traditionally think about. There are tons of cool online videos specializing in ambient sounds. For example, I found one video that puts you directly in a cafe in the comfort of your own personal workspace (creative thinking). I'm also partial to a nine-hour washing machine video (critical thinking).

Open Spaces

Large open spaces have the best influence on creativity. The more open the room or taller the ceiling, the more open your thinking will be.

The opposite is true for critical thinking. Small confined spaces like the infamous library desk are great for detail-oriented tasks.

	Creative Thinking	Critical Thinking
Color	Green and blue	Red
Lighting	Dim	Bright
Noise	Moderate (≈70 dB)	Quiet (<70 dB)
Space	Large and open	Narrow and confined

Creativity Begets Creativity

According to Nancy Rivenburgh, Professor of Global Communication at the University of Washington, our output is primed by our input:

> When people visit an art exhibit, pay attention to public art, go to a concert, watch a chef's demonstration, listen to a street musician, or view prize-winning photography online, it enhances their own capacity to be creative.

You can use this to your advantage when you are engineering your workspace.

Place stimulating pictures in your workspace. Research suggests that abstract visual images, such as geometric patterns and shapes, and drawings or photos of nature prompt the most creative thinking. In addition, you can improve your creative thinking by taking breaks to watch video clips of others doing creative acts. Finally, if you're working on a tough problem and need a break, leave your workspace to check out a local art and music events to prime your mind. If you spend an afternoon working at a cafe, take some time to look at the art hanging on the walls (believe it or not, the art pieces may inspire you to connect the dots in your own work).

Other factors to consider when thinking about your workspace:

Not too hot, not too cold: The temperature of your workspace contributes to your productivity. According to research conducted at Cornell University, study participants made 44% fewer errors and 150% more keystrokes when the temperature in the room was raised from 20 °C (68 °F) to 25 °C (77 °F). If you are starting to feel sluggish and cold, try putting on an extra layer or turning up the thermostat and get to work!

Eye strain/fatigue: Set up your environment to reduce eye strain and fatigue. The average American adult stares at a screen for about

11 hours a day. This invariably leads to visual strain (and walking around like a cartoon whose eyes are dilated). One nifty (and free) application that works well for reducing eye strain during nighttime use is F.lux, a program that changes your screen's color temperature based on the time of day.

You can also use the 20-20-20 rule. This rule suggests that every 20 minutes you take a break from your computer for at least 20 seconds and look at objects that are 20 feet away.

Other tips include covering reflective surfaces, using indirect lighting whenever possible, and maximizing natural light. If that all fails, you can always invest in those geeky computer glasses I talk about in Part 2.

Key Takeaways

o   Your space impacts the type of thinking you will be able to do best. Creative thinking is best done in environments with blues and greens, while critical thinking is best done in environments with reds.

o   Low lighting is better for creative thinking. Low noise is better for critical thinking.

o   Less errors are made in rooms with slightly elevated temp-eratures.

o   Reduce eye strain and fatigue by taking a break from your screen every twenty minutes and looking twenty feet away.

GOAL FOR TODAY: Make a list of places you can work for creative and critical work, respectively. Make a list of ways you can reinforce creative and critical thinking in your office at work or at home. Is there a way you can modify your workplace to reinforce creative work AND critical work?

OVERTHINKING, OVERTHINKING

Don't think, just do.
— HORACE

Don't Panic.
— DOUGLAS ADAMS, *The Hitchhiker's Guide to the Galaxy*

For about five years, I played bass guitar in death metal bands in Grand Rapids, MI. One of the popular music venues that catered to local bands in the mid-to-late 2000s was the adolescent-friendly safe haven: Skelletones. Before I played on their stage, I grew up spending as much time as I could mingling with aspiring bands and the off-beat, we're-so-counter-culture-we-hate-counter-culture crowd. At 15, the only dream I had was to play on their stage. At 19, I got my chance. The difference between Skelletones and other small venues I had played was the novelty of playing where I discovered my love for music. It was the winter of 2008 and Mirf, the owner of Skelletones, was talking to my band on stage from the sound booth, adjusting our mic levels during the soundcheck. That is when it sunk in: This. Is. Real. I knew I shouldn't be nervous, but my body wasn't responding to my brain. I started counting my breaths up to four to slow my breathing, but it was no use. My hands, slick with perspiration, slid down the neck of the guitar. My fingers, then legs, started trembling so rapidly I had a hard time tuning my bass. "This is it," I kept thinking. This is it.

When I have to speak or perform in public, my heart beats so hard I swear I can feel my brain rattle. My vision goes blurry and my blood turns to cement. I step outside of myself and only watch myself react. This is probably because all my energy is going directly into my head, throwing it into overdrive.

It's not only public speaking, it's also when I'm on my way to meet new people. When I was single, I felt this way before asking someone out on a date. I feel it the night before a big project is due, and I'm hunched over my laptop scanning every line for a defect or searching for something I know I'm missing—a flaw people will see that I can't see. Three hours later, with half-moons caressing my bloodshot eyes, my dark horse (Change, page 39) sits in the middle of the road not wanting to move. It tells me I shouldn't turn it in because everyone is going to think it's dumb and a waste of time. It says: "you don't have anything to say, get off the stage." It says: "Why bother? Sure, you could play a song, write a book/blog post, give a speech, speak your mind, but what if everyone hates you? Or worse, what if people like you so much you have to do it again?"

On stage at Skelletones, I'm overthinking again. If you could crawl into my ear and listen to my thoughts it would go something like this: *My bass is in tune—I think—but what if it's not exactly tuned right with the other guitars? My hands are sweaty, really sweaty. Is that why my mouth is so dry? Because all the moisture in my body is going to my hands? What happens if I puke? That's pretty metal, I guess; so if I puke I'll just go with it. Oh! I have to remember to talk about our Myspace page. Am I blinking? ...because I can't feel my face.*

Overthinking leads to fabricated fears, and because fear calls on all our homemade monsters, creative people can easily imagine extraordinary negative outcomes: *What if I knock over an amp and it falls on the drummer? What if I hit a light with my bass when I swing it around my neck and it starts a fire? Is it possible to puke and evacuate my bowels at the same time? What if we play so badly we get booed off the stage—I'll never be able to come back here.*

As this is all running through my head, on stage left, toward the top of the ceiling, I see a sign that I have never noticed before because you can only get a good view of it from on stage. It says: "don't even THINK about it." These were exactly the right words I needed. Don't think about it. Mirf and Skelletones knew exactly what young bands needed for encouragement OR Mirf was saying: Don't even think about swinging from this pipe because it can't support the weight of a human body (hanging upside down from piping was usually fair game). Regardless of the true reason, the handmade sign made me aware of my overthinking. Instead of it taking control of me, I tried to control it. It prompted me to do six important things I still do whenever I am too nervous to speak or do anything in front of the public.

1. Slow Down

When you're overthinking, you're overstimulated and need to find a way to calm down. I focus in on a single point in the room and slowly take it all in. This slows down my thinking and helps me become more mindful of where I am so I can confirm what I'm doing. For me, focusing in on one concrete object moves me back into my body and places me in control of my breathing. I think, I am here, this is what I am doing, and I am in control of my body.

At Skelletones, I thought: *I am here at Skelletones! A place I feel comfortable in. I am playing music I love; I can feel my body and can feel my hands on my guitar; and I am in control of my body, breathing, and I am present in this moment.*

2. Validate Your Support

Everyone in the room is cheering for you, even if you don't know them. Think about a time when you watched someone in the spotlight who you could tell was struggling. You wanted them to pull through, right? This is because we have something called mirror neurons, which makes an audience respond to what they are seeing as if it were happening to them. Researchers have hypothesized that mirror neurons play a key role in empathy. Since we do not want to fail ourselves, we hope the person we are watching is successful, too.

Another thing you can do is think about all the people you have who may not be there with you, your friends and family, who are pulling for you. At home, your friends and family want you to be successful.

At Skelletones, I thought: *I am surrounded by people I trust and love. My bandmates have always had my back, and the crowd is full of people who are looking forward to watching me play well.*

3. Confirm Your Skill

Give yourself some credit. Think about how much you have done to prepare for this event. You have nothing to worry about because you have all the information inside of you already.

At Skelletones, I thought: *I have played in front of crowds larger than this one, so this isn't anything I can't manage. I can play all the songs with my eyes closed—it's all muscle memory by now. I can do this practically without thinking about it. Now is my time to have a little fun with it.*

4. Ask: What's the Worst That Could Happen?

If you are like me and you create elaborate stories about how badly you could fail, ask yourself: What is the worst thing that could happen? Honestly? Too often, we overestimate the probability of something going wrong and underestimate our ability to adapt to an unexpected challenge. If something does not go according to plan, you will recover. And if you don't recover, most people won't notice or care because we have all made mistakes.

At Skelletones, I thought: *The worst thing that could happen, honestly, is knocking something over with the neck of my bass and breaking the tuning key. If I make a mistake, I will recover. It's not the end of the world. If something breaks, I'm friends with some of the other bands playing tonight and they will help up out. (Side note: At a show a few months later, my bass broke a couple songs into our set. Fortunately, I was able to borrow a bass from another band.)*

5. Remember

Recall a time when you were nervous and then remember how you felt afterwards. It's never as bad as you think it's going to be, right? Fear is only as big as your imagination.

At Skelletones, I thought: *Remember back to the first show you played. After the first song, you were out of breath, but it was a good kind of exhaustion, like a runner's high. You got into the groove of playing and that's all you wanted to do the rest of the night. You felt sad when playing the last song because you didn't want it to be over.*

6. Stand Tall

This was something I learned when I rowed crew in high school: If you get tired, focus on your posture. Columbia and Harvard researchers agree. A recent study found that standing tall with good posture directly influences our biochemistry by increasing testosterone and decreasing cortisol, resulting in a feeling of confidence.

At Skelletones: *I took a deep breath, put out my chest, and maintained good posture.*

"Don't even THINK about it." When I read the sign, I found my breath again and calmed my racing thoughts. Nobody died, I didn't puke on stage, and the band and I ended up having a decent show, good enough to be invited back to play the following month.

If you are uncomfortable or nervous, acknowledge what you are feeling and challenge yourself to work through it. What you're feeling are growing pains, and if you push through it your self-confidence will grow. Your fears are never as bad as you think, and the more you practice facing your fears, the more confident you will be. Good luck, and remember: Don't even think about it.

Key Takeaways

○ Overthinking can lead to overstimulation, which can lead to doubting yourself and panic.

○ If you find this happening, slow down, validate the support you are being given, and reaffirm that you're skilled enough to succeed.

○ Ask yourself what's the worst that could happen and visualize a time when you were nervous and succeeded.

○ Standing tall, with good posture, releases chemicals that will make you more confident and help you calm down.

GOAL FOR TODAY: Put together a plan to follow when you start overthinking. What are a few ways you can calm yourself down and see things from a level perspective? If you have a few strategies ahead of time, you can call on them when you realize you're heading down the path of overthinking.

GAINING KNOWLEDGE

The future belongs to the curious. The ones who are not afraid
to try it, explore it, poke at it, question it, and turn it inside out.
— ANONYMOUS

I am neither clever nor especially gifted. I am only very, very
curious.
— ALBERT EINSTEIN

Brilliance thrives in a culture of curiosity. The more knowledge
you have, the more connections you will be able to make, and the
more diverse your skills and problem solving will be. Although it's
more important knowing what to do with knowledge once you
have it, gathering it is the first step. That's why when I started
college as a freshman in 2008, I decided to read 100 books every
year, a large number for someone who has struggled with reading
and had not read a book of any kind in years.

What I found was, once I learned the tools to reading quickly,
reading two or three books a week was easy. Let me save you
some legwork and tell you how I am able to read well over 100
books every year.

Audiobooks

One of the first things people tell me when they walk in my home is, "I wish I had more time to read." Books are strewn across the kitchen table and stacks clutter my desk, taking up most of the tabletop except for a small section where I can set my laptop and cup of earl grey tea. Floor-to-ceiling shelves line my office (with the additional shelf add-on option) and flow over into the living room. There are books in between spice racks in the kitchen (honestly, that was my wife's idea, they look nice as decoration—hey, where'd my Vonnegut book go?). The bedroom nightstand looks like Annie Hall's apartment—you get the picture. A lot of fuel if there was a fire (my dream is to have a miniature bookshelf in the bathroom, but my wife hasn't given in...yet).

Here's my confession. About 80% of the books I read are audiobooks. I am a slow reader—always have been—and because reading didn't come naturally to me, I hated it growing up. I hated English class in high school and avoided books, magazines, and even email. At breakfast, I was terrified when the back of the cereal box was facing me. It wasn't until I found audiobooks that I fell in love with reading.

Listening to an audiobook (at 2x speed) along with the physical book is my preference. This allows me to scan each line and make notes if there is an interesting portion I want to return to later. When I am not interested in a book's style or plot structure and I am only interested in the content, I don't bother sitting down with a physical book. I listen to these books when I am running, on the bus, cleaning, and walking from one appointment to the next. Research suggests there is little difference in comprehension between reading and listening to a text. In fact, we are conditioned to listen and are more likely to continue listening to a book than to keep reading it.

Math Breakdown

It is easy to read well over 100 books per year using audiobooks without changing your daily schedule. If you listen to an audiobook while you are doing something you don't have to think about (i.e. running, commuting, doing laundry), you can do two tasks at the same time. Here's how I break down my audiobook listening: if an average audiobook is 8 hours long, and if I listen to it at 2x speed, each book takes four hours to complete.

- Daily run (40 minutes + 20 minute cool down) = 1 hour/day

- Bus/commute = 1 hour/day

- Miscellaneous (cleaning/doing laundry/making dinner/washing dishes) = ½-1 hour/day

In a 5-day work week of commuting to work and exercising for an hour a day, that's 12.5 hours of listening, which is roughly 2.5 books per week. 52 weeks multiplied by 2.5 = 130 books per year.

Where to Find Audiobooks

There are four ways to acquire audiobooks: the library, subscription plans, pay as you go, and in the public domain.

The library. I am a big supporter of my local library and using them is your cheapest option. If I listen to 100 audiobooks a year, it would cost me about $2500 if I bought each audiobook individually or $1000 on a subscription plan. Since you already pay for your library card through taxes, every book in their catalogue is free to you. If there is a popular title, you do need to wait in line, but with thousands of books eager to be read, you'll have a lot to keep yourself busy.

Cassette tapes and Audio CDs are mostly a thing of the past, although I'm sure your local library has a cassette tape or two if you are going to fire up the old Pinto this summer. If you haven't been to your local library in a while, things might have changed. Most library books and audiobooks are hosted on the library website in an electronic library (e-audio and e-book). You can download them directly to your phone, tablet, or laptop in seconds using the app OneClickDigital and/or OverDrive. Both programs work on Mac/Windows/Android computers, tablets, and smartphones. I like Overdrive a little better because it is more user-friendly, and it allows me to increase the speed up to 2x.

If you do not have access to a decent library or prefer to own your audiobooks, the following options may be best for you.

A subscription. The four most common subscription sites are Audible, Audiobook.com, Scribd, and Simplyaudio. At the time of this writing, Audible owns a majority of this market. However, there will be other companies breaking in. One of those companies is Playster. For about $15 a month, you can listen to as many audiobooks as you want. Best of all, you can stream it so the audiobooks don't take up a whole lot of room on your phone. This is by far my favorite service yet!

Pay as you go. You can purchase audiobooks individually in CD format and as a direct download through Audible, Audiobook stand, Barnes and Noble, and iTunes.

The public domain. In the United States, a book enters the public domain 70 years after the death of the author. If the book is a work of corporate authorship, it enters the public domain 95 years from publication or 120 years from creation, whichever expires first. Once a book enters the public domain, it can be reproduced by anyone, meaning people can make an audiobook version without having to get the rights from the author or publisher.

- **Librivox** is a non-profit organization specializing in volunteer-read books in the public domain. You can download them fast and for free! The only downsides are that you can't speed up the reading, and sometimes there's a different reader for every chapter. However, you can speed up the downloaded audio file using QuickTime.

- **Internet archive** is similar to Librivox but more focused on audiobooks and recordings that were recorded earlier. The audio enters the public domain. For example, there is a recording of B.F. Skinner reading his book, *Walden Two*!

Speed Reading

Despite what anyone tells you, we are reading more than ever. *What* we read is changing. In addition to reading books and magazines, we are reading blog posts, online articles, e-books, and online research journals–not to mention the hundreds of emails that arrive in your inbox each week. And text messages. And social media posts. And online discussion boards. And...

During my apprenticeship at Sustainable Evolution Inc., they taught me that an informed worker should read one million words per week. That's the same as reading *War and Peace* by Leo Tolstoy twice! It's not so surprising when you add up all the reading: your emails, journal articles, online communities/social media, business books, and your own personal reading (the books you read for fun). If the average person reads 200 words per minute, it takes 5,000 minutes to read 1 million words. Or, about 83 hours.

If you double your reading speed, you will earn 40 hours of your time back—that's an entire work week! Imagine if you can triple it or more. Speed reading is an essential skill in the workplace, and that's why I chose to include it in this book. When it comes to speed reading, here are the six most important tips I learned.

Tip #1: Do Not Read Every Word

Our eyes work like a still camera, recording four or five times each second. If you add it up, that's about 240-300 snapshots per minute, so if you are reading one word per snapshot, you are maxed out at 300 words per minute. Instead of reading every word, you should chunk groups of words together. You do this by starting to read the first sentence and then increasing your speed, so you are scanning chunks instead of reading individual words. Focusing on every third word will make the text scannable and lump the word behind and in front to give your brain enough context. Doing this can increase your read time by a multiple of three.

Tip #2: Lose Your Inner Voice

In order to scan quickly, you need to lose your inner voice that reads to you. DO NOT say every word you read in your head. Instead, look for the ideas, not the words. You can think about it like this: you are absorbing ideas, not processing words.

Tip #3: Focus and Control Your Speed

Before you start reading, spend one minute thinking deeply so you can gather your focus and clear your mind. Next, spend one minute reading in a sprint—this will loosen your reading muscles. After the one minute is up, slow down a bit. It will feel like you are going slow, but in comparison to your "normal" speed, you are still going very fast. Just like when you are driving a car and exit a freeway: you are still going fast, but it feels a lot slower.

Tip #4: Tracking

When you start reading, use a pen or pencil to track your location. The faster you move the pen over the line, the faster your brain will work to make sense of the content.

When something in the text stands out to you, use the pen or pencil to place a single dot next to the line or paragraph. At the end of the chapter, go back to the beginning and reread the marked locations ONLY. Doing this will pull together the main points of the piece.

Tip #5: Forests, Not Trees

There is a technique I use called "three read". First, I quickly scan the document to get a sense of the narrative and to look for anything that is bolded or bulleted (you can do this in a few seconds). Next, I go through a second time to see if any information stands out (sometimes, content jumps or "flashes" out). During the third read, I have a good idea of what the main points are, and I closely read the parts that jumped out at me during the second read.

Tip #6: Read with Intent

Most industry or business-related content is written for a large audience, so not all of it will resonate with you. This means that you do not need to read all of it. Zoom in on content that applies to you and skip over anything that is not applicable. If something sparks your interest, stop and apply it to your existing knowledge. The more connections you make, the easier it will be to retain.

Reading quickly is a skill that is learned. As with any other skill, you will get better with practice. One million words may be intimidating now, but if you follow these tips and practice, you will increase your reading speed and open up hours of extra time in your schedule.

Keeping Track of Your Books

It's a good idea to write a few notes about every book you read, including both audio and print books. I find that writing a summary sentence after each chapter helps me recall the main points later. At the end of the book, you will have a full paragraph summarizing your impressions of the major themes. Not only will it help you understand the content as you read, it will also create associations so you can recall the information later. When you finish a book, the website Goodreads is a great way to keep track of the books you have read, post reviews, find new books, and connect with others who have similar interests.

Key Takeaways

o   Building a strong foundation includes gaining a broad level of knowledge. Accelerate your learning by shifting how you consume knowledge.

o   Use audiobooks to listen and learn as you are doing other, more physical or less focused tasks, such as exercising or vacuuming.

○ Use speed reading techniques to quickly gain understanding and identify the information that is important to you.

○ Keep track of what you are learning and where you are finding information by jotting a quick note about what you read or listened to in your notebook.

GOAL FOR TODAY: Visit your local library and sign up for a library card. You're already paying for it with your tax dollars, why not stop in for a visit? P.S. Librarians are some of the greatest human beings on the planet. My local librarians at the Nokomis Library in Minneapolis have a great sense of humor and are always willing to answer any questions I have.

MONEY

We buy things we don't need with money we don't have to impress people we don't like.
— DAVE RAMSEY

When I was in college, the first two weeks of every term killed me. I was on pins and needles with all the other students waiting for their financial aid, grants, or scholarships to kick in. I quickly learned that money can cause an immense amount of stress, and that stress caused me to become so distracted my grades always dipped in the first two weeks. It was an uphill battle the rest of the term.

Thankfully, now that I'm out of school, I don't have to worry about being dropped from a class because my funding didn't come through, but I do need to make sure my income can cover all my living expenses. One benefit of scraping by in college with loans, scholarships, and a part-time job was learning how to make a budget, and it took a few tight months for me to learn my lesson. When I reached the limit of my food budget and all the money remaining for the month was tied to my rent due the following week, eating rice, beans, and carrots for a week and a half taught me to save and be more thrifty the following month (it took more than one or two rough months to correct my spending). During those rice and carrot days, I often thought: once I get a job, a real nine-to-five job with benefits, I won't ever have to worry about money again.

A couple months after graduating, I received a friendly email reminding me that my first student loan payment was due, and it wasn't cheap. Loans, along with paying for my housing, food, clothing, transportation, and all the things I want to live comfortably, lead me back to square one: the monthly budget, a skill I am happy I learned early, even if it was the hard way.

With easy credit cards—especially for those with a college degree or a full-time job, and multiple lenders offering you student loans—it's easy to live comfortably for a few years without stumbling into the budgeting lesson I had to learn. Think about the following professions: doctors, investment professionals, professional athletes, and celebrities. What do they all have in common? They are all in high money-making professions. Arguably, many would say that people in these professions are intelligent and have achieved a level of success beyond the average person. Anything else? According to an article in the Fiscal Times, they are four of the most vulnerable careers that are likely to lead to bankruptcy. Why? Because they never learned how to manage their money.

In the book *The Millionaire Next Door*, Thomas J. Stanley and William D. Danko argue that most millionaires are first generation rich who live among the middle class and who know the value of being frugal. The authors go on to say that many high-income-producing households are asset poor. Meaning, if you make $200,000/year, and spend $250,000/year, you're on your way to the bankruptcy, and quick. It is the middle class who, historically, has understood the value of paying off debts to avoid paying interest and learned the craft of being thrifty.

I am in no way, shape, or form a millionaire. I am 27, have student loan debt, a mortgage, and my expenses are growing as my family grows. I never formally learned how to manage my money because it was left out of my public education (I'm sure your schools didn't cover it either). I have, however, had the privilege of being around some people who are very smart with money and I soaked in as much financial wisdom from them as I could. With their advice, I am on a good track to paying off my debt and saving for the future. Below are the five steps I'm using that you can use to become more money savvy.

Step 1: Track Your Spending for an Entire Month
Before making a budget, you should track your spending so you have a baseline for your budget. You will get a better idea of what your

spending trends are after tracking them for a few months, but one month is all you need to get started.

A lot of my friends spend until they hit a certain number in their checking account and then they take it easy until their next paycheck comes. When I ask my friends where their money goes, most of them have no idea and, as one of my more animated friends put it: "It's more or less a cluster-f*ck of spending in the moment."

Use a notebook, Excel document, or a notes application on your phone to write down each expense. When you see where your money is going, you become aware of your choices. When you are in charge of your choices, the power shifts in your favor.

Step 2: Save for Your Emergency Fund

What will you do if your employer has to let your whole department go? Or you get sick and can't go to work? What happens when you get a speeding ticket, or need to purchase new tires for your car, or your washing machine breaks and ruins your floor? Not sure? According to Dave Ramsey, the first thing you need to do is start saving for an emergency fund. Your fund should be able to cover three to six months of expenses (three minimum, six maximum), so when something unexpected happens, you can use your emergency fund instead of going into debt. Debt is easily obtained and slow to pay off. One bad week might take a year or more to recover from.

Step 3: Make a Budget

Once you are aware of how much you are spending and where, you can start planning your month's budget.

1. Break your spending down into categories and subcategories. You can make your budget as simple or complex as you would like. Here's one way to break it down:

Category	Subcategories
Housing	mortgage/rent, internet, water/sewer, gas, electricity, waste removal
Transportation	vehicle payment, fuel, insurance, parking, public transportation fees
Daily Living	groceries, eating out, clothing
Children	medical, clothing, tuition, school supplies, lunch money, allowance, childcare, sports/clubs
Entertainment	video streaming services, concerts, sporting events, spending money
Pets	food, medical, grooming, toys

Gifts & Donations	presents, charity, flowers
Financial Obligations	student loans, credit cards, taxes
Savings & Investments	savings, stock, retirement (such as a 401K)

2. For each category and/or subcategory, use past data you have gathered through Step 1 to create an estimate amount (make sure to factor in your total income so you are not overspending).

3. Start tracking and try to stay within your budget.

Go to vertex42.com/ExcelTemplates/family-budget-planner.html for a free template you can edit and make your own.

Keep in mind that throughout this process, you will discover places where you can cut your spending and start putting money where you see the need. For example, my wife and I tracked our expenses for three months and saw that we were consistently spending $100 over what we had budgeted for food. Since food quality is important to us, we did not want to reduce the amount we were spending. We also saw that we over-budgeted in our clothing allowance. In our fourth month, we revised our budget by adding $100 to groceries and reduced our clothing allowance by $100.

When thinking about a budget, always put money into savings apart from your emergency fund. Think about it this way: When you save, it's like sending a small gift to your future self. Do you really need to spend your money on a small expense this month (like buying coffee or going to the movies) or would you rather save for a time in the future when you want to buy a big item (like buying a car, boat, or going on a vacation)?

Planning ahead gives you flexibility and allows you to regain financial control when an unexpected event or circumstance creeps into your life. Don't let poor financial planning cause you stress—you have more important things to think about.

Step 4: Invest in Your Future
Your money should be working for you, and you can do this by thinking of your spending as investing. I invest in the health of my body (quality food and exercise), the health of my brain (education and meditation), and the health of my finances (smart buying practices and making my money work for me).

Step 5: Diversify Your Savings

A good rule is to never have more than 20% of your wealth in one asset. You have the same amount of wealth invested, you are just changing what it looks like. Here's why: If you have all your savings in a bank account, what happens if the dollar is devalued? Unfortunately, U.S. currency is not backed by gold, but that's not entirely a bad thing. You can invest in gold (or another precious metal) so if the dollar tanks, your gold will hold its value. Other good places to invest your wealth besides cash and metal are property (i.e. your house) and stock or mutual funds. When you get into stocks, you can diversify in a number of different industries, so if one dries up, you will have others to fall back on.

Easy Ways to Cut Down on Your Expenses and Save Money

- **Bring your lunch.** I don't spend $12 on a salad or sandwich I know I can make for $5 at home with locally grown organic produce. It's cheaper, healthier, and I get to make it the way I like it.

- **Have just one credit card.** I never carry a balance on my credit card. I use one credit card to earn points, aka free money, and paying off my balance every month builds up my credit.

- **Visit the bar less.** Alcohol and drugs are expensive. If you are trying to save money, they should be the first to go. If you want an eye opener, start doing the math. A pack of cigarettes in a bigger city costs roughly $10 a pack. Let's say you smoke a pack a week because you only smoke when you're out at the bar drinking with friends, because duh, everyone knows smoking is bad for you, but it's not like you do it all the time. That alone adds up to $520/year. Let's look at your bar tab. You order a $4 microbrew and tip a dollar, so that's $5—a good number to add with. Let's say you have six drinks a week at the bar. $30/week is $1560. Add the two figures together and that's $2080 dollars a year spent in casual bar visits. Want to make $1 more per hour? In a 40-hour work week, $1 more per hour is an additional $2080 to your total yearly salary (40*52=2080).

- **Don't pay for something you can get for free.** There are benefits to having a gym membership, but if you need to save money and still want to stay fit, running outside is free. This also applies to free internet, movies, and books you can get at the library. You can even grow your own produce (and use it to share or barter with others). If you put your mind to it, there are a lot of ways to legally get something for free that you might already be paying for.

- **Buy used.** The quickest way to lose a few thousand dollars is to buy a new automobile. According to Stanley and Danko, Millionaires buy used cars, because they know that as soon as a new car leaves the dealer parking lot it drops thousands of dollars in value.

- **Buy, don't rent**. When I was renting an apartment, my money was going directly into someone else's pocket. Now that I have a mortgage, some of the money I pay goes back to me. If I sell my house 10 years after buying it, more than likely I will make back what I paid. I'm only out the money I paid in interest.

- **Buy in bulk.** Go 50/50 with a friend on a big box store membership like Costco or Sam's Club. The portions are crazy big, but in the long run you will save.

The majority of millionaires became wealthy one dollar at a time, not all at once. Right now is the best time to start learning frugal spending habits. If you have any outstanding debt, put a plan together to start aggressively paying it off. And finally, start saving a little every month. Your future self will thank you.

Key Takeaways

- Your personal finances can put you under a lot of stress that will impact areas of your personal and work life. Learning to budget and live within a budget is critical, regardless of how much you make.

- Start the budgeting process by base-lining your monthly spending habits.

- Identify what is necessary and what is nice, and create a grouped list of budget areas you need to account for.

- Find ways to reduce what you spend without impacting your daily life too much—do you really need a $5 coffee and to eat out for lunch every day?

GOAL FOR TODAY: Make a list of your current monthly expenses and figure out how much you need to put aside for your emergency fund.

Four Final Rules

As you flip to the final pages of the book, I want to leave you with some soft skills I'm constantly working on. I call them rules, because they're behaviors I try to follow every day, but they are easily forgotten, especially under stress.

1. Everything is a gift.

When someone offers help through time, advice, or funding, it is a gift. They are going out of their way to help you for the sole purpose of making you a strong or better human being. It is not something you are entitled to, it is truly a gift, and one you can give back to others. If someone has helped you, the best way to thank them is to help others as they have helped you.

2. Respect others because you respect yourself.

Respect is something that is earned. Before someone has earned your respect or after they have lost it all, treat them with decency because of the respect you have for yourself. When you are rude, cruel, mean, disengaged, or hold a grudge, you are only hurting yourself—you hold yourself back from your own progress. Whatever you do, do it respectfully, because how you treat others starts with how you treat yourself.

3. Practice empathy.

Everyone you meet has something on their mind they are working through. No matter where you go, inside of every person there is a tragedy and a comedy fighting for center stage. This is why I try to be especially kind to people who are rude, because there is a real struggle at play in their hearts, and their body is only responding as any of ours would. Be kind, and part of being kind is knowing when to stick with or pull out of a project, knowing when to close the gap or distance a friendship. Be patient, and when you can't be patient, be kind.

ALWAYS DO YOUR BEST
(Rule Four)

I want to end with my favorite passage from Don Miguel Ruiz's book, *The Four Agreements*.

Always Do Your Best. Your best is going to change from moment to moment; it will be different when you are healthy as opposed to sick. Under any circumstance, simply do your best, and you will avoid self-judgment, self-abuse and regret.
—DON MIGUEL RUIZ

All other rules follow this one rule: Always do your best. Always. You cannot buy integrity, you cannot buy years of knowledge, you cannot buy a skill, and you cannot buy your reputation. These are all things you build, and always doing your best is the quickest way there.

ALWAYS DO YOUR BEST
PART 2

This is YOUR best, not someone else's. Every person is on a separate path leading to their own unique goal. Never compare yourself to others, because their goal is not your goal. Your pasts are just as different as your respective futures. When your paths cross, always do your best, and encourage them to do their best. If you find that your half-hearted effort is as good as their best, be patient and lead by example. Your focus should always be on doing YOUR personal best.

ALWAYS DO YOUR BEST
PART 3

When you are always doing your best, you see failure as an opportunity to learn.

When you are always doing your best, you don't live in regret.

When you are always doing your best, you don't care if you look like an amateur, because you know that's how you learn.

When you are always doing your best, you are kind to others, not because they have earned your respect, but because you respect yourself.

When you are always doing your best, you only focus on what is in your control.

When you are always doing your best, you are honest with yourself about your skills and goals.

When you are always doing your best, you inspire others to do their best.

When you are always doing your best, the task itself is the only motivation you need.

When you are always doing your best, you feel connected to a larger purpose.

When you are always doing your best, every tool and skill you learned in this book fits together thoughtlessly.

When you are always doing your best, everything falls into place as it needs to. Always.

When you are always doing your best, you are always doing your best work because you're learning something new every day.

When you are always doing your best, you are answering the question Benjamin Franklin asked himself every morning: *What good shall I do this day?*

What is your passion? Your career goal? Life goal? It's what motivates you to get up every morning and do your best. That should be your **GOAL FOR TODAY** and your goal **EVERY DAY.**

AFTERWORD

If you read this book from start to finish, you just constructed a great building: you laid a foundation, built structure, and added reinforcement. You have all the makings of a good home, but you're not finished yet. This book only provided you with the bones of the building—inside, it's completely empty. It's up to you to fill it with your own personal dreams and experiences. One thing will lead to another, and you will add on to your house, tear some structures down, and build new, stronger reinforcements. Your life is under constant construction, and the day you call it finished is the day you start working on another part of the house.

Unfortunately, this is my stop and I have to get off so I can hop on the next train. This isn't a "good-bye, good-bye" it's only a "see you later" farewell. You can keep up-to-date by visiting my blog at http://andrewjwilt.com/blog.

Finally, let me leave you with the words of one of my favorite writers: I wish you way more than luck.

Take care & talk soon,

Andrew J. Wilt

SUGGESTED READING & LISTENING

BOOKS

<u>Business</u>

TED Talks: The Official TED Guide to Public Speaking, by Chris Anderson

The 4-Hour Workweek, by Timothy Ferriss

Blink, by Malcolm Gladwell

David and Goliath, by Malcolm Gladwell

The Tipping Point, by Malcolm Gladwell

What the Dog Saw, by Malcolm Gladwell

Tribes, by Seth Godin

The $100 Startup, by Chris Guillebeau

Side Hustle, by Chris Guillebeau

Outwitting the Devil, by Napoleon Hill

Think and Grow Rich, by Napoleon Hill

Blue Ocean Strategy, by W. Chan Kim and Renee Mauborgne

The Phoenix Project, by Gene Kim, Kevin Behr, and George Spafford

Business Model Generation, by Alexander Osterwalder and Yves Pigneur

To Sell Is Human, by Daniel H. Pink

Practical Genius, by Gina Amaro Rudan

The Fifth Discipline, by Peter M. Senge

Start with Why, by Simon Sinek

Scrum, by Jeff Sutherland
Networking Is a Contact Sport, by Joe Sweeney
Hit Makers, by Derek Thompson

Career
The New Rules of Work, by Alexandra Cavoulacos and Kathryn Minshew
Mastery, by Robert Greene
The Dip by Seth Godin
Business Model You, by Alexander Osterwalder, Tim Clark, and Yves Pigneur
The Element, by Ken Robinson
Getting There, by Gillian Zoe Segal

Change
Transitions, by William Bridges
Switch, by Chip Heath and Dan Heath
Change Anything, by Kerry Patterson, Joseph Grenny, David Maxfield, Ron McMillan, and Al Switzler

Communication
If I Understood You, Would I Have This Look on My Face?, by Alan Alda
The Lost Art of Listening, by Michael P. Nichols
Getting to Yes, by Roger Fisher and William Ury

Emotional Intelligence
Emotional Intelligence 2.0, by Travis Bradberry
Emotional Intelligence, by Daniel Goleman

Gamification
Level Up Your Life, by Steve Kamb
Reality is Broken, by Jane McGonigal
SuperBetter, by Jane McGonigal

Health
Head Strong, by Dave Asprey
The 4-Hour Body, by Timothy Ferriss
In Defense of Food, by Michael Pollan
The Omnivore's Dilemma, by Michael Pollan
The Dorito Effect, by Mark Schatzker
Anticancer, by David Servan-Schreiber
Sleep Smarter, by Shawn Stevenson
Good Calories, Bad Calories, by Gary Taubes

The Sleep Solution, by W. Chris Winter, MD

Mindfulness
The Miracle of Mindfulness, by Thich Nhat Hanh
Waking up, by Sam Harris (note: this is a book for the nonreligious-nonspiritual)
Wherever You Go, There You Are, by Jon Kabat-Zinn
Catching the Big Fish, by David Lynch
Mindfulness at Work, by Stephen McKenzie
The Buddha Walks into a Bar, by Lodro Rinzler

Money
Dave Ramsey's Complete Guide to Money, by Dave Ramsey
The Millionaire Next Door, by Thomas J. Stanley and William D. Danko
The Millionaire Mind, Thomas J. Stanley

Motivation
The Willpower Instinct, by Kelly Mcgonigal
Essentialism, by Greg McKeown
Drive, by Daniel H. Pink
Do the Work, by Steven Pressfield
Turning Pro, by Steven Pressfield
The War of Art, by Steven Pressfield
Willpower, by John Tierney and Roy Baumeister

Neuro-Linguistic Programming
NLP: The Essential Guide to Neuro-Linguistic Programming, by Susan Sanders, Tom Dotz, and Tom Hoobyar
NLP: principles in practice, by Lisa Wake

Philosophy of Living
The Consolations of Philosophy, by Alain de Botton
The Pleasures of Sorrows of Work, by Alain de Botton
Status Anxiety, by Alain de Botton
Daily Rituals, by Mason Currey
The Art of Living, by Epictetus
Man's Search for Meaning, by Viktor E. Frankl
The Autobiography of Benjamin Franklin, by Benjamin Franklin
The Icarus Deception, by Seth Godin
Mastery, by George Leonard
The Subtle Art of Not Giving a F*ck, by Mark Manson
Five Dialogues: Euthyphro, Apology, Crito, Meno, Phaedo, by Plato

The Four Agreements, by Don Miguel Ruiz
The Death of Ivan Ilyich and *Confession,* by Leo Tolstoy
The Book, by Alan Watts
The Wisdom of Insecurity, by Alan Watts

Practice
Talent is Overrated, by Geoff Colvin
The Little Book of Talent, by Daniel Coyle
The Talent Code, by Daniel Coyle
Outliers, by Malcolm Gladwell
Steal Like an Artist, by Austin Kleon
Bounce, by Matthew Syed

Psychology
Grit, by Angela Duckworth
The Power of Habit, by Charles Duhigg
Mindset, by Carol S. Dweck
Moonwalking with Einstein, by Joshua Foer
A Whole New Mind, by Daniel H. Pink
Why We Work, by Barry Schwartz
The Happiness Track, by Emma Seppala

Writing
Writing Down the Bones, by Natalie Goldberg
Bird by Bird, by Anne Lamott
On Writing, by Stephen King
The Elements of Style, Fourth Edition, by William Strunk Jr. and E.B. White

BLOGS

Dave Asprey blog.bulletproof.com/
Leo Babauta: zenhabits.net/
Tim Ferriss: tim.blog/
Seth Godin: sethgodin.typepad.com/
Chris Guillebeau: chrisguillebeau.com/
Lara Callender Hogan: larahogan.me/blog/
Steve Kamb (Nerd Fitness): nerdfitness.com/
Mark Manson: markmanson.net/archive
The Muse: themuse.com/advice
Paula Pant: affordanything.com/blog/
Gary Vaynerchuk: garyvaynerchuk.com/blog/
My blog: ageofagility.com/blog

PODCASTS

The James Altucher Show: jamesaltucher.com/category/the-james-altucher-show/

Melissa Ambrosini: melissaambrosini.com/podcast/

Dave Asprey's Bulletproof Radio: blog.bulletproof.com/bulletproof-radio-episodes-directory/

Lisa Chow's StartUp: gimletmedia.com/startup/

The Tim Ferriss Show: tim.blog/podcast/

Freakonomics Radio: freakonomics.com/archive/

Chris Guillebeau's Side Hustle: sidehustleschool.com/podcasts/

10% Happier with Dan Harris: tunein.com/radio/10-Happier-with-Dan-Harris-p860860/

John Henry's Open for Business: creative.gimletmedia.com/shows/open-for-business/

Marketplace: marketplace.org/

Ana Melikian's Mindset Zone: anamelikian.com/mindsetzone/

NPR's How I Built This: npr.org/podcasts/510313/how-i-built-this

NPR's Modern Love: npr.org/podcasts/469516571/modern-love

NPR's Planet Money: npr.org/planetmoney

NPR's TED Radio Hour: npr.org/programs/ted-radio-hour/

Optimal Finance Daily: optimallivingdaily.com/category/optimalfinancedaily/

Optimal Health Daily: optimallivingdaily.com/category/optimalhealthdaily/

Optimal Living Daily: optimallivingdaily.com/category/optimallivingdaily/

Optimal Relationships Daily: optimallivingdaily.com/category/optimal-living-daily-relationships/

Optimal StartUp Daily: optimallivingdaily.com/category/optimalstartupdaily/

The Pitch: gimletmedia.com/thepitch/

Success: success.com/podcasts

TEDTalks Business: player.fm/series/tedtalks-business

Lea Thau's Strangers: storycentral.org/strangers/

Emily Thompson & Kathleen Shannon's Being Boss: beingboss.club/category/podcast/full-episodes

On Being with Krista Tippett: onbeing.org/

Benjamen Walker's Theory of Everything: toe.prx.org

Robert Wright's Meaning of Life: meaningoflife.tv/

NOTES & REFERENCES

INTRODUCTION

The Age of Agility

Lifelong careers are something of the past

Card, J. (2017, March 30). Douglas Coupland: 'The nine to five is barbaric' Retrieved June 10, 2017, from https://www.theguardian.com/small-business-network/2017/mar/30/douglas-coupland-the-nine-to-five-is-barbaric

Cavoulacos, A., & Minshew, K. (2017). *The new rules of work: the modern playbook for navigating your career.* New York: Crown Business.

U.S. Bureau of Labor and Statistics: Employee Tenure Summary. (2016, September 22). Retrieved June 10, 2017, from https://www.bls.gov/news .release/tenure.nr0.htm

Thomas Frey

Frey, T. (2011, November 11). 55 Jobs of the Future. Retrieved June 10, 2017, from http://www.futuristspeaker.com/business-trends/55-jobs-of-the-future/

Tweet quoted from @ThomasFrey, 9:30AM - 11 Nov 2011

Journal

Why? What's the Point?

Wright, R. (1995). *The moral animal: evolutionary Psychology and everyday life.* New

York, NY: Vintage Books.

I first learned of Darwin's use of notebooks and journals in the book, *The Moral Animal*, by Robert Wright. I continued researching and found an excellent article published in *BioScience* in 2009. Below is the citation and a short excerpt of my findings.

Costa, J. T. (2009). The Darwinian Revelation: Tracing the Origin and Evolution of an Idea. *BioScience,59*(10), 886-894. doi:10.1525/bio.2009.59.10 .10

Darwin reopened the notebook he was working on during the last leg of the *Beagle* voyage (his "Red Notebook") soon after hearing Lyell's presidential address in mid-February 1837 (Sulloway 1982b). His first evolutionary musings in this notebook, probably dating to the time of his meeting with Gould in March 1837, pertain to how species might change, ... By that summer, Darwin opened a new notebook dedicated to transmutation, designated his "B Notebook".

Darwin first published his theory in 1959—more than 20 years after first writing about it.

What Should You Write?

Gilbert, E. (2016). *Big Magic*. Penguin USA.

In-text quote and related information can be found in Elizabeth Gilbert's book, *Big Magic*.

PART 1: LAYING A FOUNDATION

Change

The Internal Battle

P., Woodruff, P., & Nehamas, A. (1995). *Phaedrus*. Indianapolis: Hackett.
The idea for the flying horses and charioteer come directly from *Phaedrus* by Plato.

How Does Change Work

Heath, C., & Heath, D. (2010). *Switch: how to change things when change is hard*. New York: Broadway Books.

This section was inspired by *Switch* by Chip and Dan Heath. They use a similar metaphor in their book: the elephant and rider, which is a play on Socrates and Plato's horse and chariot. In addition, the see, feel, change, description of the change process I write about is also in *Switch* and it is the very same one used in NLP, however, it may be coincidence since they never acknowledge NLP in any of their work. NLP is often used in business, but rarely spoken of. If the strategy is spoken about, many choose to call it by a different name.

Hoobyar, T., Dotz, T., & Sanders, S. (2013). *NLP: the essential guide to neuro-linguistic programming*. New York: William Morrow.

I described the change process using The Structure of Experience on page. This is a common description of change in NLP, and the authors do a great job explaining it.

Change

Change your environment: Wansink, B. (2006). *Mindless eating: why we eat more than we think*. New York: Bantam Books.

Talent

Muggsy Bogues

About Me – The Official Site of Muggsy Bogues. (n.d.). Retrieved March 30, 2017, from http://www.muggsybogues.com/about-me/

Hajek, D. (2014, October 25). No Small Feat: The NBA's Shortest Player Never Gave Up. Retrieved March 30, 2017, from http://www.npr.org/2014/10/25/358358540/the-nbas-shortest-player-never-gave-up

Peralta, K. (2016, April 23). How being an underdog drove ex-Hornet Muggsy Bogues to succeed. Retrieved March 30, 2017, from http://www.charlotteobserver.com/news/business/article97442447.html

Nurture vs. Nature

Sincero , S. (n.d.). Nature and Nurture Debate. Retrieved March 30, 2017, from https://explorable.com/nature-vs-nurture-debate

Mindset

Coyle, D. (2009). *The talent code: greatest isn't born, it's grown, here's how*. New York: Bantam Books.

Dweck, C. S. (2008). *Mindset: the new psychology of success:*. New York: Ballantine Books.

Failure

Your Network is a Safety Net

Hill, N. (1999). *Think and grow rich*. No. Hollywood, CA: Wilshire Book Co.

Emotional Resilience

Emotional Resilience. Illinois Math and Science Academy. (n.d.). Retrieved April 4, 2017, from https://www.imsa.edu/sites/default/files/upload/emotional%20resilience_0.pdf

There are a lot of great resources for emotional resilience. My definition comes from a resource put together by the Illinois Math and Science Academy.

Botton, A. D. (2001). *The consolations of philosophy*. New York: Vintage Books.

The idea behind "emotional resilience and beliefs" & "changing a belief will remove a roadblock." comes from Seneca the Elder, who said that we respond to a set of ideas based on reasoning. Essentially, if we are responding poorly, our reasoning is poor. Here is a description of the theory in Alain de Botton's *The Consolations of Philosophy*.

P; 82-83: Reason does not always govern our actions, he conceded: if we are sprinkled with cold water, our body gives us no choice but to shiver; if fingers are flicked over our eyes, we have to blink. But anger does not belong in the category of involuntary physical movement, it can only break out on the back of certain rationally held ideas; if we can only change the ideas, we will change our propensity to anger. ... How badly we react to frustration is critically determined by what we think of as normal. We may be frustrated that it is raining, but our familiarity with showers means we are unlikely ever to respond to one with anger. Our frustrations are tempered by what we understand we can expect from the world, by our experience of what it is normal to hope for. We aren't overwhelmed by anger whenever we are denied an object we desire, only when we believe ourselves entitled to obtain it. Our greatest furies spring from events which violate our sense of the ground rules of existence.

P. 100: It's tempting when we are hurt, to believe that the thing which hurt us intended to do so.

Vielife. (n.d.). *Emotional Resilience and Productivity of the Working Age Population*. Business Action on Health. Business in the Community. Retrieved April 4, 2017, from http://www.bitc.org.uk/sites/default/files/emotional_resilience_and_productivity.pdf

Information about how emotional resilience affects your career comes from the UK-based Health Risk Assessment and research company Vielife.

Practice Failing

Shontell, A. (2014, August 10). *Why Everyone Should Purposely Sit In The Wrong Seat On An Airplane At Least Once*. Retrieved April 04, 2017, from http://www.businessinsider.com/noah-kagans-coffee-challenge-helps-you-get-over-fear-2014-8/

This is an article about the challenge in business insider. The original Noah Kagan Coffee Challenge video can be viewed here: https://www.youtube.com/watch?v=_9PdepKEG6c

Learning Styles

E., & Verwey, S. (n.d.). The VARK Modalities. Retrieved April 04, 2017, from http://vark-learn.com/introduction-to-vark/the-vark-modalities/

This is a description of the VARK Model.

Learning Zone

The Learning Zone Model. (n.d.). Retrieved April 04, 2017, from http://www.thempra.org.uk/social-pedagogy/key-concepts-in-social-peda gogy/the-learning-zone-model/

Watling, S. (2016, February 26). Posts about Senninger's Learning Zone Model on digital academic. Retrieved April 04, 2017, from https://digitalacademicblog.wordpress.com/tag/senningers-learning-zone-mode

I have two unconventional sources in this section. Let me explain.

Hugh MacLeod's book *The Art of Not Sucking*, is not for sale, yet. I read a draft of it in 2013 when he released it on his website at this URL https://www.gapingvoid.com/blog/2013/02/21/notsuck/. The quote I referenced is in the introduction (still at this URL) but the good stuff is out of print. Hopefully he publishes it in full, soon. You can still read a portion of the book here: https://gapingvoid.pressbooks.com/chapter /part-one/

Andy Catlin taught me about the learning zone and panic zone during one of our weekly coffee mentoring sessions between 2009 and 2012. When I wrote this chapter, I searched for his source and these two do a good job explaining Senninger's Learning Zone Model.

WORK AND SCHOOL ARE MISSING SOMETHING

Watts, A. (1989). The book on the taboo against knowing who you are. New York, NY: Vintage Books.

Alan Watts is one of my favorite philosophers. This quote comes from page 80.

Lead or Follow

Patton

Michael. (2016, August 10). George S Patton - Leadership Profile. Retrieved April 30, 2017, from http://www.leadershipgeeks.com/george-s-patton-leadership/

Businessman and Fisherman Fable

Edberg, H. (n.d.). The Story of the Mexican Fisherman. Retrieved April 04, 2017, from http://www.positivityblog.com/the-story-of-the-mexican-fisherman/

Like all fables, this story has been told and retold so many times it's hard to decipher the origin. In the text I reference above, the author suggests that Heinrich Böll was probably the first person to bring the story to modern Western culture (adding his own personal touch). Where Böll first heard the story requires more digging. My best guess is that it is an Eastern fable because it resembles stories in Eastern philosophy, specifically Buddhist fables (others have also come to this same conclusion). Paulo Coelho, international best-selling author of *The Alchemist* (as well as many others) believes it to be a Brazilian story, but this is likely because he is Brazilian and he first heard the fable in his native land. Coelho's version of the story is cited below.

Coelho, P. (2015, September 04). 1 MIN READING: The fisherman and the businessman. Retrieved April 04, 2017, from http://paulocoelho blog.com/2015/09/04/the-fisherman-and-the-businessman/

Career Goals

Finding Your Passion

This section was inspired by conversations I had with Andy Ruth during my apprenticeship at Sustainable Evolution Inc.

Visualize Your Future

This section was inspired by conversations I had with Jason Benchimol at the University of Washington.

Tolstoy, L., Carson, P., & Beard, M. (2015). The death of Ivan Ilyich and Confession. New York: Liveright Publishing Corporation.

The deathbed reflection example was inspired by *The Death of Ivan Ilyich* and Leo Tolstoy's commentary on life, living, and death, in his essay *Confession*.

Make Two Lists

Rudan, G. (2011). *Practical genius: the real smarts you need to get your talents and passion working for you.* New York: Simon & Schuster.

This section was inspired by a conversation with Andy Ruth about the book *Practical Genius* by Gina Amaro Rudan. On page 25, she writes about your "other G spot."

Light/Heavy Test

Richard Webb taught me the light/heavy test over coffee at SoulFood Books in the summer of 2012.

What We Talk About When We Talk About Goals

Two Data Points

Beaton, C. (2016, March 29). Never Good Enough: Why Millennials Are Obsessed With Self-Improvement. Retrieved April 06, 2017, from https://www.forbes.com/sites/carolinebeaton/2016/02/25/never-good-enough-why-millennials-are-obsessed-with-self-improvement/#6d2bd3587efa

Mulvey, K. (2017, January 03). 80% of New Year's resolutions fail by February - here's how to keep yours. Retrieved April 06, 2017, from http://www.businessinsider.com/new-years-resolutions-courses-2016-12

Neuro-Linguistic Programming

Smith, R. (n.d.). Nlp (neuro-linguistic programming). Retrieved April 06, 2017, from http://www.businessballs.com/nlpneuro-linguistic programming.htm

Definitions

I chose these definitions based on their simplicity and readability.

Neuro. (n.d.). *Dictionary.com Unabridged.* Retrieved April 6, 2017 from Dictionary.com website http://www.dictionary.com/browse/neuro

Linguistics. (n.d.). *Dictionary.com Unabridged.* Retrieved April 6, 2017 from Dictionary.com website http://www.dictionary.com/browse/linguistics

Programming. (n.d.). *Dictionary.com Unabridged.* Retrieved April 6, 2017 from Dictionary.com website http://www.dictionary.com/browse /programming

Science and study of NLP

Wake, L. (2010). *NLP: principles in practice.* Ecademy Press.

Hoobyar, T., Dotz, T., & Sanders, S. (2013). NLP: the essential guide to neuro-linguistic programming. New York: William Morrow.

Language in action example #2

When you're watching a movie, you know when something is about to jump out at you if the music causes the hair on the back of your neck to rise. In language, word choice is the same music that taps your nerve. Here's my second example—some readers might find it a little graphic. Only read if you are ok with being a little grossed out.

Megan creaks open the oven and grabs a pot holder from the drawer. The pie is nearly finished. The recipe is a tart cherry pie she found between two pages in her grandmother's journal. Steam rises steadily out of the crust where she had cut lines to vent the hot air. She lifts the pie out of the oven and places it on a rack on top of the stove top.

Inside the oven, the pie left a noticeable discharge. Cherry chunks cling to the bottom in a stringy mess, like smeared curds left on a hospital floor by a vomiting fetus. In the heat, the liquid pie phlegm continues to fester. It gurgles, popping and snapping into the air, and begins to smoke. As the oven cools, the sticky mess falls back onto itself and yawns open into a doughy bubble. Like a healing scab, there is a distinct smell and the feeling of wanting to be scratched. A small pin-prick of a hole tears opens, defusing its insides. A steady stream of milky cherry puss begins oozing over the crusty burnt crumbs.

Positive Outcome Strategy

Hill, N. (1999). *Think and grow rich*. No. Hollywood, CA: Wilshire Book Co.

> This strategy was pieced together using the NLP theory in the texts already cited in this chapter combined with Napoleon Hill's intention setting theories in *Think and Grow Rich*.

Accomplishing Your Goals

Set a Deadline

Parkinson's law: Parkinson's Law. (1955, November 19). Retrieved April 06, 2017, from http://www.economist.com/node/14116121

Hofstadter, D. R. (1980). *Godel, Escher, Bach: an eternal golden braid*. Harmondsworth: Penguin. P. 160.

Set a Strategy

Sutherland, J. (2014). *Scrum: the art of doing twice the work in half the time*. New York: Crown Business.

Set an Intention

Intention setting and the six steps are both found in *Think and Grow Rich* by Napoleon Hill.

Hill, N. (1999). *Think and grow rich*. No. Hollywood, CA: Wilshire Book Co.

Motivation

Machiavelli, N., & Thompson, N. H. (1992). *The prince*. New York. N.Y.: Dover. P. 43

Microsoft

Auerbach, D. (2013, August 26). A Firsthand Account of Microsoft's Employee-Ranking System. Retrieved April 17, 2017, from http://www.slate.com/articles/business/moneybox/2013/08/microsoft_ceo_steve_ballmer_retires_a_firsthand_account_of_the_company_s.html

Bort, J. (2012, May 23). Microsoft Is Filled With Abusive Managers And Overworked Employees, Says Tell-All Book. Retrieved April 30, 2017, from http://www.businessinsider.com/microsoft-is-filled-with-abusive-managers-and-overworked-employees-says-tell-all-book-2012-5

Bort, J. (2014, August 27). This Is Why Some Microsoft Employees Still Fear The Controversial 'Stack Ranking' Employee Review System. Retrieved April 19, 2017, from http://www.businessinsider.com/microsofts-old-employee-review-system-2014-8

Eichenwald, K. (2015, January 29). How Microsoft Lost Its Mojo: Steve Ballmer and Corporate America's Most Spectacular Decline. Retrieved April 17, 2017, from http://www.vanityfair.com/news/business/2012/08/Microsoft-lost-mojo-steve-ballmer

Kwoh, L. (2012, January 31). 'Rank and Yank' Retains Vocal Fans. Retrieved April 17, 2017, from https://www.wsj.com/articles/SB1000142405297020 3363504577186970064375222

Nisen, M. (2015, September 17). A lawsuit claims Microsoft's infamous stack rankings made things worse for women. Retrieved April 17, 2017, from https://qz.com/504507/a-lawsuit-claims-microsofts-infamous-stack-rankings-made-things-worse-for-women/

Pepitone, J. (2013, November 13). Microsoft axes controversial employee-ranking system. Retrieved April 17, 2017, from http://money.cnn.com /2013/11/13/technology/enterprise/microsoft-stack-ranking/

Pareto Principle

Chapman, A. (n.d.). Pareto's principle. Retrieved April 17, 2017, from http://www.businessballs.com/pareto-principle-80-20-rule.htm

Simon, K. (n.d.). Pareto Principle (80/20 Rule). Retrieved April 19, 2017, from https://www.isixsigma.com/tools-templates/pareto/pareto-principle-8020-rule/

Problems with stack ranking

McGregor, J. (2013, November 20). For whom the bell curve tolls. Retrieved April 17, 2017, from https://www.washingtonpost.com/news /on-leadership/wp/2013/11/20/for-whom-the-bell-curve-tolls/

3M

Goetz, K. (2011, February 01). How 3M Gave Everyone Days Off and Created an Innovation Dynamo. Retrieved April 19, 2017, from https://www.fastcodesign.com/1663137/how-3m-gave-everyone-days-off-and-created-an-innovation-dynamo

Srinivas, V. G. (2014, August 07). The Innovation Mindset in Action: 3M Corporation. Retrieved April 18, 2017, from https://hbr.org/2013/08/the-innovation-mindset-in-acti-3

Google

Mediratta, B. (2007, October 20). The Google Way: Give Engineers Room. Retrieved April 17, 2017, from http://www.nytimes.com/2007/10/21/jobs/21pre.html

Tate, R. (2013, August 21). Google Couldn't Kill 20 Percent Time Even if It Wanted To. Retrieved April 18, 2017, from https://www.wired.com/2013/08/20-percent-time-will-never-die/

Definitions

Definitions for extrinsic motivation and intrinsic motivation from businessdictionary.com

Extrinsic Motivation (n.d.) *BusinessDictionary*. In BusinessDictionary. Retrieved April 6, 2017, from http://www.businessdictionary.com/definition/extrinsic-motivation.html

Intrinsic Motivation. (n.d.) *BusinessDictionary*. In BusinessDictionary. Retrieved April 6, 2017, from http://www.businessdictionary.com/definition/intrinsic-motivation.html

Sources that inspired the chapter

Robinson, K., & Aronica, L. (2009). *The element: how finding your passion changes everything*. New York: Penguin Books.

Pink, D. H. (2012). *Drive: the surprising truth about what motivates us*. New York: Riverhead Books.

Time Management

Strategies in this section came from trial and error while I was in the Sustainable Evolution Inc. Apprenticeship Program.

Self-Management

O. Henry

Current-Garcia, Eugene (1993). *O. Henry: A Study of the Short Fiction*. New York, New York: Twayne Publishers, Macmillan Publishing Co. p. 123.

Miller, J. J. (2010, June 08). His Writers' Workshop? A Prison Cell. Retrieved April 11, 2017, from https://www.wsj.com/articles/SB10001424052748704852004575258824174766374

2-hour days

Ferriss, T. (2007). *The 4-hour workweek: escape 9-5, live anywhere, and join the new rich*. New York, NY: Crown.

Reduced hour days and the recovering in the hospital comes from Timothy Ferriss in the above citation.

Wikipedia example: O. Henry, Banana Republic

Banana republic. (2017, March 25). Retrieved April 11, 2017, from https://en.wikipedia.org/wiki/Banana_republic

> I think Wikipedia is a great source and it has been shown to be the most accurate online encyclopedia. Many scholars, however, don't agree. That's why this citation is only used in the Banana Republic joke.

Do not take anyone's monkey

Wass, W. O., & McCarthy, T. S. (1999, Nov. & dec.). *Management Time: Who's Got the Monkey?* Retrieved April 11, 2017, from https://hbr.org/1999/11/management-time-whos-got-the-monkey

Getting Started

Try a different format

Rohde, M. (2013). *The sketchnote handbook: the illustrated guide to visual note taking.* Berkeley, CA: Peachpit Press.

Play a game

McGonigal, J. (2012). *Reality is Broken: Why Games Make Us Better and How They Can Change the World.* London: Vintage.

Shower shock

Michelson, M. (2012, June 06). The Cold-Shower Performance Enhancer. Retrieved April 23, 2017, from http://www.mensjournal.com/health-fitness/exercise/the-cold-shower-performance-enhancer-20120606

Do a SFD

Lamott, A. (1997). *Bird by Bird.* New York: Anchor Books.

> View PDF of the SFD chapter here: https://wrd.as.uky.edu/sites/default/files/1Shitty%20First%20Drafts.pdf

Smile

Strack, Fritz; Martin, Leonard L.; Stepper, Sabine *Journal of Personality and Social Psychology*, Vol 54(5), May 1988, 768-777. http://dx.doi.org/10.1037/0022-3514.54.5.768

> Inhibiting and facilitating conditions of the human smile: A nonobtrusive test of the facial feedback hypothesis.

Get a little zen

76 Scientific Benefits of Meditation. (2017, April 14). Retrieved April 23, 2017, from http://liveanddare.com/benefits-of-meditation-2/

Pick your posture

5 famous writers who stood while they worked. (2011, May 27). Retrieved April 11, 2017, from https://www.prdaily.com/Main/Articles/5_famous_writers_who_stood_while_they_worked_8390.aspx

Brunner, B. (2014, January 07). 7 Famous Authors Who Wrote Lying Down. Retrieved April 11, 2017, from http://www.huffingtonpost.com/bernd-brunner/famous-author-who-wrote-l_b_4555808.html

Building Relationships

Tickle-Degnen, L., & Rosenthal, R. (1990). The Nature of Rapport and Its Nonverbal Correlates. *Psychological Inquiry*, 1(4), 285-293. Retrieved from http://www.jstor.org/stable/1449345

Emotional Intelligence

Joel Pumper's story is used with permission. Information was gathered in interviews in March, 2017. Content and quotes have been verified and approved by Joel.

Kessler, G. (2014, January 27). Do nine out of 10 new businesses fail, as Rand Paul claims? Retrieved May 01, 2017, from https://www.washingtonpost.com/news/fact-checker/wp/2014/01/27/do-9-out-of-10-new-businesses-fail-as-rand-paul-claims/

After four years, about 50% of businesses are still open

What Is Intelligence?

Csikszentmihalyi, M. (2009). *Flow: the psychology of optimal experience.* New York: Harper Perennial Modern Classics.

McKinlay, G. (2017, April 13). IQ Test: Where Does It Come From and What Does It Measure? Retrieved May 01, 2017, from https://edubloxtutor.com/history-iq-test/

Robinson, K., & Aronica, L. (2009). *The element: how finding your passion changes everything.* New York: Penguin Books. P. 37-39

Shenk, D. (2010, February 01). What Is "Smart?". Retrieved May 01, 2017, from https://www.theatlantic.com/national/archive/2010/02/what-is-smart/35106/

Emotional intelligence content

Bradberry, T., Greaves, J., & Lencioni, P. (2009). *Emotional intelligence 2.0: the world's most popular emotional intelligence test.* San Diego (California): TalentSmart.

Emotional Intelligence. Goleman, D. (1995). *Emotional intelligence: Why it can matter more than IQ.* New York: Bantam Books.

Lucas, S. (2017, February 22). Why EQ Could Be More Important Than IQ.

Retrieved May 01, 2017, from https://www.business.com/articles/why-eq-could-be-more-important-than-iq/

Salovey, P., & Sluyter, D. J. (2001). *Emotional development and emotional intelligence: educational implications.* New York: BasicBooks.

Remembering Names

Cohen, G. and Faulkner, D. (1986), Memory for proper names: Age differences in retrieval. *British Journal of Developmental Psychology,* 4: 187–197. doi:10.1111/j.2044-835X.1986.tb01010.x

Foer, J. (2011). *Moonwalking with Einstein: a journey through memory and the mind.* London: Allen Lane.

How to Avoid Miss. Communication

Sheffert, M. (2001, April). Ventures. Poor Communication Can Cost You. Retrieved May 04, 2017, from http://www.manchestercompanies.com/news_views/Manchester-April2001.htm

Listening & Being Heard

Keysar, B., & Henly, A. (2002). Speakers' Overestimation of Their Effectiveness. *Psychological Science, 13*(3), 207-212. Retrieved from http://www.jstor.org/stable/40063708

Schonwlad, J. (2002, May 09). Researchers show people overestimate ability to effectively communicate ambiguous information. Retrieved May 07, 2017, from http://chronicle.uchicago.edu/020509/keysarresearch.shtml

Being understood

Nichols, M. P. (2009). *The lost art of listening: how learning to listen can improve relationships.* New York: Guilford Press. P. Whole book, specifically P. 33-99

Language Patterns

Hoobyar, T., Dotz, T., & Sanders, S. (2013). *NLP: the essential guide to neuro-linguistic programming.* New York: William Morrow.

and & but

Gladwell, M. (2013). *Blink: the power of thinking without thinking.* New York: Back Bay Books.

Lisitsa, E. (2017, February 09). The Four Horsemen: Criticism, Contempt, Defensiveness, and Stonewalling. Retrieved May 07, 2017, from https://www.gottman.com/blog/the-four-horsemen-recognizing-criticism-contempt-defensiveness-and-stonewalling/

We Are Still Children…Kind of…

Botton, A. D. (2016). *The course of love: a novel.* New York, NY: Simon &

Schuster.

Nichols, M. P. (2009). *The lost art of listening: how learning to listen can improve relationships.* New York: Guilford Press.

Whole book, specifically P. 114

Listen First, And Maybe Only Listen

Nichols, M. P. (2009). *The lost art of listening: how learning to listen can improve relationships.* New York: Guilford Press.

Body Language

Yaffe, P. (2011). The 7% rule. *Ubiquity,* 2011(October), 1-5. doi:10.1145/2043155.2043156

> The above citation is one study discussing the 7% rule. It discusses the 1971 book *Silent Messages* by Albert Mehrabian. In the book, Mehrabian studied salespeople and argues that 55% of their communication came from body language and 38% came from the tone and music of their voice, leaving only 7% to the actual words.

Eastman, B. (n.d.). How much of communication is really nonverbal? Retrieved May 09, 2017, from http://www.nonverbalgroup.com/2011/08/how-much-of-communication-is-really-nonverbal

> The 60-90% number is in the data discussed in the first citation and is confirmed by the Nonverbal Group. Scholars still debate what the exact percentage is—if you read the first book on my Suggested Reading & Listening page, *TED Talks: The Official TED Guide to Public Speaking,* by Chris Anderson, he will give you a different critique of the study—despite the debate, all sides agree that nonverbal communication is as important as the words being spoken (if not more).

Thinking with Your Body & Eye Movement

Knight, S. (2010). *NLP at Work: The Essence of Excellence (People skills for professionals).* Nicholas Brealey Publishing.

Information in these sections come from Chapter 4.

Mirroring

Hoobyar, T., Dotz, T., & Sanders, S. (2013). *NLP: the essential guide to neuro-linguistic programming.* New York: William Morrow.

Young, P. (2004). *Understanding NLP: principles and practice.* Carmarthen: Crown House.

Meta-mirroring is explained in Chapter 12.

PART 2: BUILDING STRUCTURE

Introduction to the Dock

Robert Standefer taught me how to prioritize my life. Thanks Rob. I still haven't read *The Stranger* by Albert Camus in French. It's currently not a priority to learn French just so I can experience his beautiful prose in the language it was written in. For now, I'll stick to the less-beautiful English translation. Gotta love those opening lines, though: Aujourd'hui, maman est morte. Ou peut-être hier, je ne sais pas.

Image: Maslows Hierarchy of Needs from Wikimedia Commons, the free media repository. https://commons.wikimedia.org/wiki/File:Maslows HierarchyOfNeeds.svg

Health

Sleep

People who prioritize sleep

Hall, A. (2014, April 28). 14 Highly Successful People Who Prioritize A Good Night's Sleep. Retrieved July 19, 2017, from http://www.huffington post.com/2014/04/28/successful-people-who-sle_n_5201290.html
Dalai Lama: ch. 43: sleep, "…getting a full night's sleep will make your 'daytime calm, relaxed."

Hersey, B. (2014). The practice of nada yoga: meditation on the inner sacred sound. Rochester, VT: Inner Traditions.

Arianna Huffington: Huffington, A. S. (2016). The sleep revolution: transforming your life, one night at a time. New York: Harmony.

Ellen Degeneres: The Importance of a Good Night's Sleep on Ellen Show. (2014, April 25). Retrieved July 20, 2017, from https://www.youtube.com /watch?v=TGLDaHMZ2As

Bill Gates: Zetlin, M. (n.d.). 8 Highly Effective Habits That Helped Make Bill Gates the Richest Man on Earth. Retrieved July 20, 2017, from https://www.region10.org/r10website/assets/File/8%20Highly%20Effecti ve%20Habits%20That%20Helped%20Make%20Bill%20Gates%20the%20 Richest%20Man%20on%20Earth.pdf

Warren Buffett: Huffington, A. S. (2016). The sleep revolution: transforming your life, one night at a time. New York: Harmony.

Buffet said: "When forced to choose, I will not trade even a night's sleep for the chance of extra profits." From a 2008 letter to shareholders of Berkshire Hathaway p. 243.

Sleep seven hours or more per night

Watson, N. F., Badr, M. S., Belenky, G., Bliwise, D. L., Buxton, O. M., Buysse, D., . . . Tasali, E. (2015). Recommended Amount of Sleep for a

Healthy Adult: A Joint Consensus Statement of the American Academy of Sleep Medicine and Sleep Research Society. *Journal of Clinical Sleep Medicine.* doi:10.5664/jcsm.4758

Cognitive Performance

Alhola, P., & Polo-Kantola, P. (2007). Sleep deprivation: Impact on cognitive performance. *Neuropsychiatric Disease and Treatment*, 3(5), 553–567.

Lots of health problems are brewing, even if you don't see it yet

Institute of Medicine (US) Committee on Sleep Medicine and Research; Colten HR, Altevogt BM, editors. *Sleep Disorders and Sleep Deprivation: An Unmet Public Health Problem.* Washington (DC): National Academies Press (US); 2006. 3, Extent and Health Consequences of Chronic Sleep Loss and Sleep Disorders. Available from: https://www.ncbi.nlm.nih.gov/books/NBK19961/

Ju, Y. S., Ooms, S. J., Sutphen, C., Macauley, S. L., Zangrilli, M. A., Jerome, G., . . . Holtzman, D. M. (2017). Slow wave sleep disruption increases cerebrospinal fluid amyloid-beta levels. *Brain.* doi:10.1093/brain/awx148

Marie , L., & Weiler, P. (2015, August 31). Short Sleepers Are Four Times More Likely to Catch a Cold. Retrieved July 22, 2017, from https://www.ucsf.edu/news/2015/08/131411/short-sleepers-are-four-times-more-likely-catch-cold

Sprecher, K. E., Koscik, R. L., Carlsson, C. M., Zetterberg, H., Blennow, K., Okonkwo, O. C., . . . Bendlin, B. B. (2017). Poor sleep is associated with CSF biomarkers of amyloid pathology in cognitively normal adults. *Neurology.* doi:10.1212/wnl.0000000000004171

Winter, W. C. (2017). *The sleep solution: why your sleep is broken and how to fix it.* New York: New American Library. P.20.

Not sleeping is the same as alcohol intoxication

Fryer, B. (2014, July 31). Sleep Deficit: The Performance Killer. Retrieved July 19, 2017, from https://hbr.org/2006/10/sleep-deficit-the-performance-killer

Williamson, A. M., & Feyer, A. M. (2000). Moderate sleep deprivation produces impairments in cognitive and motor performance equivalent to legally prescribed levels of alcohol intoxication. *Occupational and Environmental Medicine*, 57(10), 649-655. doi:10.1136/oem.57.10.649

You are sleeping, even if you are unaware of it. (microsleep)

Co-activated yet disconnected-Neural correlates of eye closures when trying to stay awake. Ju Lynn Ong, Danyang Kong, Tiffany T. Y. Chia, Jesisca Tandi, B. T. Thomas Yeo, Michael W. L. Chee *Neuroimage.* 2015 Sep; 118:

553–562. Published online 2015 May 24. doi: 10.1016/j.neuroimage.2015 .03.085

Gregoire, C. (2016, March 12). What's Happening In Your Brain During 'Microsleep'. Retrieved July 22, 2017, from http://www.huffingtonpost.com /entry/microsleep-brain-sleep-deprivation_us_56d9ed81e4b0ffe6f8e958e6

Winter, W. C. (2017). *The sleep solution: why your sleep is broken and how to fix it.* New York: New American Library. P.25.

Set a bedtime (circadian rhythm)

Aschoff, J. (1965). Circadian Rhythms in Man: A self-sustained oscillator with an inherent frequency underlies human 24-hour periodicity. *Science*, 148(3676), 1427-1432. doi:10.1126/science.148.3676.1427

See also: https://www.mpg.de/943613/S003_Flashback_060_061.pdf

Duffy, J. F., & Czeisler, C. A. (2009). Effect of Light on Human Circadian Physiology. *Sleep Medicine Clinics*, 4(2), 165–177. http://doi.org/10.1016/ j.jsmc.2009.01.004

Individual Variation and the Genetics of Sleep. (n.d.). Retrieved July 23, 2017, from http://healthysleep.med.harvard.edu/healthy/science/ variations/individual-variation-genetics

Cut out blue light before bed

Gooley, J. J., Chamberlain, K., Smith, K. A., Khalsa, S. B. S., Rajaratnam, S. M. W., Van Reen, E., ... Lockley, S. W. (2011). Exposure to Room Light before Bedtime Suppresses Melatonin Onset and Shortens Melatonin Duration in Humans. *The Journal of Clinical Endocrinology and Metabolism*, 96(3), E463–E472. http://doi.org/10.1210/jc.2010-2098

Publications, H. H. (2015, September 02). Blue light has a dark side. Retrieved July 24, 2017, from http://www.health.harvard.edu/staying-healthy/blue-light-has-a-dark-side

Robinson, M. (2015, October 30). This app has transformed my nighttime computer use. Retrieved July 24, 2017, from http://www.businessinsider. com/flux-review-2015-10

Rosen, L. (2015, August 31). Relax, Turn Off Your Phone, and Go to Sleep. Retrieved July 24, 2017, from https://hbr.org/2015/08/research-shows-how-anxiety-and-technology-are-affecting-our-sleep

Schmerler, J. (2015, September 01). Q&A: Why Is Blue Light before Bedtime Bad for Sleep? Retrieved July 24, 2017, from https://www.scient ificamerican.com/article/q-a-why-is-blue-light-before-bedtime-bad-for-sleep/

More about f.lux here: https://justgetflux.com/research.html (see also in

Part III, Workspace: Eye strain/Fatigue)

Why we like scrolling

Brookshire, B. (2013, July 03). What Is Dopamine for, Anyway? Love, Lust, Pleasure, Addiction? Retrieved July 24, 2017, from http://www.slate.com /articles/health_and_science/science/2013/07/what_is_dopamine_love_lu st_sex_addiction_gambling_motivation_reward.html

Dreifus, C. (2017, March 06). Why We Can't Look Away From Our Screens. Retrieved July 24, 2017, from https://www.nytimes.com/2017/03/ 06/science/technology-addiction-irresistible-by-adam-alter.html

McGuire, H. (2015, December 26). Why can't we read anymore? Retrieved July 24, 2017, from http://www.sfchronicle.com/business/article/Why-can-t-we-read-anymore-6720404.php?t=50fc85d59d3ac39e4f&cmpid=twit ter-premium

Weinschenk, S. (2012, September 11). Why We're All Addicted to Texts, Twitter and Google. Retrieved July 24, 2017, from https://www.psychology today.com/blog/brain-wise/201209/why-were-all-addicted-texts-twitter-and-google

Only two things in bed

"Every sleep doctor with his or her weight in foam earplugs will tell you the bed is for two things: sex and sleep." P. 114

From : Winter, W. C. (2017). *The sleep solution: why your sleep is broken and how to fix it.* New York: New American Library.

Caffeine, coffee, alcohol, nicotine

Coffee & Health. (2014, February 28). Retrieved July 17, 2017, from https://www.hsph.harvard.edu/news/multimedia-article/benefits/

This is an interactive infographic.

Drake, C., Roehrs, T., Shambroom, J., & Roth, T. (2013). Caffeine Effects on Sleep Taken 0, 3, or 6 Hours before Going to Bed. *Journal of Clinical Sleep Medicine,* 9(11). doi:10.5664/jcsm.3170

Ebrahim, I. O., Shapiro, C. M., Williams, A. J., & Fenwick, P. B. (2013). Alcohol and Sleep I: Effects on Normal Sleep. *Alcoholism: Clinical and Experimental Research,* 37(4). doi:10.1111/acer.12006

Ferré, S., & O'Brien, M. C. (2011). Alcohol and Caffeine: The Perfect Storm. *Journal of Caffeine Research,* 1(3), 153–162. http://doi.org/10.1089/jcr. 2011.0017

Urinary and Kidney Team . (2016, November 15). Adults Booze = Bedwetting? Here's Why It Happens to You. Retrieved July 25, 2017, from https://health.clevelandclinic.org/2016/11/adults-booze-bedwetting-heres-happens/

Note on coffee:

When I wrote the first and second draft of this book, I was still a tea-only guy (earl grey, baby). Right now, as I'm revising AoA for a third time, I'd like to make a confession: I've recently started drinking one cup of Bulletproof coffee in the morning. My life has gotten a little more hectic so I added an extra boost in the morning. I drink Dave Asprey's Bulletproof coffee with grass-fed butter and brain octane oil (the brain octane oil is important, even if the name sounds gimmicky). Bulletproof coffee helps me be laser-focus in the morning so I can get all my heavy lifting done. One cup. That's it. It also works great with my intermittent fasting.

You can learn more about Bulletproof coffee here: https://blog.bullet proof.com/how-to-make-your-coffee-bulletproof-and-your-morning-too/

Pro Tip: I usually don't buy directly from the Bulletproof website. The company is growing, which is great for them, but one of their growing pains is shipping and customer support. In a world where 2-day shipping is standard, I can't wait an entire week: two days processing, five days ground. Thankfully, it's Prime on Amazon, and I can get it in two hours if I really need it.

P.S. I'm not getting paid to write about the brands I like. I like Dave and a few of his products, and I'm going to keep doing what works for me and my budget. You should do the same, and that might be another product. Do what works for you, and, as always, feel free to share it with me—maybe I'll like it too!

Water/lemon water

Insider, B. (2016, September 23). Why top executives swear by a 30-second morning habit anyone can adopt. Retrieved July 25, 2017, from http://www.businessinsider.com/executives-drink-water-when-they-wake-up-2016-9

Zamon, R. (2017, January 16). Lemon Water Can Really Improve Your Morning (And Day). Retrieved July 25, 2017, from http://www.huffington post.ca/2014/03/17/lemon-water-benefits_n_4980265.html

REM

Brain Basics: Understanding Sleep. (n.d.). Retrieved July 25, 2017, from https://www.ninds.nih.gov/Disorders/Patient-Caregiver-Education/Understanding-Sleep#2

Nicotine

Winter, W. C. (2017). *The sleep solution: why your sleep is broken and how to fix it.* New York: New American Library. P.117-119.

Short mid-day naps are okay

Goleman, D. (1989, September 11). Feeling Sleepy? An Urge to Nap Is Built In. Retrieved July 26, 2017, from http://www.nytimes.com/1989/09/12/science/feeling-sleepy-an-urge-to-nap-is-built-in.html?pagewanted=all

Gregoire, C. (2013, May 28). Napping Tips: 7 Expert Strategies For Maximizing Your Naptime. Retrieved July 26, 2017, from http://www.huffingtonpost.com/2013/05/28/napping-tips-expert-strat_n_3320571.html

Lahl, O., Wispel, C., Willigens, B., & Pietrowsky, R. (2008). An ultra short episode of sleep is sufficient to promote declarative memory performance. *Journal of Sleep Research,* 17(1), 3-10. doi:10.1111/j.1365-2869.2008.00622.x

Winter, W. C. (2017). *The sleep solution: why your sleep is broken and how to fix it.* New York: New American Library, p.197-210.

Eat Food

Brody, J. E. (2010, February 01). Rules Worth Following, for Everyone's Sake. Retrieved July 27, 2017, from http://www.nytimes.com/2010/02/02/health/02brod.html

Pollan, M. (2014). *Cooked: a natural history of transformation.* New York: Penguin Books. P.164.

Pollan, M. (2009). *In defense of food: an eaters manifesto.* London: Penguin Books.

Pollan, M. (2008). *The omnivores dilemma: a natural history of four meals.* New York: Penguin Books.

Schatzker, M. (2016). *The Dorito effect: the surprising new truth about food and flavor.* New York: Simon & Schuster Paperbacks.

Cut out refined sugar and rely on complex carbohydrates, proteins, and fats as your fuel source

Carbohydrates and Blood Sugar. (2016, July 25). Retrieved August 14, 2017, from https://www.hsph.harvard.edu/nutritionsource/carbohydrates/carbohydrates-and-blood-sugar/

Leung, C. W., Laraia, B. A., Needham, B. L., Rehkopf, D. H., Adler, N. E., Lin, J., . . . Epel, E. S. (2014). Soda and Cell Aging: Associations Between Sugar-Sweetened Beverage Consumption and Leukocyte Telomere Length in Healthy Adults From the National Health and Nutrition Examination Surveys. *American Journal of Public Health,* 104(12), 2425-2431. doi:10.2105/

ajph.2014.302151

Oaklander, M. (2014, October 17). Sugar and Soda: It May Age You As Much As Smoking. Retrieved August 14, 2017, from http://time.com/3513875/soda-may-age-you-as-much-as-smoking/

Servan-Schreiber, D. (2010). *Anticancer: a new way of life.* New York: Viking.

The truth about fats: the good, the bad, and the in-between. (2015, August 07). Retrieved August 16, 2017, from https://www.health.harvard.edu/staying-healthy/the-truth-about-fats-bad-and-good

Valdes, A., Andrew, T., Gardner, J., Kimura, M., Oelsner, E., Cherkas, L., .. . Spector, T. (2005). Obesity, cigarette smoking, and telomere length in women. *The Lancet,* 366(9486), 662-664. doi:10.1016/s0140-6736(05)66630-5

Slowly decomposing bodies

Gammill, J. (2017, February 15). The bodies in the past 30 years have not been decomposing. See why and what's the problem with it... Retrieved August 13, 2017, from http://iheartintelligence.com/2015/07/02/bodies-have-not-been-decomposing/

Leidig, M. (2003, November 16). Dust to dust (but not if your dearly departed is buried in Germany). Retrieved August 13, 2017, from http://www.telegraph.co.uk/news/worldnews/europe/germany/1446872/Dust-to-dust-but-not-if-your-dearly-departed-is-buried-in-Germany.html

Slow body decomposition is a new problem, and as such, the scientific community is still investigating causes for this issue, that's why it's largely labeled as inconclusive. Those who have observed an issue in delayed decomposition cite food preservatives, cosmetics (make up, mouthwash, etc.), and environmental factors like pollution, for the abnormalities. **Many in the scientific community think this is an urban legen**d (as noted in the text) and bodies are decaying at the same rate as they always have. I included this story because I think it's a fun anecdote, regardless if it's true or not. The focus of this section is about food preservatives and their FDA approval process.

Cut out processed products

Neltner, T. G., Alger, H. M., Leonard, J. E., & Maffini, M. V. (2013). Data gaps in toxicity testing of chemicals allowed in food in the United States. *Reproductive Toxicology,* 42, 85-94. doi:10.1016/j.reprotox.2013.07.023

Ruddock, V. (n.d.). Dangers of Food Additives and Preservatives. Retrieved August 13, 2017, from http://greenliving.lovetoknow.com/dangers-food-additives-preservatives

Get your vitamins from plants, not pills

Guallar E, Stranges S, Mulrow C, Appel LJ, Miller ER. Enough Is Enough:

Stop Wasting Money on Vitamin and Mineral Supplements. *Ann Intern Med.* 2013; 159:850–851. doi: 10.7326/0003-4819-159-12-201312170-00011

Publications, H. H. (2014, March). Do multivitamins make you healthier? Retrieved August 13, 2017, from https://www.health.harvard.edu/menshealth/do-multivitamins-make-you-healthier

Avoid diets, cleanses, detoxes, and other health buzzwords

Aamodt, S. (2016). *Why Diets Make Us Fat: The Unintended Consequences of Our Obsession with Weight Loss.* Penguin Group.

Fain, J. (2016, June 07). A Neuroscientist Tackles 'Why Diets Make Us Fat'. Retrieved August 14, 2017, from http://www.npr.org/sections/thesalt/2016/06/07/481094825/a-neuroscientist-tackles-why-diets-make-us-fat

Klein, A. V., & Kiat, H. (2014). Detox diets for toxin elimination and weight management: a critical review of the evidence. *Journal of Human Nutrition and Dietetics,* 28(6), 675-686. doi:10.1111/jhn.12286

Steen, J. (2017, January 18). So, 'Detoxes' Or 'Cleanses' Don't Work. Here's Why. Retrieved August 14, 2017, from http://www.huffingtonpost.com.au/2017/01/18/so-detoxes-or-cleanses-dont-work-heres-why_a_21657800/

Know your labels

Decoding Food Labels. (2013, June 17). Retrieved August 14, 2017, from http://wtcafe.com/decoding-food-labels/

FDA Basics - What is the meaning of 'natural' on the label of food? (n.d.). Retrieved August 14, 2017, from https://www.fda.gov/aboutfda/transparency/basics/ucm214868.htm

Humane certifications. (n.d.). Retrieved August 14, 2017, from https://www.humaneitarian.org/what-is-humanely-raised-meat/humane-certifications/

Rock, A. (2016, January 29). Peeling Back the 'Natural' Food Label. Retrieved August 14, 2017, from https://www.consumerreports.org/food-safety/peeling-back-the-natural-food-label/

Tanner, K. (2011, January 21). Getting to Know Your Meat Labels. Retrieved August 14, 2017, from https://cuesa.org/article/getting-know-your-meat-labels

Buy healthy organic food

Are organic foods worth the price? (2017, April 18). Retrieved August 17, 2017, from http://www.mayoclinic.org/healthy-lifestyle/nutrition-and-healthy-eating/in-depth/organic-food/art-20043880?pg=1

Freedman, Bill. "Biomagnification." The Gale Encyclopedia of Science, edited by K. Lee Lerner and Brenda Wilmoth Lerner, 5th ed., Gale, 2014.

Science in Context, link.galegroup.com/apps/doc/CV2644030285/SCIC?
u=albertak12&xid=8bc4ff8d. Accessed 25 Aug. 2017.

Hapke, H. (1996). Heavy metal transfer in the food chain to humans.
Fertilizers and Environment, 431-436. doi:10.1007/978-94-009-1586-2_73

Proceedings of the International Symposium "Fertilizers and
Environment"

Stop grazing

Ohkawara, K., Cornier, M.-A., Kohrt, W. M., & Melanson, E. L. (2013).
Effects of Increased Meal Frequency on Fat Oxidation and Perceived
Hunger. *Obesity* (Silver Spring, Md.), 21(2), 336–343. http://doi.org/10.1002
/oby.20032

Start (intermittent) fasting

Anson, R. M., Guo, Z., de Cabo, R., Iyun, T., Rios, M., Hagepanos, A., …
Mattson, M. P. (2003). Intermittent fasting dissociates beneficial effects of
dietary restriction on glucose metabolism and neuronal resistance to injury
from calorie intake. *Proceedings of the National Academy of Sciences of the United
States of America*, 100(10), 6216–6220. http://doi.org/10.1073/pnas.10357
20100

Asprey, D. (2017, July 18). How To Kick More Ass with Bulletproof
Intermittent Fasting! Retrieved August 25, 2017, from https://blog.bullet
proof.com/bulletproof-intermittent-fasting-the-definitive-guide/#ref-4

Cameron, J. D., Cyr, M., & Doucet, É. (2009). Increased meal frequency
does not promote greater weight loss in subjects who were prescribed an 8-
week equi-energetic energy-restricted diet. *British Journal of Nutrition*, 1.
doi:10.1017/s0007114509992984

Drayer, L. (2017, February 03). Are 'food comas' real or a figment of your
digestion? Retrieved August 25, 2017, from http://www.cnn.com/2017/
02/03/health/food-comas-drayer/index.html

Fontana, L., & Partridge, L. (2015). Promoting Health and Longevity
through Diet: From Model Organisms to Humans. *Cell*, 161(1), 106-118.
doi:10.1016/j.cell.2015.02.020

Kamb, S. (2017, July 15). A Beginner's Guide to Intermittent Fasting.
Retrieved August 25, 2017, from https://www.nerdfitness.com/blog/a-
beginners-guide-to-intermittent-fasting/

Kinsey, A. W., & Ormsbee, M. J. (2015). The Health Impact of Nighttime
Eating: Old and New Perspectives. *Nutrients*, 7(4), 2648–2662.
http://doi.org/10.3390/nu7042648

Roeder, A. (2013, August 29). Skip the juice, go for whole fruit. Retrieved

August 23, 2017, from http://news.harvard.edu/gazette/story/2013/08/reduce-type-2-diabetes-risk/

Swaminathan, N. (2008, April 28). Why Does the Brain Need So Much Power? Retrieved August 23, 2017, from https://www.scientificamerican.com/article/why-does-the-brain-need-s/

Drink water.

Stone, J. (2014, June 19). How to calculate how much water you should drink. Retrieved August 14, 2017, from https://www.umsystem.edu/-calculate-how-much-water-you-should-drink/

The Powdered Life

Food in Space. (n.d.). Retrieved August 17, 2017, from https://airandspace.si.edu/exhibitions/apollo-to-the-moon/online/astronaut-life/food-in-space.cfm

National Aeronautics and Space Administration. (n.d.). Space Food and Nutrition.EG-199-02-115-HQ. https://www.nasa.gov/pdf/143163main_Space.Food.and.Nutrition.pdf/bibliographies/220069312?new=true

Matcha/green tea

Chacko, S. M., Thambi, P. T., Kuttan, R., & Nishigaki, I. (2010). Beneficial effects of green tea: A literature review. *Chinese Medicine*, 5, 13. http://doi.org/10.1186/1749-8546-5-13. https://www.ncbi.nlm.nih.gov/pmc/articles/PMC2855614/

Maca

Gonzales, G. F. (2012). Ethnobiology and Ethnopharmacology of Lepidium meyenii (Maca), a Plant from the Peruvian Highlands. *Evidence-Based Complementary and Alternative Medicine : eCAM*, 2012, 193496. http://doi.org/10.1155/2012/193496. https://www.ncbi.nlm.nih.gov/pmc/articles/PMC3184420/

Cacao

Pucciarelli, D. (2013). Cocoa and Heart Health: A Historical Review of the Science. *Nutrients*, 5(10), 3854-3870. doi:10.3390/nu5103854
Nehlig, A. (2013). The neuroprotective effects of cocoa flavanol and its influence on cognitive performance. *British Journal of Clinical Pharmacology*, 75(3), 716–727. http://doi.org/10.1111/j.1365-2125.2012.04378.x

Wheat grass, alfalfa grass, and barley grass

Gore, R. D., Palaskar, S. J., & Bartake, A. R. (2017). Wheatgrass: Green Blood can Help to Fight Cancer. *Journal of Clinical and Diagnostic Research : JCDR*, 11(6), ZC40–ZC42. http://doi.org/10.7860/JCDR/2017/26316.

10057

Mannion, C., Page, S., Bell, L. H., & Verhoef, M. (2011). Components of an Anticancer Diet: Dietary Recommendations, Restrictions and Supplements of the Bill Henderson Protocol. *Nutrients*, 3(1), 1–26. http://doi.org/10.33 90/nu3010001

Wheat grass Nutrition Facts & Calories. (n.d.). Retrieved August 25, 2017, from http://nutritiondata.self.com/facts/custom/900675/2

Chia

McDougall, C. (2011). *Born to run: a hidden tribe, superathletes, and the greatest race the world has never seen.* New York: Vintage Books. p.44

Mohd Ali, N., Yeap, S. K., Ho, W. Y., Beh, B. K., Tan, S. W., & Tan, S. G. (2012). The Promising Future of Chia, Salvia hispanica L. *Journal of Biomedicine and Biotechnology*, 2012, 171956. http://doi.org/10.1155/2012/ 171956

Moringa

Jung, I. L. (2014). Soluble Extract from Moringa oleifera Leaves with a New Anticancer Activity. *PLoS ONE*, 9(4). doi:10.1371/journal.pone.0095492

Kumar, H. D. (2004). Management of Nutritional and Health Needs of Malnourished and Vegetarian People in India. *Advances in Experimental Medicine and Biology Complementary and Alternative Approaches to Biomedicine*, 311-321. doi:10.1007/978-1-4757-4820-8_23

Mbikay, M. (2012). Therapeutic Potential of Moringa oleifera Leaves in Chronic Hyperglycemia and Dyslipidemia: A Review. *Frontiers in Pharmacology*, 3, 24. http://doi.org/10.3389/fphar.2012.00024

Change food culture

Haspel, T. (2015, December 28). 10 things we should do to fix our broken food system. Retrieved August 16, 2017, from https://www.washingtonpost .com/lifestyle/food/10-things-we-should-do-to-fix-our-broken-foodsystem /2015/12/28/ea720336-a8f7-11e5-9b92-dea7cd4b1a4d_story.html?utm_ter m=.7a9ebd26eff4Paul, E. (2016, March 23).

Millennials Have the Power to Change Our Food System-Why Aren't We? Retrieved August 16, 2017, from https://greatist.com/eat/millennials-have-the-power-to-change-food-policy

Nicholas Taleb

Taleb, N. N. (2014). *Antifragile: things that gain from disorder.* New York: Random House Trade Paperbacks.

I am citing from the text below:

I, for my part, resist eating fruits not found in the ancient Eastern Mediterranean (I use "I" here in order to show that I am not narrowly generalizing to the rest of humanity). I avoid any fruit that does not have an ancient Greek or Hebrew name, such as mangoes, papayas, even oranges. Oranges seem to be the postmedieval equivalent of candy; they did not exist in the ancient Mediterranean. Apparently, the Portuguese found a sweet citrus tree in Goa or elsewhere and started breeding it for sweeter and sweeter fruits, like a modern confectionary company. Even the apples we see in the stores are to be regarded with some suspicion: original apples were devoid of sweet taste and fruit corporations bred them for maximal sweetness—the mountain apples of my childhood were acid, bitter, crunchy, and much smaller than the shiny variety in U.S. stores said to keep the doctor away.

As to liquid, my rule is drink no liquid that is not at least a thousand years old—so its fitness has been tested. I drink just wine, water, and coffee. No soft drinks. Perhaps the most possibly deceitfully noxious drink is the orange juice we make poor innocent people imbibe at the breakfast table while, thanks to marketing, we convince them it is "healthy." (Aside from the point that the citrus our ancestors ingested was not sweet, they never ingested carbohydrates without large, very large quantities of fiber. Eating an orange or an apple is not biologically equivalent to drinking orange or apple juice.) From such examples, I derived the rule that what is called "healthy" is generally unhealthy, just as "social" networks are antisocial, and the "knowledge"-based economy is typically ignorant.

John Locke / bowel movements

Locke, J., & Grant, R. W. (1996). Some thoughts concerning education; Of the conduct of the understanding. Indianapolis (Ind.): Hackett.

Access to online text here: https://archive.org/stream/somethoughts conc00lockuoft/somethoughtsconc00lockuoft_djvu.txt and here: http:/ /oll.libertyfund.org/titles/locke-the-works-vol-8-some-thoughts-concerning-education-posthumous-works-familiar-letters

Text citation of this section:
24. It being an indisposition I had a particular reason to inquire into, and not finding the cure of it in books, I set my thoughts on work, believing that greater changes than that, might be made in our bodies, if we took the right course, and proceeded by rational steps.
1. Then I considered, that going to stool was the effect of certain motions of the body, especially of the peristaltic motion of the guts.
2. I considered, that several motions that were not perfectly voluntary, might yet, by use and constant application, be brought to be habitual, if by an unintermitted custom they were at certain seasons endeavoured to

be constantly produced.

3. I had observed some men, who, by taking after supper a pipe of tobacco, never failed of a stool; and began to doubt with myself, whether it were not more custom than the tobacco, that gave them the benefit of nature; or at least, if the tobacco did it, it was rather by exciting a vigorous motion in the guts, than [24] by any purging quality; for then it would have had other effects.

Having thus once got the opinion, that it was possible to make it habitual; the next thing was to consider, what way and means were the likeliest to obtain it.

4. Then I guessed, that if a man, after his first eating in the morning, would presently solicit nature, and try whether he could strain himself so as to obtain a stool, he might in time, by a constant application, bring it to be habitual.

25. The reasons that made me choose this time, were:

1. Because the stomach being then empty, if it received any thing grateful to it, (for I would never, but in case of necessity, have any one eat, but what he likes, and when he has an appetite,) it was apt to embrace it close by a strong constriction of its fibers; which constriction, I supposed, might probably be continued on in the guts, and so increase their peristaltic motion: as we see in the ileus, that an inverted motion being begun any-where below, continues itself all the whole length, and makes even the stomach obey that irregular motion.

2. Because when men eat, they usually relax their thoughts; and the spirits, then free from other employments, are more vigorously distributed into the lower belly, which thereby contribute to the same effect.

3. Because, whenever men have leisure to eat, they have leisure enough also to make so much court to madam Cloacina, as would be necessary to our present purpose; but else, in the variety of human affairs and accidents, it was impossible to affix it to any hour certain; whereby the custom would be interrupted: whereas men in health seldom failing to eat once a day, though the hour be changed, the custom might still be preserved.

Food for thought: whose meal plan are you more likely to trust? A Harvard MBA grad or a state school grad who has a master's in dietetics? Just because someone graduated with an advanced degree from a well-known school doesn't make them knowledgeable in every subject. For more on Ivy Leagues, education, and the fallacy of an Ivy League providing a better education than a state school, read the article, *Getting In*, by Malcolm Gladwell www.newyorker.com/magazine/2005/10/10/getting-in

Food ethics commentary, notes on human progress and future reading suggestions.

Food is no doubt a huge debate. I may have written something in the section that you disagree with, and I welcome you to share your opinion with me. I believe that one should always be open to revising their ideas, so I am open to revising my ideas if you lay out a well-structured argument backed by evidence and peer-reviewed sources. As you can probably guess, I personally avoid consuming unnecessary food additives and GMOs, though, I know many people are a big fan of both. If this is you, you are the one ultimately responsible for what is at the end of your fork, and you should eat what you think is best for your body, mind, and spirit. I have come across many people who would rather eat GMOs, factory farmed meat, and processed foods, and enjoy themselves, even if it puts them at a higher risk of life-threatening disease. If your argument for GMOs revolves around solving world hunger, consider this: According to the United Nations, it will cost about $30 Billion/year to solve world hunger. (See: http://www.nytimes.com/2008/06/04/ news/04iht-04food.13446176.html or http://articles.latimes.com/ 2008/jun/23/opinion/ed-food23). To put this in perspective, the U.S. spends $611 Billion/year on defense (http://www.pgpf.org/chart-archive/0053_defense-comparison) and U.S. citizens give more than $82.5 billion to religious organizations every year. (https://www.wash ingtonpost.com/news/wonk/wp/2013/08/22/you-give-religions -more-than-82-5-billion-a-year/?utm_term=.36e1fc3ac2c1). If the U.S. or any other developed nation wanted to end world hunger, we could with the resources we currently have available. Easy. We could end poverty. We could solve a lot of our world problems, but unfortunately, it's not a priority. Further reading: *Famine, Affluence, and Morality* by Peter Singer, Foreword by Bill and Melinda Gates.

If your argument for use of food additives and GMOs is one concerning human progress, there are two books I've read recently—one for the idea of human progress and one against it—and both are worth mentioning. Whenever I bring up a sensitive topic, I try to suggest two books that present good opposing arguments. For example, every time I recommend *Atlas Shrugged* by Ayn Rand, I also recommend *The Jungle* by Upston Sinclair (and vice versa). There is usually some truth in each side of the argument—the key is trying to understand each argument before forming an opinion. Besides, if you never read what your enemy is reading, you will never be able to predict their next move (some wisdom adapted from *The Art of War* by Sun Tzu).

The first book is *Eating People* by Andy Kessler.

Argument:

1) Human progress is measured by having a higher standard of living than previous years.

2) Advancements in technology eliminates menial jobs and create new

jobs in sectors that increase the standard of living.

3) We currently have the highest standard of living in human history, and to continue raising the standard of living, we must invest in technology that eliminates jobs (and creates new jobs that seek to find solutions that will eliminate more jobs).

4) Technology and automation (and, in the future, machine learning) will replace most jobs we have today so we can live in a world with the highest standard of living of any culture in the history of humanity.

For more info, you can read my notes here: http://www.sustainableevolution
.com/notes-eat-people

The second book is *Straw Dogs* by John Gray.

Argument:

1) Even rational human beings cannot escape self-delusion.

2) All "progress" has come with great damage to the environment our species.

3) We have the same problems we did thousands of years ago, the only difference is that through technology, our problems express themselves in different forms.

4) Since we are delusional, we think: Technology = Progress, but technology hasn't solved any of our problems. We still have war, famine, disease, we still don't get along with others, we are selfish, egotistical, have poor means of communication, … et al.

5) There is no such thing as human progress, there is only change and change is not progress.

I like to entertain both ideas simultaneously. Our technology is improving, we are living longer, but most of the technological advances deal with entertaining ourselves. The root of humanity's problems remains the same. We still have conflict in all sizes from war to family arguments at holiday dinners. They are the same problems, only packaged in different cultural wrapping paper.

For more info, you can read an interview here: http://thequietus.com/articles/
12496-john-gray-silence-of-animals-interview

<u>Move</u>

Just Move

Bergouignan, A., Legget, K. T., Jong, N. D., Kealey, E., Nikolovski, J., Groppel, J. L., . . . Bessesen, D. H. (2016). Effect of frequent interruptions of prolonged sitting on self-perceived levels of energy, mood, food cravings and cognitive function. *International Journal of Behavioral Nutrition and Physical Activity*, 13(1). doi:10.1186/s12966-016-0437-z

Chobdee, J., & Elton, K. (n.d.). 50 Tips to Move More at Work. Retrieved September 16, 2017, from https://wellness.ucr.edu/docs/movemore/movemore_50tips.pdf

Diaz, K. M., Howard, V. J., Hutto, B., Colabianchi, N., Vena, J. E., Safford,

M. M., . . . Hooker, S. P. (2017). Patterns of Sedentary Behavior and Mortality in U.S. Middle-Aged and Older Adults. *Annals of Internal Medicine.* doi:10.7326/m17-0212

Macewen, B. T., Macdonald, D. J., & Burr, J. F. (2015). A systematic review of standing and treadmill desks in the workplace. *Preventive Medicine*, 70, 50-58. doi:10.1016/j.ypmed.2014.11.011

Thorp, A. A., Kingwell, B. A., Owen, N., & Dunstan, D. W. (2014). Breaking up workplace sitting time with intermittent standing bouts improves fatigue and musculoskeletal discomfort in overweight/obese office workers. *Occupational and Environmental Medicine*, 71(11), 765-771. doi:10.1136/oemed-2014-102348

Types of Movement

7 tips for a safe and successful strength-training program. (n.d.). Retrieved September 19, 2017, from https://www.health.harvard.edu/exercise-and-fitness/7-tips-for-a-safe-and-successful-strength-training-program

Andersen, J. C. (2005). Stretching Before and After Exercise: Effect on Muscle Soreness and Injury Risk. *Journal of Athletic Training*, 40(3), 218–220.

Boutcher, S. H. (2011). High-Intensity Intermittent Exercise and Fat Loss. *Journal of Obesity*, 2011, 868305. http://doi.org/10.1155/2011/868305

Irving, B. A., Davis, C. K., Brock, D. W., Weltman, J. Y., Swift, D., Barrett, E. J., ... Weltman, A. (2008). Effect of exercise training intensity on abdominal visceral fat and body composition. *Medicine and Science in Sports and Exercise*, 40(11), 1863–1872. http://doi.org/10.1249/MSS.0b013e3181801 d40

Laskowski, E. (2016, August 20). How much exercise do you really need? Retrieved September 19, 2017, from http://www.mayoclinic.org/healthy-lifestyle/fitness/expert-answers/exercise/faq-20057916

Schuenke, M., Mikat, R., & Mcbride, J. (2002). Effect of an acute period of resistance exercise on excess post-exercise oxygen consumption: implications for body mass management. *European Journal of Applied Physiology*, 86(5), 411-417. doi:10.1007/s00421-001-0568-y

Move More: 3 Kinds of Exercise That Boost Heart Health. (n.d.). Retrieved September 19, 2017, from Aerobic vs Anaerobic Respiration. (n.d.). Retrieved September 19, 2017, from http://www.diffen.com/difference/ Aerobic_Respiration_vs_Anaerobic_Respiration

How Movement Increases Health & Productivity

Adams, O. P. (2013). The impact of brief high-intensity exercise on blood glucose levels. *Diabetes, Metabolic Syndrome and Obesity: Targets and Therapy*, 6, 113–122. http://doi.org/10.2147/DMSO.S29222

Alban, D. (2016, March 29). Anandamide: Putting The Bliss Molecule To Work For Your Brain. Retrieved September 21, 2017, from http://reset. me/story/anandamide-putting-the-bliss-molecule-to-work-for-your-brain/

Benefits of exercise – reduces stress, anxiety, and helps fight depression, from Harvard Men's Health Watch. (2011, February). Retrieved September 21, 2017, from https://www.health.harvard.edu/press_releases/benefits-of-exercisereduces-stress-anxiety-and-helps-fight-depression

Blumenthal, J. A., Smith, P. J., & Hoffman, B. M. (2012). Is Exercise a Viable Treatment for Depression? *ACSM's Health & Fitness Journal*, 16(4), 14–21. http://doi.org/10.1249/01.FIT.0000416000.09526.eb

Colberg, S. R., Sigal, R. J., Fernhall, B., Regensteiner, J. G., Blissmer, B. J., Rubin, R. R., … Braun, B. (2010). Exercise and Type 2 Diabetes: The American College of Sports Medicine and the American Diabetes Association: joint position statement. *Diabetes Care*, 33(12), e147–e167. http://doi.org/10.2337/dc10-9990

Cornelissen, V. A., & Smart, N. A. (2013). Exercise Training for Blood Pressure: A Systematic Review and Meta-analysis. *Journal of the American Heart Association:* Cardiovascular and Cerebrovascular Disease, 2(1), e004473.http://doi.org/10.1161/JAHA.112.004473

Craft, L. L., & Perna, F. M. (2004). The Benefits of Exercise for the Clinically Depressed. Primary Care Companion to *The Journal of Clinical Psychiatry*, 6(3), 104–111.

Erickson, K. I., Voss, M. W., Prakash, R. S., Basak, C., Szabo, A., Chaddock, L., … Kramer, A. F. (2011). Exercise training increases size of hippocampus and improves memory. *Proceedings of the National Academy of Sciences of the United States of America*, 108(7), 3017–3022. http://doi.org/10.1073/pnas.1015950108

Exercise is an all-natural treatment to fight depression. (2013, August). Retrieved September 21, 2017, from https://www.health.harvard.edu /mind-and-mood/exercise-is-an-all-natural-treatment-to-fight-depression

Fahmy , S. (2008, February 28). Low-intensity exercise reduces fatigue symptoms by 65 percent, study finds. Retrieved September 21, 2017, from http://news.uga.edu/releases/article/low-intensity-exercise-reduces-fatigue-symptoms-by-65-percent-study-finds/

Hötting, K., Schickert, N., Kaiser, J., Röder, B., & Schmidt-Kassow, M. (2016). The Effects of Acute Physical Exercise on Memory, Peripheral BDNF, and Cortisol in Young Adults. *Neural Plasticity*, 2016, 1-12. doi:10 .1155/2016/6860573

Fuss, J., Steinle, J., Bindila, L., Auer, M. K., Kirchherr, H., Lutz, B., & Gass, P. (2015). A runner's high depends on cannabinoid receptors in mice.

Proceedings of the National Academy of Sciences, 112(42), 13105-13108. doi:10. 1073/pnas.1514996112

Godman, H. (2016, November 29). Regular exercise changes the brain to improve memory, thinking skills. Retrieved September 21, 2017, from https://www.health.harvard.edu/blog/regular-exercise-changes-brain-improve-memory-thinking-skills-201404097110

Gomez-Pinilla, F., & Hillman, C. (2013). The Influence of Exercise on Cognitive Abilities. *Comprehensive Physiology*, 3(1), 403–428. http://doi.org /10.1002/cphy.c110063

Itoh, T., Imano, M., Nishida, S., Tsubaki, M., Hashimoto, S., Ito, A., & Satou, T. (2010). Exercise increases neural stem cell proliferation surrounding the area of damage following rat traumatic brain injury. *Journal of Neural Transmission*, 118(2), 193-202. doi:10.1007/s00702-010-0495-3

Lees, C., & Hopkins, J. (2013). Effect of Aerobic Exercise on Cognition, Academic Achievement, and Psychosocial Function in Children: A Systematic Review of Randomized Control Trials. *Preventing Chronic Disease*, 10, E174. http://doi.org/10.5888/pcd10.130010

Loh, H. H., Tseng, L. F., Wei, E., & Li, C. H. (1976). beta-endorphin is a potent analgesic agent. *Proceedings of the National Academy of Sciences of the United States of America*, 73(8), 2895–2898.

Mejri, M. A., Hammouda, O., Tayech, A., Yousfi, N., Chaouachi, A., & Souissi, N. (2017). Comment on "Interrelationship between Sleep and Exercise: A Systematic Review". *Advances in Preventive Medicine*, 2017, 1-1. doi:10.1155/2017/7301676

News, J. L. (2015, October 08). New Brain Effects behind "Runner's High". Retrieved September 21, 2017, from https://www.scientificamerican.com/ article/new-brain-effects-behind-runner-s-high/

Nokia, M. S., Lensu, S., Ahtiainen, J. P., Johansson, P. P., Koch, L. G., Britton, S. L., & Kainulainen, H. (2016). Physical exercise increases adult hippocampal neurogenesis in male rats provided it is aerobic and sustained. *The Journal of Physiology*, 594(7), 1855–1873. http://doi.org/10.1113/JP271 552

Puetz, T. W., Flowers, S. S., & O'connor, P. J. (2008). A Randomized Controlled Trial of the Effect of Aerobic Exercise Training on Feelings of Energy and Fatigue in Sedentary Young Adults with Persistent Fatigue. *Psychotherapy and Psychosomatics*, 77(3), 167-174. doi:10.1159/000116610

Punia, S., Kulandaivelan, S., Singh, V., & Punia, V. (2016). Effect of Aerobic Exercise Training on Blood Pressure in Indians: Systematic Review. *International Journal of Chronic Diseases*, 2016, 1370148. http://doi.org/10. 1155/2016/1370148

Schwarz, U. V., & Hasson, H. (2011). Employee Self-rated Productivity and Objective Organizational Production Levels. *Journal of Occupational and Environmental Medicine*, 53(8), 838-844. doi:10.1097/jom.0b013e31822589c2

Sears, M. E., Kerr, K. J., & Bray, R. I. (2012). Arsenic, Cadmium, Lead, and Mercury in Sweat: A Systematic Review. *Journal of Environmental and Public Health*, 2012, 184745. http://doi.org/10.1155/2012/184745

Breathe

Congleton, C., Hölzel, B., & Lazar, S. (2015, January 08). Mindfulness Can Literally Change Your Brain. Retrieved September 02, 2017, from https://hbr.org/2015/01/mindfulness-can-literally-change-your-brain

Fisher, N. (2016, February 02). Stress raising your blood pressure? Take a deep breath. Retrieved September 04, 2017, from https://www.health.harvard.edu/blog/stress-raising-your-blood-pressure-take-a-deep-breath-201602159168

Goyal, M., Singh, S., Sibinga, E. M. S., Gould, N. F., Rowland-Seymour, A., Sharma, R., ... Haythornthwaite, J. A. (2014). Meditation Programs for Psychological Stress and Well-being: A Systematic Review and Meta-analysis. *JAMA Internal Medicine*, 174(3), 357–368. http://doi.org/10.1001/jamainternmed.2013.13018

Hölzel, B. K., Carmody, J., Vangel, M., Congleton, C., Yerramsetti, S. M., Gard, T., & Lazar, S. W. (2011). Mindfulness practice leads to increases in regional brain gray matter density. *Psychiatry Research*, 191(1), 36–43. http://doi.org/10.1016/j.pscychresns.2010.08.006

Kabat-Zinn, J. (2014). *Wherever you go, there you are: mindfulness meditation in everyday life*. New York: Hachette Books.

Seppala, E. (2016). *The happiness track: how to apply the science of happiness to accelerate your success*. New York, NY: HarperOne, an imprint of HarperCollins. P. 58

Tello , M. (2016, October 16). Regular meditation more beneficial than vacation. Retrieved September 04, 2017, from https://www.health.harvard.edu/blog/relaxation-benefits-meditation-stronger-relaxation-benefits-taking-vacation-2016102710532

Meditation and mindfulness:

David Lynch, famous for his TV series, *Twin Peaks,* and award-winning films, *Mulholland Drive* and *Eraserhead* (*Lost Highway* is my personal favorite), started his own transcendental meditation foundation with a focus on healing traumatic stress and raising performance in at-risk populations. According to research on their page (https://www.davidlynchfoundation.org/research.html), transcendental meditation, sometimes just "TM", increases high school graduation rates, improves GPA, reduces symptoms of PTSD and depression, decreases insomnia, and improves quality of life in abused women and girls.

If only Lynch could quit smoking cigarettes and remake *Dune*, then he might be a model citizen we could look up to. :-)

More info about the benefits of meditation from the From the National Institutes of Health: https://nccih.nih.gov/health/meditation/overview.htm#hed6

Better Air

Daisey, J. M., Angell, W. J., & Apte, M. G. (2003). Indoor air quality, ventilation and health symptoms in schools: an analysis of existing information. *Indoor Air*, 13(1), 53-64. doi:10.1034/j.1600-0668.2003.00153.x

Largo-Wight, E., Chen, W. W., Dodd, V., & Weiler, R. (2011). Healthy Workplaces: The Effects of Nature Contact at Work on Employee Stress and Health. *Public Health Reports*, 126(Suppl 1), 124–130.

Lichtenfeld, S., Elliot, A. J., Maier, M. A., & Pekrun, R. (2012). Fertile Green. *Personality and Social Psychology Bulletin*, 38(6), 784-797. doi:10.1177/0146167212436611

Mergel, M. (2011, July 06). A Small Dose of Solvents. Retrieved September 03, 2017, from http://www.toxipedia.org/display/toxipedia/A Small Dose of Solvents

NASA: A study of interior landscape plants for indoor air pollution abatement: https://archive.org/details/nasa_techdoc_19930072988

Salleh, M. R. (2008). Life Event, Stress and Illness. *The Malaysian Journal of Medical Sciences*: MJMS, 15(4), 9–18.

Selecting the right house plant could improve indoor air (animation). (2013, August 24). Retrieved September 03, 2017, from https://www.acs.org/content/acs/en/pressroom/newsreleases/2016/august/selecting-the-right-house-plant-could-improve-indoor-air-animation.html

TailSmart. (2016, February 22). 11 Detoxifying Plants that are Safe for Cats and Dogs. Retrieved September 03, 2017, from http://www.tailsmart.com/11-detoxifying-plants-that-are-safe-for-cats-and-dogs/

See also (videos):

American Chemical Society: Reducing Indoor Air Pollution with Houseplants - Headline Science: https://www.youtube.com/watch?v=HdOibycDIA4&feature=youtu.be

Scientific American: Indoor Plants Can Clean Your Air https://www.youtube.com/watch?v=y6sDb48pIBg

Practice

Brauneis , W. (1991/1992). "Dies irae, dies illa – Day of wrath, day of wailing": Notes on the commissioning, origin, and completion of Mozart's Requiem. *Jahrbuch des Vereins für Geschichte der Stadt Wien*, 33-50. Retrieved October 3, 2017, from http://www.datasheets.tips/people-and-self/walther-brauneis-dies-irae-dies-illa-a%C2%80%C2%93-day-of-wrath-day-of-wailing-notes-on-the-commissioning-origin-and-completion-of-mozarts-requiem-kv-626/

Clear, J. (2017, September 18). Vince Lombardi on the Power of Mastering the Fundamentals. Retrieved October 08, 2017, from http://jamesclear.com/vince-lombardi-fundamentals

Colvin, G. (2010). *Talent is overrated: what really separates world-class performers from everybody else*. New York: Portfolio.

Coyle, D. (2012). *The little book of talent: 52 tips for improving your skills*. New York: Bantam Books.

Coyle, D. (2009). *The talent code: greatness isn't born: it's grown, here's how*. New York: Bantam Books

Documents Suggest Mozart Wasn't Poor. (n.d.). Retrieved October 03, 2017, from http://www.billboard.com/articles/news/58873/documents-suggest-mozart-wasnt-poor

$42,000/year in 2006 is about $51,500 in 2017 (via https://www.dollartimes.com/inflation/inflation.php?amount=42000&year=2006)

Gardner, H. (2011). *Creating minds: an anatomy of creativity seen through the lives of Freud, Einstein, Picasso, Stravinsky, Eliot, Graham, and Gandhi*. New York: BasicBooks.

Gaiman, N. (2016). *The view from the cheap seats: selected nonfiction*. New York, NY: William Morrow.

Gladwell, M. (2013). *Outliers: the story of success*. New York: Back Bay Books, Little, Brown and Company.

Hendricks, D. (2014, July 24). 6 $25 Billion Companies That Started in a Garage. Retrieved October 09, 2017, from https://www.inc.com/drew-hendricks/6-25-billion-companies-that-started-in-a-garage.html

Howe, M. J. (2001). *Genius explained*. Cambridge: Cambridge University Press.

Johnson, T. (2016, September 06). Americans Spend an Average of 17,600 Minutes Driving Each Year. Retrieved October 02, 2017, from http://newsroom.aaa.com/2016/09/americans-spend-average-17600-minutes-driving-year/

See also: https://www.aaafoundation.org/sites/default/files/American DrivingSurvey2015.pdf

Judit Polgar new captain of the Hungarian National Men's Chess Team | Chessdom. (2015, June 12). Retrieved October 07, 2017, from http://www.chessdom.com/judit-polgar-new-captain-of-the-hungarian-national-mens-chess-team/

Kavalek, L. (2005, August 08). Chess. Retrieved October 07, 2017, from http://www.washingtonpost.com/wp-dyn/content/article/2005/08/08/AR2005080800302_pf.html

Kleon, A. (2012). *Steal like an artist: 10 things nobody told you about being creative.* New York: Workman.

Maurer, L., Zitting, K.-M., Elliott, K., Czeisler, C. A., Ronda, J. M., & Duffy, J. F. (2015). A new face of sleep: The impact of post-learning sleep on recognition memory for face-name associations. *Neurobiology of Learning and Memory*, 126, 31–38. http://doi.org/10.1016/j.nlm.2015.10.012

Menand, L. (2017, June 19). Believer. Retrieved October 14, 2017, from https://www.newyorker.com/magazine/2005/03/07/believer

Originally published in print March 7, 2005

Olympians who swam at the North Baltimore Aquatic Club listed here: http://www.nbac.net/TabGeneric.jsp?_tabid_=50027&team=msnbac

O'Keeffe, A. (2005, December 31). A musical genius? No, Mozart was just a hard-working boy. Retrieved October 03, 2017, from https://www.the guardian.com/uk/2006/jan/01/arts.music

Parham, J. (2016, October 20). 15 Tech Companies Created In Dorm Rooms. Retrieved October 09, 2017, from http://www.complex.com/pop-culture/2013/01/15-tech-companies-created-in-dorm-rooms/

Passell, P. (1991, December 10). Economic Scene; Mozart's Money Misunderstanding. Retrieved October 03, 2017, from http://www.nytimes.com/1991/12/11/business/economic-scene-mozart-s-money-misund erstanding.html

Polgar, S. (2005). *Breaking through: how the Polgar sisters changed the game of chess.* London: Gloucester Pub.

Porterfield , C. (1984, September 30). The Trouble' With Gifted Children Does Talent Have to Mean Terror?. *The Times Herald from Port Huron, Michigan*, pp. 134-135.

Reilly, L. (2017, January 11). How Stephen King's Wife Saved Carrie and Launched His Career. Retrieved October 09, 2017, from http://mentalfloss.com/article/53235/how-stephen-kings-wife-saved-carrie-and-launched-his-career

SI Wire. (2017, February 5). How many Super Bowls has Tom Brady won? Retrieved October 08, 2017, from https://www.si.com/nfl/2017/02/05/tom-brady-super-bowl-total-wins

Syed, M. (2011). *Bounce: Mozart, Federer, Picasso, Beckham, and the science of success*. New York: Perennial.

Taylor, C. (2015). *How Star wars conquered the universe: the past, present, and future of a multibillion dollar franchise*. New York: Basic Books, a member of the Perseus Books Group.

Terry Pratchett. (2008, July 22). Retrieved October 14, 2017, from https://www.theguardian.com/books/2008/jun/12/terrypratchett

Reel, J. (2016, April 01). A Reexamination of Leopold Mozart's Famous Violin Pedagogy. Retrieved October 03, 2017, from http://stringsmaazine.com/a-reexamination-of-leopold-mozarts-famous-violin-pedagogy/

Ross, A. (2017, June 19). The Storm of Style. Retrieved October 03, 2017, from https://www.newyorker.com/magazine/2006/07/24/the-storm-of-style

    Originally published in the July 24, 2006 issue.

U.S. Department of Transportation Federal Highway Administration. July 13, 2016. Licensed Drivers by Age and Sex (In Thousands). Retrieved October 02, 2017, from https://www.fhwa.dot.gov/ohim/onh00/bar7.htm

Winters, E. (2015, May 20). The New York Times Company. Retrieved September 26, 2017, from https://www.nytimes.com/roomfordebate/2015/05/20/the-benefits-and-pressures-of-being-a-young-genius/often-child-prodigies-do-not-grow-into-adult-genius?mcubz=3

Zaslaw, Neal. (1992). Mozart as a Working Stiff. 102-112.

    Note: Collected in book: Morris, J. M. (1995). *On Mozart*. Washington, D.C.: Woodrow Wilson Center Press.

Play

Sleep

Knutson, K. L., Van Cauter, E., Rathouz, P. J., DeLeire, T., & Lauderdale, D. S. (2010). Trends in the Prevalence of Short Sleepers in the USA: 1975–2006. *Sleep*, 33(1), 37–45.

Winter, W. C. (2017). *The sleep solution: why your sleep is broken and how to fix it*. New York: New American Library, p.33.

Full-time workers working longer hours

Saad, L. (2014, August 29). The "40-Hour" Workweek Is Actually Longer --

by Seven Hours. Retrieved August 26, 2017, from http://www.gallup.com/poll/175286/hour-workweek-actually-longer-seven-hours.aspx

Organizations like the Organization for Economic Co-operation and Development (OECD) (https://stats.oecd.org/Index.aspx?Data SetCode=ANHRS#) take into account short-time workers and part-time workers, which skew the results for full-time workers. The Gallup poll only takes into consideration full-time workers.

Put it on the shelf

Inspired by conversations with Dr. Sue Dilsworth, owner of Heart's Journey Wellness Center: http://heartsjourneywellness.com/

Play (general)

Bherer, L., Erickson, K. I., & Liu-Ambrose, T. (2013). A Review of the Effects of Physical Activity and Exercise on Cognitive and Brain Functions in Older Adults. *Journal of Aging Research*, 2013, 657508. http://doi.org/10.1155/2013/657508

Brown, S. (2008). Play is more than just fun. Retrieved August 26, 2017, from https://www.ted.com/talks/stuart_brown_says_play_is_more_than_fun_it_s_vital/discussion#t-480993

Brown, S. L., & Vaughan, C. C. (2010). *Play: how it shapes the brain, opens the imagination, and invigorates the soul.* New York: Avery.

Coleman, A. (2016, February 11). Is Google's model of the creative workplace the future of the office? Retrieved September 01, 2017, from https://www.theguardian.com/careers/2016/feb/11/is-googles-model-of-the-creative-workplace-the-future-of-the-office

Creative Mornings. (2013, October 13). Shaun Huberts: Why are children better at play than adults? Retrieved August 26, 2017, from https://www.youtube.com/watch?v=Yg0z-aMin4A

Delaney, P. (2009, April). Play's the Thing - Study Shows "Free Play" Is Highly Important to Human Social Development boston college researcher: modern focus on competition, drive to win may have contributed to economic woes. Retrieved August 26, 2017, from http://www.bc.edu/offices/pubaf/journalist/Gray_Play.html

Gaiman, N., & McKean, D. (2012). *Coraline.* New York: Harper.

Quote from G.K. Chesterton.

Gaiman, N. (2016). *The view from the cheap seats: a collection of introductions, essays, and assorted writings.* New York, NY: William Morrow. P.41

Gaiman, N. (2011, September 02). Week three: Neil Gaiman on writing American Gods. Retrieved August 13, 2017, from https://www.theguardian

.com/books/2011/sep/02/american-gods-neil-gaiman-bookclub

Hallowell, E. M. (2011). *Shine: using brain science to get the best from your people.* Boston, MA: Harvard Business Review Press.

Hannaford, C. (2005). *Smart moves why learning is not all in your head.* Salt Lake City, UT: Great River Books.

Johnson, S. (2016). *Wonderland: how play made the modern world.* New York: Riverhead Books.

McGonigal, J. (2016). *Super Better: the power of living gamefully.* NY, NY: Penguin Books.

Pink, D. H. (2012). *Drive: the surprising truth about what motivates us.* New York: Riverhead Books. p 1-4.

Robinson, L., Smith, M., Segal, J., & Shubin, J. (2017, April). The Benefits of Play for Adults. Retrieved August 26, 2017, from https://www.helpguide.org/articles/mental-health/benefits-of-play-for-adults.htm

The Science. (n.d.). Retrieved August 26, 2017, from http://www.nifplay.org/science/overview/

Seinfeld, S., Figueroa, H., Ortiz-Gil, J., & Sanchez-Vives, M. V. (2013). Effects of music learning and piano practice on cognitive function, mood and quality of life in older adults. *Frontiers in Psychology*, 4, 810. http://doi.org/10.3389/fpsyg.2013.00810

Swafford, J. (2009, February 03). When music critics attack. Retrieved October 06, 2017, from http://www.slate.com/articles/arts/music_box/2009/02/great_composers_lousy_reviews.html

Voosen, P. (2015, November 08). Bringing Up Genius. Retrieved November 13, 2015, from http://www.chronicle.com/article/Bringing-Up-Genius/234061

See also: http://web.chessdailynews.com/wp-content/uploads/2015/11/Bringing-Up-Genius-The-Chronicle-of-Higher-Education1.pdf

Watts, Alan: https://www.youtube.com/watch?v=Qx4fUpalvTU

Text (from transcript) cited below:

The art of washing dishes is that you only have to wash one at a time. If you're doing it day after day, you have in your mind's eye an enormous stack of filthy dishes that you have washed up in years past, and an enormous stack of filthy dishes which you will wash up in years future. But if you bring in your mind to the state of reality which just is - as I have pointed out to you - only Now. This is where we are. There is only Now. You only have to wash one dish! It's the only dish you ever have to wash, this one! You ignore all the rest, because in reality there is no past, and there is no future, there is only this one!

Yenigun, S. (2014, August 06). Play Doesn't End With Childhood: Why Adults Need Recess Too. Retrieved August 26, 2017, from http://www.npr.org/sections/ed/2014/08/06/336360521/play-doesnt-end-with-childhood-why-adults-need-recess-too

Reflection

Barry, M. (2000). *Syrup: a novel.* New York: Penguin Books.

Dickens, C. (1991). *A Christmas Carol.* New York: Dover Publications.

Gates, B. (2006, April 07). How I Work: Bill Gates. Retrieved September 21, 2017, from http://money.cnn.com/2006/03/30/news/newsmakers/gates_howiwork_fortune/

Godin, S. (2014, December 27). Is your niche too small? Retrieved September 24, 2017, from http://sethgodin.typepad.com/seths_blog/2014/12/is-your-niche-too-small.html

Guth, R. A. (2005, March 28). In Secret Hideaway, Bill Gates Ponders Microsoft's Future. Retrieved August 10, 2017, from https://www.wsj.com/articles/SB111196625830690477

Karnjanaprakorn, M. (2014, April 22). How Skillshare's CEO Cultivates And Applies Creativity (Taking Cues From Bill Gates and Chuck Close). Retrieved August 10, 2017, from https://www.fastcompany.com/3024934/how-skillshares-ceo-cultivates-and-applies-creativity-taking-cues-from-b

Nobel, C. (2014, May 05). Reflecting on Work Improves Job Performance. Retrieved September 24, 2017, from http://hbswk.hbs.edu/item/reflecting-on-work-improves-job-performance

Polgár, J., Marin, M., & Shaw, J. (2012). *How I beat Fischers record.* Glasgow: Quality Chess.

Stefano, G. D., Gino, F., Pisano, G. P., & Staats, B. R. (2014). Learning by Thinking: How Reflection Aids Performance. *SSRN Electronic Journal.* doi:10.2139/ssrn.2414478

This is a working paper published by the Harvard Business School. The paper is in draft form and can be viewed at http://www.sc.edu/usc connect/doc/Learning%20by%20Thinking,%20How%20Reflection%20Aids%20Performance.pdf

Skillshare: I write about Michael Karnjanaprakorn and Skillshare in this chapter and I want to take a moment to say that Skillshare is really freakin' awesome. It is an online learning community where anyone can take or teach a class about just about anything from the arts to business. It's not free, but it's affordably priced (and there's a free trial). Skillshare was created to fill the gap between school and industry, and its online platform is changing how we think of education. In an interview, Karnjanaprakorn said: "The skills kids need today—problem solving, creativity, and collaborating—a lot of our classes are targeted to that realm." (via https://www.inc.com/best-industries-2013/april-joyner /skillshare-education-gap.html) Take some time and visit Skillshare (I'm going to put it in bold so it stands out and pops when you are flipping through these back pages): **https://www.skillshare.com/**

Building Your Dock

AtGoogleTalks. (2016, August 01). Tim Ferriss: "How to Cage the Monkey Mind" | Talks at Google. Retrieved October 20, 2017, from https://www. youtube.com/watch?v=I7Foam6oKPI

Baer, D. (2015, April 28). The scientific reason why Barack Obama and Mark Zuckerberg wear the same outfit every day. Retrieved October 21, 2017, from http://www.businessinsider.com/barack-obama-mark-zucker berg-wear-the-same-outfit-2015-4

Barauta, L. (n.d.). Triggers and Habits. Retrieved October 20, 2017, from https://zenhabits.net/triggers-and-habits/

Baumeister, R., & Tierney, J. (2012). *Willpower: Rediscovering the Greatest Human Strength*. Penguin USA.

Brewer, J., & Kabat-Zinn, J. (2017). *The craving mind: from cigarettes to smartphones to love - why we get hooked and how we can break bad habits*. New Haven: Yale University Press.

Cherkovski, N. (1999). *Bukowski: a life*. South Royalton, VT: Steerforth Press.

Danziger, S., Levav, J., & Avnaim-Pesso, L. (2011). Extraneous factors in judicial decisions. *Proceedings of the National Academy of Sciences*, 108(17), 6889-6892. doi:10.1073/pnas.1018033108

Duhigg, C. (2012). *The Power of habit: why we do what we do in life and business*. Random House.

Gaiman, N., & Kidd, C. (2013). *Make good art*. New York: Harper Collins.

Gawande, A. (2010). *The checklist manifesto: how to get things right*. New York: Picador.

Isaacson, W. (2011). *Steve Jobs*. New York: Simon & Schuster.

Kamb, S. (2016). *Level up your life: how to unlock adventure and happiness by becoming the hero of your own story*. New York: Rodale Books.

Lally, P., Jaarsveld, C. H., Potts, H. W., & Wardle, J. (2009). How are habits formed: Modelling habit formation in the real world. *European Journal of*

Social Psychology, 40(6), 998-1009. doi:10.1002/ejsp.674

Thank you to James Clear and his post https://jamesclear.com/new-habit for linking me to this data.

McGonigal, K. (2012). *The Willpower Instinct: How Self-Control Works, Why It Matters, and What You Can Do to Get More of It*. New York, NY: Avery.

McRaven, W. (2015, December 14). Adm. McRaven Urges Graduates to Find Courage to Change the World. Retrieved October 19, 2017, from https://news.utexas.edu/2014/05/16/mcraven-urges-graduates-to-find-courage-to-change-the-world

Sweeney, J., & Yorkey, M. (2015). *Moving the needle: get clear, get free, and get going in your career, business, and life*. Hoboken, NJ: John Wiley & Sons, Inc.

TEDx talks. Nerd Fitness and Resetting the Game of Life: Steve Kamb at TEDxEmory 2012. (2012, June 25). Retrieved August 31, 2017, from https://www.youtube.com/watch?v=kcYEivl-NIM

Tierney, J. (2011, August 17). Do You Suffer From Decision Fatigue? Retrieved October 21, 2017, from http://www.nytimes.com/2011/08/21/magazine/do-you-suffer-from-decision-fatigue.html

Further reading: http://blogs.discovermagazine.com/notrocketscience/2011/04/11/justice-is-served-but-more-so-after-lunch-how-food-breaks-sway-the-decisions-of-judges/#.V-VwP5MrJE4

Image: Greek mythology: the blind giant Orion carried his servant Cedalion on his shoulders to act as the giant's eyes. [Photograph]. (n.d.). [Encyclopedic manuscript containing allegorical and medical drawings], Library of Congress, Rosenwald 4, Bl. 5r, South Germany, ca. 1410. Public domain.

See also: https://catalog.loc.gov/vwebv/citeRecord?searchId=17022&recPointer=0&recCount=25&searchType=1&bibId=14310280, https://en.wikipedia.org/wiki/Standing_on_the_shoulders_of_giants#/media/File:Library_of_Congress,_Rosenwald_4,_Bl._5r.jpg

Image description: Keith, B. (2016). *Strategic sourcing in the new economy: harnessing the potential of sourcing business models for modern procurement*. Basingstoke: Palgrave Macmillan.

PART 3: REINFORCEMENT

Mentoring: No One is 100% Self-Made

Biro, M. M. (2016, July 27). Preparing for the Retirement Boom. Retrieved June 20, 2017, from http://www.huffingtonpost.com/meghan-m-biro-/preparing-for-the-retirem_b_11208530.html

Lindenberger, J., & Stoltz-Loike, M. (2016, October 12). Why Not Use Your Baby Boomer Employees as Mentors? Retrieved June 20, 2017, from https://www.thebalance.com/mentoring-and-baby-boomers-1917840

The empire strikes back

Kurtz, G., Brackett, L., Kasdan, L., Kershner, I., Lucas, G., Hamill, M., Ford, H., ... Twentieth Century Fox Home Entertainment, Inc. (2004). Star wars: Episode V. United States: 20th Century Fox.

Hints and Pitfalls: Fat brains

Rudan, G. (2011). *Practical genius: the real smarts you need to get your talents and passion working for you.* New York: Simon & Schuster.

Interviewing as a Skill

This section is based on conversations I had with Andy Ruth and from my own personal experience.

Motivational Interviewing

Morin, A. (2014, March 31). Looking To Motivate Someone To Change? Try Motivational Interviewing. Retrieved July 01, 2017, from https://www.forbes.com/sites/amymorin/2014/03/31/looking-to-motivate-someone-to-change-try-motivational-interviewing/#3488d6fe7283

Treatment, C. F. (1999, January 01). Chapter 3-Motivational Interviewing as a Counseling Style. Retrieved July 01, 2017, from https://www.ncbi.nlm.nih.gov/books/NBK64964/

Echo Chambers and Company Cult-ure

The opening quote comes from an article in the Huffington Post by Ruth Whippman.

Whippman, R. (2012, November 24). How Corporate America Is Turning Into a Cult and Why It's Harming the American Employee. Retrieved April 10, 2017, from http://www.huffingtonpost.com/ruth-whippman/how-corporate-america-is-_b_2171040.html

Yes, smart people join cults

Dawson, Lorne L. *Comprehending Cults: the Sociology of New Religious Movements.* Toronto: Oxford UP Canada, 1998. Print.

Excerpt of text cited below:

"[W]ith few exceptions studies have found that recruits to NRMs [new religious movements] are on average markedly better educated than the general public" (87).

Cults and culture

Berger, A. A. (2000). The Meanings of Culture. *M/C Journal*, 3(2). Retrieved June 22, 2017, from http://journal.media-culture.org.au/0005/meaning.php

See also: https://en.wiktionary.org/wiki/cult#English for etymology of cult.

Thiel, P. (2017, June 03). You Should Run Your Startup Like a Cult. Here's How. Retrieved June 24, 2017, from https://www.wired.com/2014/09/run-startup-like-cult-heres/

Thiel, P. A., & Masters, B. (2015). *Zero to one: notes on startups, or how to build the future.* London: Virgin Books.

Gen Y & startups

Robehmed, N. (2013, August 13). Why Recent Grads Are Swarming Startups. Retrieved June 25, 2017, from https://www.forbes.com/sites/natalierobehmed/2013/08/13/why-recent-grads-are-swarming-startups/#48de2410442b

"Cult-Thinking" Causes an Echo-Chamber Effect

Martin, A. (2016, May 23). The web's 'echo chamber' leaves us none the wiser. Retrieved June 25, 2017, from http://www.wired.co.uk/article/online-stubbornness

Pentland, A. %. (2017, March 20). Beyond the Echo Chamber. Retrieved June 25, 2017, from https://hbr.org/2013/11/beyond-the-echo-chamber

Confirmation bias definition

Confirmation. (n.d.). Retrieved June 29, 2017, from http://www.dictionary.com/browse/confirmation-bias?s=t

Great YouTube video about confirmation bias: https://www.youtube.com/watch?v=jOjIAiJCNIk

See also: *To Serve God and Wal-Mart: The Making of Christian Free Enterprise* by Bethany Moreton

How to Write a Blog

Personal branding resource

https://www.quicksprout.com/the-complete-guide-to-building-your-personal-brand/

Engage Often

Seth Godin, write a blog every day: https://blog.hubspot.com/marketing/writing-tips-seth-godin

Titles are 80% of Your Piece

Dahl, G. (2007). *Advertising For Dummies*, 2nd Edition. John Wiley & Sons.

Pictures/Media/Copyrights

Mawhinney, J. (2017, January 3). 42 Visual Content Marketing Statistics You Should Know in 2017. Retrieved June 20, 2017, from https://blog.hubspot.com/marketing/visual-content-marketing strategy?__hstc=228091842.d8e90f424b789248cafab9b03c97d602.1481194545949.1481194545949.1481194545949.1&__hssc=228091842.1.1481194545949&__hsfp=2105749059

How to cite Creative Commons licensed material

https://wiki.creativecommons.org/wiki/Best_practices_for_attribution

Workspace

Casinos

Finlay, K., Marmurek, H. H., Kanetkar, V., & Londerville, J. (2009). Casino Decor Effects on Gambling Emotions and Intentions. *Environment and Behavior*, 42(4), 524-545. doi:10.1177/0013916509341791

Lehrer, J. (2015, February 25). Royal Flush. Retrieved April 11, 2017, from http://www.newyorker.com/magazine/2012/03/26/royal-flush-2

Grocery Stores

Coupland, D. (2016, January 8). Douglas Coupland: The power of smell. Retrieved April 11, 2017, from https://www.ft.com/content/84c54b7a-b4b3-11e5-8358-9a82b43f6b2f

Duhigg, C. (2014). *Power of habit: why we do what we do in life and business*. New York: Random House Trade Paperbacks. P. 185

The way the brain buys. (2008, December 20). Retrieved April 11, 2017, from http://www.economist.com/node/12792420

Two Types of Thinking

Jorlen, %. A. (2016, March 04). Five Types of Creative Thinking. Retrieved April 11, 2017, from https://adamjorlen.com/2013/06/10/five-types-of-creative-thinking/

Progress, W. I. (2012, September 26). How to Develop 5 Critical Thinking Types. Retrieved April 11, 2017, from https://www.forbes.com/sites/work-in-progress/2012/03/27/how-to-develop-5-critical-thinking-types/#a7dc833ef0a8

Green, Blue, Red

Belluck, P. (2009, February 05). Reinvent Wheel? Blue Room. Defusing a Bomb? Red Room. Retrieved April 11, 2017, from http://www.nytimes.com/2009/02/06/science/06color.html

Landkammer, F., & Sassenberg, K. (2016). Competing while cooperating with the same others: The consequences of conflicting demands in co-opetition. *Journal of Experimental Psychology*: General, 145(12), 1670-1686. doi:10.1037/xge0000232

Lichtenfeld, S., Elliot, A. J., Maier, M. A., & Pekrun, R. (2012). Fertile Green. *Personality and Social Psychology Bulletin*, 38(6), 784-797. doi:10.1177/0146167212436611

Mehta, R., & Zhu, R. (. (2009, February 27). Blue or Red? Exploring the Effect of Color on Cognitive Task Performances. Retrieved April 11, 2017, from http://science.sciencemag.org/content/323/5918/1226

Ng, L. (2016, February 25). Plant Wellness. Retrieved April 11, 2017, from http://www.planteddesign.com/planteddesign/2016/2/25/plant-wellness

Shandrow, K. L. (2015, March 09). How the Color of Your Office Impacts Productivity (Infographic). Retrieved April 11, 2017, from https://www.entrepreneur.com/article/243749

Lighting

Johnson, D. (2009, October 01). Light Your Office Properly to Avoid Fatigue, Improve Productivity. Retrieved April 30, 2017, from http://www.cbsnews.com/news/light-your-office-properly-to-avoid-fatigue-improve-productivity/

Noise

Mehta, R., Zhu, R., & Cheema, A. (2012). Is Noise Always Bad? Exploring the Effects of Ambient Noise on Creative Cognition. *Journal of Consumer Research*, 39(4), 784-799. doi:10.1086/665048

O'connor, A. (2013, June 20). How the Hum of a Coffee Shop Can Boost Creativity. Retrieved April 28, 2017, from http://well.blogs.nytimes.com/2013/06/21/how-the-hum-of-a-coffee-shop-can-boost-creativity/?_r=0

Coffee shop noises, for your listening pleasure :-)- https://www.youtube.com/watch?v=BOdLmxy06H0

Washing machine (washing cycle only)- https://www.youtube.com/watch?v=e2ShIbugdzs

Not Too Hot, Not Too Cold

Hedge A. Linking environmental conditions to productivity. Power Point presentation. (2004) Cornell University. http://ergo.human.cornell.edu/Conferences/EECE_IEQ%20and%20Productivity_ABBR.pdf

Lang, B. S. (2004, October 19). Study links warm offices to fewer typing errors and higher productivity. Retrieved April 28, 2017, from http://www.news.cornell.edu/stories/2004/10/warm-offices-linked-fewer-typing-errors-higher-productivity

Seppanen, O.; Fisk, W.J.; & Lei, Q.H.(2006). Room temperature and productivity in office work. Lawrence Berkeley National Laboratory. Lawrence Berkeley National Laboratory: Lawrence Berkeley National Laboratory. Retrieved from: http://escholarship.org/uc/item/9bw3n707

Open Spaces

Myers-Levy, J., Zhu, R., & John Deighton served as editor and Gavan Fitzsimons served as associate editor for this article. (2007). The Influence of Ceiling Height: The Effect of Priming on the Type of Processing That People Use. *Journal of Consumer Research*, 34(2), 174-186. doi:10.1086/519146

Eye Strain/Fatigue

Brown, M. (2015, March 13). Nielsen reports that the average American adult spends 11 hours per day on gadgets. Retrieved April 30, 2017, from http://www.geekwire.com/2015/nielsen-reports-that-the-average-american-adult-spends-11-hours-per-day-on-gadgets/

This is where you can download F.lux: https://justgetflux.com/ (See also f.lux in sleep, Dock Model, Pillar 1, Part II)

Creativity Begets Creativity

This section was inspired by a class I took on creativity at the University of Washington taught by Nancy Rivenburgh. The information in this section is used with permission from Nancy.

Overthinking Overthinking

Everyone wants you to do well

Coupland, D. (2015, December 04). Douglas Coupland: Tips for public speaking. Retrieved April 11, 2017, from https://www.ft.com/content/cb450f26-9943-11e5-95c7-d47aa298f769

Mirror Neurons

Acharya, S., & Shukla, S. (2012). Mirror neurons: Enigma of the metaphysical modular brain. *Journal of Natural Science, Biology, and Medicine*, 3(2), 118–124. http://doi.org/10.4103/0976-9668.101878

Posture

Cuddy, Amy J.C., Caroline A. Wilmuth, and Dana R. Carney. "The Benefit of Power Posing Before a High-Stakes Social Evaluation." Harvard Business School Working Paper, No. 13-027, September 2012.

This is a working paper. You can read the pull text here: http://data colada.org/wp-content/uploads/2015/05/Carney-Cuddy-Yap-2010.pdf

Gaining Knowledge

Khazan, O. (2011, October 03). Is Listening to Audio Books Really the Same as Reading? Retrieved April 25, 2017, from https://www.forbes.com /sites/olgakhazan/2011/09/12/is-listening-to-audio-books-really-the-same-as-reading/2/#680295a32251

Money

Cole, M. (2015, April 14). 4 High-Earning Careers Surprisingly Likely to Lead to Bankruptcy. Retrieved April 12, 2017, from http://www.thefiscal times.com/2015/04/14/4-High-Earning-Careers-Surprisingly-Likely-Lead-Bankruptcy

Stanley, T. J., & Danko, W. J. (1996). *The millionaire next door: the surprising secrets of America's wealthy*. Atlanta: Longstreet Press.

"High-income-producing households are asset poor" this section is found on page 56, though, the theme is weaved throughout the entire book.

Step 2: Save for Your Emergency Fund

A Quick Guide to Your Emergency Fund. (n.d.). Retrieved April 12, 2017, from http://www.daveramsey.com/blog/quick-guide-to-your-emergency-fund

Baby Step 1. (n.d.). Retrieved April 12, 2017, from https://www.daveramsey .com/baby-ste

About the Author

Andrew J. Wilt has been working in education and workforce development since 2012. From cubicles in skyscrapers to office trailers at ethanol plants, Andrew's diverse resume includes talent development in the Pacific Northwest technology sector and apprenticeship programs in the Midwest skilled trades.

Andrew currently lives in Minneapolis, Minnesota with his super-cool wife, Megan, their newborn son, Atlas, and their cats, Harriet, Scout, and Charlotte. When Andrew is not working he enjoys writing fiction (for Megan and Atlas) and poetry (for the cats).

If you have any questions or comments, you can email Andrew at andrew.wilt@sustainableevolution.com and find him on Twitter: @andrewjwilt

About the Publisher

Sustainable Evolution Inc. is a people-building company specializing in education and business development. SEI believes in nurturing and educating the whole worker, including both hard and soft skills, so they can reach their full potential, whatever that may be.

For more information, visit sustainableevoultion.com and follow us on Twitter: @SevolutionInc. You can also follow the book @TheAgeofAgility.

Thank you for supporting my work and Sustainable Evolution Inc. Please consider leaving a review wherever you bought the book and on social media sites for book lovers like GoodReads. Every review provides us with beneficial feedback and promotes the skills we believe are valuable to growing the next generation.

Made in the USA
Monee, IL
26 October 2020